Applied Theatre: Women and the Criminal Justice System

The **Applied Theatre** series is a major innovation in applied theatre scholarship, bringing together leading international scholars that engage with and advance the field of applied theatre. Each book presents new ways of seeing and critically reflecting on this dynamic and vibrant field. Volumes offer a theoretical framework and introductory survey of the field addresses, combined with a range of case studies illustrating and critically engaging with practice.

https://www.bloomsbury.com/uk/series/applied-theatre/

Series Editors

Michael Balfour (University of New South Wales, Australia)
Sheila Preston (University of East London, UK)

Selected Titles

Applied Practice: Evidence and Impact in Theatre, Music and Art
Matthew Reason and Nick Rowe
ISBN 978-1-4742-8383-0

Applied Theatre: Economies
Molly Mullen
ISBN 978-1-3500-0170-1

Applied Theatre: Performing Health and Wellbeing
Veronica Baxter and Katharine E. Low
ISBN 978-1-4725-8457-1

Applied Theatre: Research Radical Departures
Peter O'Connor and Michael Anderson
ISBN 978-1-4725-0961-1

www.bloomsbury.com

Applied Theatre: Women and the Criminal Justice System

Caoimhe McAvinchey

Series Editors
Michael Balfour and Sheila Preston

methuen | drama
LONDON · NEW YORK · OXFORD · NEW DELHI · SYDNEY

METHUEN DRAMA
Bloomsbury Publishing Plc
50 Bedford Square, London, WC1B 3DP, UK
1385 Broadway, New York, NY 10018, USA
29 Earlsfort Terrace, Dublin 2, Ireland

BLOOMSBURY, METHUEN DRAMA and the Methuen Drama logo are
trademarks of Bloomsbury Publishing Plc

First published in Great Britain 2020
This paperback edition published in 2021

Copyright © Caoimhe McAvinchey and contributors, 2020

Caoimhe McAvinchey has asserted her right under the Copyright, Designs
and Patents Act, 1988, to be identified as the author of this work.

For legal purposes the Acknowledgements on pp. xiii–ix constitute an extension
of this copyright page.

Series design by Louise Dugdale
Cover image © Shutterstock

All rights reserved. No part of this publication may be reproduced or transmitted
in any form or by any means, electronic or mechanical, including photocopying,
recording, or any information storage or retrieval system, without prior
permission in writing from the publishers.

Bloomsbury Publishing Plc does not have any control over, or responsibility for,
any third-party websites referred to or in this book. All internet addresses given
in this book were correct at the time of going to press. The author and publisher
regret any inconvenience caused if addresses have changed or sites have ceased
to exist, but can accept no responsibility for any such changes.

A catalogue record for this book is available from the British Library.

A catalog record for this book is available from the Library of Congress.

ISBN: HB: 978-1-4742-6255-2
         PB: 978-1-3502-3598-4
      eBook: 978-1-4742-6256-9
       ePDF: 978-1-4742-6257-6

Series: Applied Theatre

Typeset by RefineCatch Limited, Bungay, Suffolk

To find out more about our authors and books visit www.bloomsbury.com
and sign up for our newsletters.

For my grandmother, Brigid Murtagh (1916–2018)

Contents

Notes on Contributors ix

Acknowledgements xiii

Introduction *Caoimhe McAvinchey* 1

Wicked (1991) 35

1 Interplay: Tracing Personal and Political Transformation through Popular Participatory Theatre in Westville Female Correctional Centre, Durban, South Africa *Miranda Young-Jahangeer* 37

'Four Walls', *Voices from Prison* (1987) 56

2 'They Pink Dress Ain't Done Shit': Sex, Dress and *Quare* Activism in a Women's Gulf Coast Prison *Lisa L. Biggs* 57

Decade (1984) 77

3 Daughters of the Floating Brothel: Engaging Indigenous Australian Women Prisoners through Participatory Radio Drama *Sarah Woodland* 79

'I am a theatre', *Voices from Prison* (1987) 105

4 What Works: The Affective and Gendered Performance of Prison *Aylwyn Walsh* 107

Extract I from *Inside Bitch* (2019) 124

5 Possible Fictions: Split Britches, Biography and Fantasy with Women in Prison *Caoimhe McAvinchey* 125

Extract I from *Killers* (1980) 141

6 Theatre as Collective Casework: Clean Break Theatre Company's *Charged* (2010) *Molly McPhee* 143

'Prison Loves, Prison Hates', *Voices from Prison* (1987) 162

viii *Contents*

7 Somebody's Daughter Theatre Company: The Arts –
   Unapologetically Transcendent   *Maud Clark AM*   163

   Extract II from *Killers* (1980)   171

8 The Meeting Place: Collaborative Learning in a
   University–Prison Partnership   *Rachel Conlon*   173

   Extract II from *Inside Bitch* (2019)   187

9 Acting Out: An Interview with Sherrin Fitzer   *Ashley Lucas*   189

   Inside a Cloud (2016)   196

10 'There Is Still Life in Me, Despite What I Have Done':
    Assuaging Woundedness through Collective Creativity
    Katharine E. Low and Clara Vaughan   197

    'Dirty Rule Makers', *Voices from Prison* (1987)   216

11 The Stella Adler Studio Outreach Programme at the Rose M.
    Singer Center for Women at Rikers Island Correctional Facility:
    An Interview with Joanne Edelmann and Tom Oppenheim
    Caoimhe McAvinchey   217

    21.23.6.15 (2018)   226

12 In Their Shoes: Participation, Social Change and Empathy in
    Open Clasp's *Key Change*   *Kay Hepplewhite*   229

    Index   245

Contributors

Lisa L. Biggs, PhD, is an actress, playwright and performance scholar. She serves as an assistant professor at Brown University in the Department of Africana Studies/Rites and Reason Theatre. Her research investigates the role of the arts in movements for social justice, in particular the impact of theatre programmes for women incarcerated in the US and in South Africa. Her articles and essays have been published in *Theatre Survey, Black Acting Methods: Critical Approaches* and *Solo/Black/Woman: Scripts, Interviews, Essays.*

Maud Clark. As co-founder Artistic Director of Somebody's Daughter Theatre, Maud has been the principal director and writer of many highly successful theatre works both inside and outside the prison. She won the Ewa Czajor Memorial Award for Directing and the Australia Council's Ros Bower Award for contribution to Community Arts. Maud was made a member of the Order of Australia in 2006 and an Honorary Fellow, Melbourne University Victorian College of the Arts in 2007. In recent years, Maud has been a lead artist in SDT's ground breaking arts led work with Education and Health where the arts become the bridge to education and inclusion for young people aged between the ages of twelve and seventeen years who are outside of the formal education system, most with histories of abuse and homelessness. This has led to the inception of SDT's official offspring's – HighWater Theatre in Albury/Wodonga and Nobody's Fool Theatre Geelong.

Rachel Conlon is Director of the Prison Partnership Project and Senior Lecturer in Theatre at York St John University. She specializes in socially engaged theatre practice, and theatre and criminal justice. Her practice investigates women's personal and collective narratives and explores the relationship women navigate between the inside and outside of prison. Her work is driven by a social justice and feminist agenda taking a therapeutic and empowering approach in its process and delivery. Rachel has worked for over twenty years in criminal justice settings.

Joanne Edelmann was a modern dancer for over twenty years, touring and performing with many modern dance theatres, including the companies of Charles Weidman and Mimi Garrard. She joined the Stella Adler Studio's movement faculty in 1984 where she ran the Teenage Conservatory and was the Director of Student Affairs for over thirteen years. Edelmann curates the Harold Clurman Poetry Reading Series bringing poets and writers from various backgrounds to the Stella Adler Studio. Gregory Pardlo, Idra Novey and Evie Shockley have read in the series, to name just three. She began her Movement Theatre and Poetry class at the Rose M. Singer Center (women's facility) on Rikers Island in 2013. The class recently performed an adaptation of *Antigone* and is currently reading the plays of Pulitzer Prize winner, Lynn Nottage.

Sherrin Fitzer is the Director of Women and Family Services at Logan Correctional Center, where she also directs the Acting Out Theater Company with incarcerated women. She has directed over twenty shows with Acting Out and has invited many guest artists, including Ashley Lucas from PCAP; Curt Tofetland, founder of Shakespeare Behind Bars; Kathryn Moller and Stacey Sotosky from Fort Lewis College in Durango CO; Janet Wilson, Director of Theatre & Dance at Illinois State University and the Illinois Shakespeare Festival Company, to work with the company inside the prison. In 2013, the Chicago Bar Association gave her the Liberty Award for helping women stay connected to their families, prepare for re-entry and assert their rights in civil cases. Multiple cats and a dog allow her to live with them in Bloomington, IL.

Kay Hepplewhite is Senior Lecturer at Northumbria University with a background in community theatre and participatory arts. Publications include book chapters in Sheila Preston, *Applied Theatre: Facilitation* (2016) and Jenny Sealey, *Reason to be Graeae: A Work in Progress* (2018), and articles in *ArtsPraxis* (NYU), *RIDE: The Journal of Applied Theatre and Performance* and *Theatre, Dance and Performance Training*. Her monograph, *The Applied Theatre Artist* (Palgrave, forthcoming), analyses practitioners at work to consider their expertise.

Katharine E. Low is a practitioner and researcher in socially engaged theatre and sexual health, with fifteen years' experience both internationally and in the UK. She is Senior Lecturer in Applied Theatre and Community Performance at the Royal Central School of Speech and Drama. As a practitioner, Katharine uses applied theatre and creative arts-based practice with communities to explore their health concerns within their wider social networks in South Africa, Tanzania and the UK. Katharine collaborates with medical practitioners and NGOs to run projects based around sexual health and other health concerns. She has published her research in a number of journals, co-edited *Applied Theatre: Performing Health and Wellbeing* (Bloomsbury, 2017) and has completed a monograph on her sexual health and applied theatre practice in South Africa for Palgrave Macmillan, *Applied Theatre and Sexual Health Communication: Apertures of Possibility*.

Contributors

Ashley Lucas is Associate Professor of Theatre and Drama and the Residential College at the University of Michigan, where she also serves as Director of the Prison Creative Arts Project. She is the author of a play about the families of prisoners, *Doin' Time: Through the Visiting Glass*, which she has performed in the US, Ireland, Brazil and Canada. Lucas is working on a book entitled *Prison Theatre: Performance and Incarceration* (Methuen Drama).

Caoimhe McAvinchey is Professor of Socially Engaged and Contemporary Theatre at Queen Mary University of London. Prior to this, she established the MA Applied Drama: Theatre in Educational, Community and Social Contexts at Goldsmiths. Previous publications include *Theatre & Prison* (2011), *Performance and Community: Case Studies and Commentary* (Methuen Drama, 2013) and, with Fabio Santos and Lucy Richardson, *Phakama: Making Participatory Theatre* (Methuen Drama, 2018). She is currently working on a book in collaboration with Clean Break, marking four decades of the theatre company's work with and about women and the criminal justice system.

Molly McPhee is a doctoral candidate in theatre at the Victorian College of the Arts, University of Melbourne. For six years (2009–15), she was a member of Clean Break Theatre Company (UK). Publications include 'Miasmatic Performance: Women and Resilience in Carceral Climates' for *Performance Research* (August 2018) and '"I don't know why she's crying": Contagion and Criminality in Clean Break's *Dream Pill* and *Little on the Inside*' in *Theatres of Contagion: Transmitting Early Modern to Contemporary Performance* (Bloomsbury 2019). She holds an MFA from the California Institute of the Arts, and was the recepient of a Fulbright grant for research at the University of Hamberg.

Tom Oppenheim has been the artistic director of the Stella Adler Studio of Acting for over twenty years. In addition to many other programmes, Tom created the Stella Adler Outreach Division in 2004. Today the division is the largest arts programme provider at Rikers Island Correctional Facility. Oppenheim studied acting at the National Shakespeare Conservatory and with his grandmother, Stella Adler. Tom co-edited *The Muses Go to School* (2012), and his writing is featured in Arthur Bartow's *Training of the American Actor* (2006).

Clara Vaughan is the Head of the Market Theatre Laboratory in Johannesburg, South Africa, and a theatre-maker, arts facilitator, arts manager, and writer. In her work at the Market Theatre Laboratory, a division of the world-famous Market Theatre, she brings together diverse theatre-practitioners and other collaborators to participate in various learning/making/experimenting/

researching processes, with an emphasis on emerging artists, and subaltern experiences, voices and identities. While the roles she plays in the arts environment are diverse, her artistic and facilitation practice is motivated by an interest in process, curiosity about alternative or experimental ways of learning and making, rigorous research, and collaborative creative methods.

Aylwyn Walsh leads the Applied Theatre and Intervention MA at the University of Leeds' School of Performance and Cultural Industries. She runs a project related to decolonial activism and performing geographies of social change. Her latest book relates to *Prison Cultures*, mapping performance, resistance and desire in women's prisons (2019). It explores theatre, television and popular culture. She has worked in prisons in South Africa and the UK for over fifteen years.

Sarah Woodland is a researcher, practitioner and educator in arts, theatre and performance. She has over twenty years' experience in the arts and cultural sectors in Australia and the UK, with a particular focus on socially engaged and participatory practices and research. Sarah is currently a Research Fellow at the Queensland Conservatorium Research Centre at Griffith University, where she undertakes research and evaluation in the arts and delivers practice-led creative research projects in prisons and community groups.

Miranda Young-Jahangeer is a Senior Lecturer in Drama and Performance Studies and the current Academic Leader for Teaching and Learning at the University of KwaZulu-Natal in Durban, South Africa. Her research is primarily in the area of Applied Theatre, Prison Theatre, African popular performance, post-colonial studies, gender and identity, and she has published widely in these areas. She has an ongoing participatory theatre programme in Westville Female Correctional Centre which has been running since 2000.

Acknowledgements

Thank you to the *Applied Theatre* Series Editors, Sheila Preston and Michael Balfour, and to Mark Dudgeon, Publisher at Methuen Drama, for inviting me to develop this book, and for their insight and care throughout the process. The team at Methuen Drama, particularly Lara Bateman and Ben Harris, has been exemplary in their attention to every detail.

Sincerest thanks to each of the contributors to *Applied Theatre: Women and the Criminal Justice System* – Lisa Biggs, Maud Clark, Rachel Conlon, Joanne Edelmann, Sherrin Fitzer, Kay Hepplewhite, Katharine Low, Ashley Lucas, Molly McPhee, Tom Oppenheim, Clara Vaughan, Aylwyn Walsh, Sarah Woodland, Miranda Young-Jahangeer – who have exposed women's experiences of structural inequality and violence through criminalization and incarceration, giving unprecedented access to international theatre and performance practices in carceral contexts and the lives, words and creative work of the women who are at the heart of this book.

Clean Break theatre company is an enduring influence in my understanding of the personal, social, cultural and political implications of the incarceration of women. Particular thanks to Anna Herrmann, Jacqueline Holborough, Jennifer Hicks, Jennifer Joseph, Róisín McBrinn and Lucy Perman for their generous conversations and permission to include archival materials, and to Sabrina Mahfouz and Sandrine Uwayo for kindly allowing us to include their work in the collection. Thanks, too, to Methuen Drama and Oberon for permission to publish extracts from *Wicked* and *Inside Bitch,* just two of the scores of published plays in Clean Break's extensive canon of new writing by women which challenge delimited societal constructions of women, crime and punishment.

I have been fortunate to work with people making extraordinary work with women in the criminal justice system: as part of *Staging Human Rights* (2002–4), Paul Heritage, Lois Weaver, Peggy Shaw, Rose Sharp, Catrin John and Yassmin V. Foster, and collaborators from HMP Highpoint, HMP and YOI Bullwood Hall in the UK, and Penitenciária Nelson Hungria and Talavera Bruce in Brazil; and as part of *Handheld* (2007), Mike Moloney from Prison Arts Foundation in Belfast, Janetka Platun, Rachel Hale and the women of HMP and YOI Hydebank Wood, Northern Ireland.

There are many other people whose reflections have informed this book: Effie Makepeace; Sylvan Baker; Kat Craft and Michelle Dahlenberg, founders of Conspire Theatre Company (USA); Edith Regier, Crossing Communities

xiv   *Acknowledgements*

(Canada); Liz Brown, Andrea Cifuentes-Poseck, Lou Heywood and Emma Smallman from Geese (UK); and Ashley Lucas, Director of the Prison Creative Arts Project at the University of Michigan.

On 4 June 2017, Clean Break and I co-curated a conference *Women, Theatre and the Criminal Justice System: International Perspectives and Practices* with financial support from QMUL's Centre for Public Engagement and School of English and Drama's Strategic Research Initiative. This event seeded many of the ideas that have since come to fruition in this book. In addition to those acknowledged as contributors to this collection, sincerest thanks to: Alison Frater, National Criminal Justice Arts Alliance; Kate Paradine, Women in Prison; Kharen Harper, Somebody's Daughter Theatre Company; Catrina McHugh, Open Clasp; Eleanor Byrne, Sarah-Jane Dent, Lorraine Faissal, Charlotte Gwinner, Sonya Hale, TerriAnn Oudjar, Ambreen Razia, Amanda Richardson, Jacqueline Stewart, Vishni Velada-Billson and Ria Zmitrowicz from Clean Break; Andy Watson, Geese Theatre Company; Sarah Colvin, University of Cambridge; and Tom Wilson, Queen Mary University of London.

My friends and colleagues in the School of English and Drama at QMUL, thank you for your unerring interest, camaraderie and humour.

As ever, there are people who have accompanied me throughout the development of the book, who know exactly the right question to ask and when to ask it. Thank you to Ali Campbell, Deborah Dean, Cass Fleming, Jen Harvie, Katja Hilevaara, Michael Hughes, Richard Ings, Kat Low, Sue Mayo, Ann McCoy, Aoife Monks, Edmond Ng, TaraMarie Perri, Samenua Sesher, Catherine Silverstone and Tiffany Watt Smith.

To my parents, Paul and Cora, thank you for all your support and love and for making days appear when they were most needed. Molly and Finn McFetridge, thank you for being your fabulously curious selves, continuing to ask useful questions about crime, punishment and how the world works – and if it's time to play. David McFetridge, thank you for everything, as ever.

Introduction

Caoimhe McAvinchey

I have been dismayed at the high prevalence of institutional misunderstanding within the criminal justice system of the things that matter to women and at the shocking level of unmet need. Yet the compelling body of research which has accumulated over many years consistently points to remedies. Much of this research was commissioned by government. There can be few topics that have been so exhaustively researched to such little practical effect as the plight of women in the criminal justice system.

Jean Corston 2007: 16

We've been talking. It's just not today and yesterday. The talking's been talked even before I went to jail. But who's listening? The people that have been in charge, that can do something about it, if they're not listening, we're just wasting our time. Don't get me twisted, if I hadn't been to prison, I wouldn't be here today, but if you want change we have to take it much further. All this talking ain't doing nothing. Someone needs to be listening otherwise what's the point.

Jennifer Joseph 2019

There are more than eleven million people incarcerated across the globe. Figures from 2017's World Female Imprisonment List reveal that 714,000 women were held in 221 prison systems – 6.9 per cent of global prison population (Walmsley 2017a: 1). This statistical snapshot reveals one fact – women are in a minority within the wider global corrections landscape – while concealing the multiple political, cultural and social implications of their incarceration. This single figure gives no context to the crimes that women are punished for, nor for the duration of their sentence. It obscures the intersectional societal disadvantages that shape the lives of many women who navigate the criminal justice system and reveals little of women's experiences of the processes, let alone the 'institutional misunderstanding' and 'shocking level of unmet need' within them (Corston 2007: 16). Research into the experience of women in the criminal justice system from law, feminist criminology and prison studies confirms that, historically, the criminological subject has been the majority – men – and, as a direct consequence, women are marginalized because of their gender, because they have been criminalized and because they are too few in number to be given specific consideration (McIvor 2004; Sharpe 2012; Agozino 1997). David Ramsbotham, Her Majesty's Chief Inspector of Prisons (1995–2001), highlighted this, stating, 'It is not merely a question of women receiving equal treatment to men; in the prison system equality is everywhere conflated with uniformity; women are treated as if they are men' (1997: para. 3.46). This is evidenced in ideologies that inform the language of the law (Kennedy 1993, 2018), the architectural design and material conditions of women's prisons (Moore and Scranton 2014) and the endemic political inertia that impedes penal reform attending to the needs of women, communities and society (Corston 2007; McCorkel 2013). It is imperative that research into theatre practices in the criminal justice system does not reiterate this lack of focus and care for the specific experience of women.

In the UK in 2006, the deaths of six women over thirteen months in HMP Styal was the tragic catalyst for a government review of the treatment of vulnerable women in the criminal justice system. Led by Jean Corston, her report (2007) detailed forty-three explicit recommendations to address failures and gaps in the system. When it was published, it was welcomed as both an exposition of successive governments' scandalous neglect and a blueprint for structural change. More than a decade later, community-based initiatives to support vulnerable women outlined in Corston's report have been decimated by government cuts undertaken in the name of austerity. During a post-show discussion for *Inside Bitch,* a Clean Break production devised and performed by women artists with experience of prison, Jennifer Joseph, one of the actors, lamented this continued lack of understanding or sustained reform: 'All this talking ain't doing nothing. Someone needs to be listening otherwise what's the point' (2019). Both Corston and Joseph's statements at the beginning of this Introduction reflect a social and political lacuna of listening, a lack of attention, a carelessness about women in prison. While these examples are situated in the specific context of the UK, they reflect wider international trends about the social and political treatment of women. *Applied Theatre: Women and the Criminal Justice System* recognizes the direct response of artists to this historical inattention and neglect.

Women, prison and the cultural imagination

Popular cultural representations of women with experience of the criminal justice system are too often reduced to a handful of recurring tropes: 'bad girls', 'monsters' and 'babes behind bars'. This phenomenon is explicitly acknowledged in the titles of television series and films such as *Bad Girls*, the long-running British television series set in the fictional HMP Larkhall (1999–2006); *Monster* (2003), a film about Aileen Wuornos, convicted for the murder of seven men and sentenced to death in the USA in 2002; and the entire Women in Prison sexploitation series, *Women in Cages* (1971), *The Big Bird Cage* (1972) and *Caged Heat* (1974). The international popular success of the American television series, *Orange Is The New Black* (2013–19), set in the fictional Litchfield Penitentiary, reaffirms the popular appeal of the women-in-prison drama, already firmly established in the cultural imagination through series including *Within These Walls* (UK, 1974–8), *Prisoner Cell Block H* (Australia, 1979–86), *Women in Prison* (USA, 1987–8), *Hinter-Gitten – Der Frauenknast* (*Behind Bars – The Women's Prison*, Germany, 1997–2007) and *Wentworth* (Australia, 2013–).

The imagery surrounding women and prison is iconic as evidenced in the marketing materials for the stage musical version of *Bad Girls* (West Yorkshire Playhouse, UK 2006). The promotional poster featured a woman's naked, toned, tanned leg, balancing on a red, metallic, high-heeled shoe with a glitter ball and chain clamped to her ankle. A shadow of prison bars framed this central image with press quotations declaring, 'These girls aren't just bad, they're wicked' (*Mail on Sunday*) and 'A hell of a lot of fun' (*Daily Telegraph*). But these cultural representations of women in prison are anything but fun – they do serious cultural, social and political work obfuscating the intersectional oppressions that shape the lives of many women navigating criminal justice systems and delimit the representational vocabulary available to a repertoire of sexualized or monstrous tropes. Tropes which have some resonance with the reductive, racist and misogynistic work of Cesare Lombrosco, considered to be one of the founders of criminology, whose *Criminal Woman, the Prostitute, and the Normal Woman*, originally published in Italian in 1893, was built on biological determinism and analysis of physical characteristics (2004).

In the early twenty-first century, prison as both a site and mode of punishment has become normalized. In *A Sin Against the Future: Imprisonment in the World* (1998), Vivien Stern acknowledges the omnipresence of prison as part of the legal, penal and social landscape: 'Everyone has them. It is as normal to have prisons as to have schools or hospitals' (1998: xx). Despite the continued growth of the global prison

4   *Applied Theatre: Women and the Criminal Justice System*

population, relatively few people will have personal experience of institutions of incarceration. However, the abundance of cultural representations of prison ensures that publics feel familiar with it. The symbolic power of prison has become 'as much a basic metaphor of our cultural imagination as it is of our penal policy' (Garland 1990: 260). Narratives about women within the structures of the criminal justice system (such as police custody, court and prisons), played out through films and television, give us the impression that we know something about the lives of individuals, collectively labelled. And, as academics in cultural criminology, particularly popular criminology, argue, we do. Nicole Rafter and Michelle Brown have written persuasively about the power of culture in generating public knowledge about crime, criminals and punishment. They urge an attentiveness to cultural artefacts – television, newspapers, rap music, novels and, especially, film – as contributors to a wider public comprehension of crime and those who commit it, proposing that 'criminology is hard at work in culture and that culture is hard at work in criminology' (2011: 1). In *The Culture of Punishment: Prison, Society, and Spectacle* (2009), Brown examines the carceral continuum that extends beyond prison into the social body, where 'citizens access punishment through cultural practices removed from formal institutions like prison in a manner which, although largely unacknowledged, massively extends throughout our social foundations' (2009: 4). In attending to the interrelationship between culture and punishment, Brown argues that subjects of the criminal justice system are framed and viewed through penal spectatorship. Ideas of a positioned spectatorship also inform Jill Dolan's work. *The Feminist Spectator in Action: Feminist Criticism for the Stage and Screen* (2013) is Dolan's call to action for those who make, consume and critique cultural work to attend to the choices we make in our practices. She reminds us that:

> Culture is not an innocent preoccupation. [...] Theatre and film show us ourselves in relation to others, or more damagingly, they persuade us of our social invisibility by not representing us at all [...] [Feminist criticism] participates in an activist project of culture-making in which we're collectively called to see what and who is stunningly, repeatedly evident and what and who is devastatingly, obviously invisible in the art and popular culture we regularly consume for edification and entertainment.
>
> Dolan 2013: 1–3

The circulation of images of women in prison, particularly in film and television, suggest that they are not invisible subjects. However, if the majority

Introduction

of visible subjects are culturally constructed within a narrow representational frame of monstrous or sexualized women, this denies awareness of and insight into the societal structural disadvantage that shapes the lived experience of many women who commit acts deemed illegal. These images and the social script they suggest, however fictionalized, are, to use Sara Ahmed's term, 'sticky' (2004), shadowing or clinging to all women, framed by penal spectatorship.

In popular criminology, there is a distinct and growing body of academic work considering film and literature, particularly novels (Rafter and Brown 2011; Baily and Hale 1998). However, there has been no consideration of how theatre and performance contribute to this discourse. This gap is due, in part, to the ontology of performance: the transience, temporality and togetherness required of both the performance-makers and audiences in this live event offer a very different proposition to the durational, often private endeavour of reading novels or watching films, cultural forms that have the potential for an individual to return to, time and again. Books and films, therefore, offer an economy of circulation that allows for an infinite audience and are more readily incorporated into globalized markets than performance (Phelan 1993). Despite significant differences between film and theatre, Rafter's work is a helpful provocation to consider issues of cultural production and intentionality, echoing Dolan's concerns about the relationship between ideology, representation and power:

> The myths, attitudes, and assumptions that we live by influence what can be said and what modes of expression can be used. What is not said is easily as important, ideologically, as what is said ... [Cultural representations] mould ideology by what they fail to show as well as by the narratives they do present, and part of my aim [...] is to point out the ideological significance of missing representations and silences.
>
> Rafter 2006: 8–9

The ideological significance of missing representations and silences is particularly acute when considering cultural representations of women in the criminal justice system. Within an economy of representation, particular representations are both abundant and amplified. These are crafted by the circulation of power, particularly, as Dolan notes, 'around the axis of not just gender, but of sexuality, race and class' (1), and continue to iterate values given to these particular subjects. The absence of alternative, nuanced and complex representations is ideological. In the wider context of theatre practices with and about women and the criminal justice system, Rafter, Brown and Dolan raise pertinent questions about the frames, methodological

6   *Applied Theatre: Women and the Criminal Justice System*

approaches and audiences for this work. What contributions do these practices offer within an activist project of culture-making? What kinds of penal spectatorship do they invite or critique? How do they contribute to wider social and political understanding about women and the criminal justice system? How do they support individual women to navigate a life marked by the stigma of criminalization?

To attend to theatre practice with and about women with experience of the criminal justice system is to attend to societal structural disadvantage shaped by intersectional considerations of gender, race, class and social mobility, particularly the feminization of poverty (Bradshaw 2002; Schnaffer Goldberg 2009), the interrelationship between poverty and punishment in neoliberal societies and the subsequent surge in the global corrections industry (Wacquant 2011). In a wider cultural landscape, where television and film images of women in prison are all too often painted from a limited palate of stereotypes, applied theatre practice can critique, expand and reframe representational vocabularies to audiences within and beyond prison walls.

The twelve essays, case studies and interviews commissioned for this book engage with a wide range of theatre practices in women's prisons in Australia, Brazil, South Africa, the United Kingdom and the United States of America. Written by artists and academics, some of whom have led sustained programmes of collaboration between universities and prisons, they reveal rich ethnographic detail about the institutional conditions – political and material – that shape women's experiences in specific cultural contexts. Each contribution considers the aesthetic, ethical and pragmatic negotiations undertaken to realize work which attends to, in Corston's words, the 'things that matter to women', that meet their needs while contributing to a wider public understanding about 'the plight of women in the criminal justice system' (2007: 16).

Women in the criminal justice system – who are they?

The political and economic imperatives for the continued growth in the global prison population are well documented (Mauer 2016; Coyle et al. 2016), reflecting an increase in the number of human behaviours identified as unlawful (particularly in relation to technology and immigration), greater intervention by law enforcement and the enduring use of incarceration as a judicial response within the multibillion-dollar global corrections industry (Davis 2003; Dreisinger 2017). Although different countries have distinctive approaches in their treatment of crime and punishment, there are particular characteristics of the prison population which are recognized globally. A disproportionate percentage of the prison population experiences social

Introduction 7

inequality through poverty, racism and limited social mobility (Mauer 1999). The interrelationship between poverty and punishment in neoliberal societies is highlighted by Wacquant who argues that 'welfare and criminal justice are two modalities of public policy toward the poor' and that 'the linked stinginess of the welfare wing and munificence of the penal wing under the guidance of moralism are profoundly injurious to democratic ideals' (2011). While Wacquant is referring directly to the USA, the punitive regulation of those who live in poverty is evident globally. Concurrently, as the poorest are criminalized and incarcerated, governments, particularly in the UK and USA, employ private companies to build and administer the increasing number of prisons required to manage them. The criminalization and incarceration of the poorest in society has become a global business (Stern 2006; Garland 2018).

The elision of welfare and penal policy means that women are particularly vulnerable to political forces of regulation, punishment and the feminization of poverty (Bradshaw 2002; Schnaffer Goldberg 2009). The socio-economic and health characteristics of women in prison reflect, largely, the profile of women who live in poverty: unemployment, homelessness and poor physical and mental health contribute to an unending cycle of hardship and distress (Fitch, Hamilton, Bassett and Davey 2011). Economic, social and health inequalities are written into the global female prison population. Self-harm and suicide attempts are disproportionately higher with women in prison than in the wider population; women in prison are more likely to have spent time in care, to have left school with few qualifications; in the UK, more than 40 per cent have reported suffering domestic violence or emotional, physical or sexual abuse in their lives (WiP 2016). Women's prisons are filled with those who are, in Corston's words, more 'troubled' than 'troublesome' (2007: 16).

Although women are less than 10 per cent of the global prison population, they are the fastest rising group within it: the number of women and girls in prison has increased by 53 per cent since the year 2000, a period in which the male world population rose by 20 per cent (Walmsley 2017a: 2). Closer consideration of this statistic reveals that this accelerated rate of incarceration is not the result of more women committing more, or more violent, crimes. Rather, it is the result of gendered sentencing: the vast majority of crimes committed by women are non-violent, primarily theft and drugs-related crimes; sentencing for women is harsher than for men; and there is a greater number of women serving shorter sentences, of less than twelve months, than men (Kennedy 1993; Gunnison and Bernat 2016). This high level of short-term sentencing has significant detrimental implications which endure long after a woman's prison sentence has been spent. When a man goes into prison, the support networks of his home and family tend to remain stable. When a woman is imprisoned, even for a short sentence, she risks losing her family and her home. In the UK, 9 per

8 Applied Theatre: Women and the Criminal Justice System

cent of the general population are single parents; however, 20 per cent of women in prison parent alone. When a mother goes into prison, 9 per cent of children are cared for by their father; 91 per cent of children are cared for by networks of family or friends or taken into care (WiP 2016).

As rates of recidivism remain stable (approximately 65 per cent in the UK and USA), there is an abundance of data which proves that prison doesn't work as a deterrent from crime or as catalyst towards rehabilitation (Carlen 2013; Genders and Player 2014). Despite the evidence of the failure of prison and its contribution to further social inequality through the decimation of families – a common, devastating and enduring consequence of women's imprisonment – the judiciary continues to default to incarceration in its sentencing (Ramsbottom 1997; Corston 2007; Walmsley 2017a). The processes of starting over – of finding a new home, employment and reconfiguring a family life disrupted by prison – are particularly difficult for women navigating life with a criminal record. While a prison sentence may be spent, it does not go away. As Joseph reflects, 'Even outside of prison, you're not allowed to forget it. You learn to live past it but it never goes' (2018). Social and political scripts write stigma and shame into a criminalized woman's identity beyond the term of their sentence: a criminal record and the limited access to employment that this ensures means that many women and their families continue to be further punished, economically and socially.

While all prisoners should be considered with care, fairness and equity, Corston's report highlighted the imperative for recognizing the distinctive needs of women within a wider socio-economic and political context:

> Equality does not mean treating everyone the same. The new gender equality duty means that men and women should be treated with equivalent respect, according to need. Equality must embrace not just fairness but also inclusivity. This will result in some different services and policies for men and women. There are fundamental differences between male and female offenders and those at risk of offending that indicate a different and distinct approach is needed for women.
>
> Corston 2007: 3

Within this book, contributors both make and examine theatre practices that attend to the 'different and distinct' needs of women.

Prison theatres

The theatre practice addressed in this book accommodates work with and about women with experience of the criminal justice system. While there is a

Introduction

considerable body of theatre practice within prisons, other important work is located in community contexts. This includes practice with those considered to be at risk of entering the criminal justice system as well as programmes specifically for people who have served sentences. This spectrum of practice is often collapsed within the term 'prison theatre'. When I use the term, it reflects an accommodation of practices both within and beyond institutional walls. In the following section I consider the characteristics of prison theatre and key areas of research in the field, and I address the book's imperative to focus on theatre and performance practices specifically with women who have experience of the criminal justice system.

There is a rich history of documented theatre practice in prisons that precedes any academic disciplinary framework of applied theatre or prison theatre. Particular institutions have a rich history of supporting a range of practices – for example, in San Quentin, California, archival photographs detail female impersonator competitions in the 1910s; newspaper reports cover Sarah Bernhardt's company performance of *Une Nuit de Noël/One Christmas Night* on a makeshift stage in the prison yard in 1913; and the San Quentin Drama Workshop, the long-running, prisoner-led company, was formed in direct response to the San Francisco Actor's Company performance of *Waiting for Godot* for 1,400 prisoners in 1957. In Volterra, Italy, the theatre director, Armando Punzo has, since 1989, led the troupe *Compagnia della Fortezza* in Volterra's maximum security state prison, Fortezza Medicea. In addition to staging performances of *Marat/Sade* (Peter Weiss 1993), *Insulti al Pubblico/Offending the Audience* (Peter Handke 1966) and works by Brecht and Shakespeare, Punzo has directed solo shows with inmates and negotiated permission from the Italian Penitentiary System to tour performances beyond the medieval prison walls (Punzo 2013). In Northern Ireland, Bill McDonnell documents 'The University of Freedom', developed by political prisoners in the Maze and the role of Paulo Freire's *Pedagogy of the Oppressed* in developing a distinctive theatre of resistance (2008).

Some theatre practices seek to make a direct intervention into the life of prison, wider penal policies and social understanding about crime and justice. Since 2007, Lebanon's Roumieh Prison has hosted Catharis, an NGO led by Zeina Daccache. During this time, Daccache, a drama therapist who also trained with Punzo in Volterra, has developed work that directly addresses additional punishments within prison. *12 Angry Lebanese,* an adaptation of the screenplay *Twelve Angry Men* (Rose 1954), contributed to an institutional review of policies which, in theory though not in practice, offered reduced sentences for good behaviour. Other projects attended to limited domestic violence laws, regulations surrounding migrant workers' relationships and the unofficial life sentences endured by inmates living with

10   *Applied Theatre: Women and the Criminal Justice System*

mental illness (Sewell 2018). *Staging Human Rights* (2002–8), a collaboration between Augusto Boal's Centro de Teatro do Oprimido and People's Palace Projects, was an extensive theatre programme across six states in Brazil, which addressed human rights issues raised by both prisoners and prison staff (Heritage 2002, 2004). In England, *Shakespeare Comes to Broadmoor* (Cox 1992) documents a collaboration between the Royal Shakespeare Company, the Royal National Theatre, Wilde Community Theatre Company and Broadmoor High Security Psychiatric Hospital, which negotiated critical questions about forensic mental health, societal perceptions of crime and mental illness and the therapeutic possibilities of theatre practices in secure settings.

Since the 1950s in the USA and UK, artists volunteering classes or projects as part of a social and political movement foregrounding prisoners' rights have contributed to a wider understanding about the benefits of arts and education within the context of institutional life (Adams, Bennett and Flanagan 1994; Brewster 2014). There are also examples of prisoner-led theatre workshops in Sweden in the 1960s (Flemsburg 2005), the UK in the 1970s (McAvinchey 2020c) and, more recently, in Colombia (Palau 2018). However, one of the most significant areas of development for theatre engaging with criminal justice has been the funding available for arts in prisons programmes, since the mid-1970s in the USA and the 1980s in the UK. Because funders require accountability for their investment, there is much greater documentation, research and evaluation of practices with reference to the specific social and economic ambitions for it: developing skills (DfES 2003), enhancing the prison environment (Brewster 1993), addressing offending behaviour (Hewish 2001) and supporting rehabilitation and resettlement (Miles 2004). Hughes's 'Doing the Arts Justice' (2005) and Gardner, Hager and Hillman's 'Prison Arts Resource Project: An Annotated Bibliography' (2014) articulate the scope and characteristics of documented work, mainly in the UK and USA, and the UK's National Criminal Justice Arts Alliance's Evidence Library provides access to over one hundred reports and evaluations which reveal something of the methodological approach of these practices and much about the political, social and economic imperatives demanded of it.[1] While there is debate and concern about framing arts in criminal justice only in terms of criminal justice outcomes (Hughes 2005; McAvinchey 2017; Chelitios 2016), there is no doubt that the arts in their broadest terms, and drama and theatre specifically, are part of institutional life. Cultural representations of prisons in television, novels and stage productions attest to the normalcy of theatre practices in criminal justice contexts; in *Orange Is the New Black* (Series 3, Episode 3, 'Empathy is a Bone

Introduction 11

Killer'), a prison counsellor runs a drama programme; Margaret Atwood's novel *Hag-Seed* (2016) is framed through the staging of Shakespeare's *The Tempest* in the fictional Fletcher County Correctional Institute; Philip Osment's play *Inside* (2010) was inspired by and stages a prison-theatre programme with fathers inside; and Phyllida Lloyd's Shakespeare Trilogy (2012–16) produced by London's Donmar Warehouse, situated *Julius Caesar, Henry IV* and *The Tempest* as plays staged by women in prison.[2]

This rich body of theatre practice in prisons, with people considered to be 'at risk' of entering them, and as part of rehabilitation programmes, is reflected in an expanded field of research. Shakespeare in Prisons is the subject of a growing body of practical and academic enquiry in Brazil, Australia, the UK and USA (Heritage 2002; Trounstine 2004; Scott-Douglass 2007; Herold 2014; Pensalfini 2016; Ward and Connolly 2018). A small number of publications focus on the work of one particular artist or company (Fraden 1994; Baim, Brooks and Mountford 2002). There are four notable edited collections which survey international theatre practices, bringing together the voices of artists, academics, prisoners and prison staff, revealing much about the development of an area of theatre practice which, despite a necessarily low public profile, has flourished in different political contexts (Balfour 2004; Thompson 1998; Shailor 2010; Lucas 2020). However, only one chapter in each of these edited collections focuses specifically on work with women in the criminal justice system. This is not surprising as, globally, men make up over 90 per cent of the prison population: there is, statistically, more opportunity to develop work with them. However, it does mean that the majority of research addressing theatre and the criminal justice system examines work with men. Theatre practices with women have not, until now, been considered alongside each other. *Applied Theatre: Women and the Criminal Justice System* offers insight into specific projects developed in particular cultural contexts while opening up a dialogue between them. Two key questions have shaped my enquiry during the development of this book: What do prison theatre practices with women reveal of both their local and wider sociopolitical context? What does work in this context reveal of the possibilities or limitations of theatre and performance?

Theatre with and about women in prison

In the following section, I identify a range of international theatre practices with and about women in the criminal justice system, identifying particular characteristics of this work, the aesthetic and social imperatives for it and

12   *Applied Theatre: Women and the Criminal Justice System*

how it is documented and shared for a wider public audience. First, I'll attend to three of the longest-running and most substantially documented companies before surveying other international practices with less available documentation.

Rhodessa Jones' The Medea Project: Theater for Incarcerated Women (USA), Teatro Yeses (Spain) and Clean Break theatre company (UK) are three companies that have developed a sustained programme of work with and about women and the criminal justice system for more than three decades. Each company has developed a distinctive approach to theatre and performance-making, reaching very different audiences within and beyond prison walls, and their work reveals both the cultural specificity of the political landscape which shapes their experiences while reiterating the intersectional oppressions that are shared beyond them.

The Medea Project: Theater for Incarcerated Women (USA)

Rhodessa Jones is, with Idris Ackamoor, Co-Artistic Director of Cultural Odyssey, a San Francisco-based performance company committed to arts as social activism. In 1989, Jones began working with women in San Francisco County Jail and, through The Medea Project: Theater for Incarcerated Women, developed an approach which directly engages with women's experiences of trauma, supporting their articulation of this through an exploration of myths and fairy tales. *Food Taboos in the Land of the Dead* (1994) was a revision of the ancient Greek myth of Demeter and Persephone, exploring the victimization and criminalization of women; Sisyphus's enduring quest was the catalyst for an examination of addiction and recovery in *A Taste of Something Else: A Place at the Table* (1994); *Buried Fire* (1996), informed by Hans Christian Andersen's fairy tale *The Ugly Duckling*, was an explicit recognition of how criminalized women negotiate a societal script of shame in the attempt to find and express a sense of self beyond this; *Slouching towards Armageddon: A Captive's Conversation/Observation on Race* (1999) engaged with the Greek myth of Pandora's Box, her curiosity and anticipation of wonders, the realization of horrors previously unknown and an acknowledgement of the possibilities of hope; and the Sumerian myths of Queen Inanna, celebrating the goddess' strength, wisdom, fearlessness and ultimately her death and rebirth, were the framework for *Can We Get There by Candlelight?* (2001), an examination of incarcerated women's release and return to their families, communities and societies (Fraden 2004; Warner 2004). The Medea Project has become an ensemble of incarcerated women, women who have served sentences and artists and activists, and the work has

Introduction 13

been staged both in prisons for prisoners' families as well as theatres and universities.

Throughout her career, Jones has declared herself 'a womanist' (Pappas and Jones 2017). She demands women's personal recognition of themselves, their choices and their bodies – their sensuality, their capacities, their beauties – and publics' recognition of the ways in which they have been abused and violated, physically and emotionally. Since 2008, The Medea Project has directly engaged with women's experience of HIV and AIDs – from education and prevention through to stigma and treatment – in a collaboration with Edward Machtinger and the University of California San Francisco, engaging wider public audiences through performances of *Dancing with the Clown of Love* (2010) (Machtinger, Lavin, Starr Hiliard, Jones, Harberer, Capito and Dawson-Rose 2015). *Birthright?* (2015), developed from conversations with the Bay Area Planned Parenthood about sexual violence, trauma, women's access to healthcare and birth control, became a public education programme. The work engages with a range of performance forms – monologues, choreographed dances, call and response prompts (Rosen 2015). Unusually for prison theatre practices, there is a substantial body of documentation about The Medea Project, including Rena Fraden's book *Imagining Medea: Rhodessa Jones and Theater for Incarcerated Women* (2004) and documentary films including *Medea Project: Concrete Jungle* (Dir. R. Jones 2006), *We Just Telling Stories* (Dir. L. Andrews 2001) and *Birthright?* (Schmiechen 2017). At the heart of all Medea projects is an exposition of the intersectional oppressions of criminalized women, a refusal to accept shame as an additional social punishment and a celebration of women's collaboration in addressing systemic injustices.

Teatro Yeses (Spain)

In 1986, Elena Cánovas, a prison officer, began a theatre workshop programme with women in Yeserías prison in Madrid, Spain, from which the company Teatro Yeses derived its name. Now based in Centro Penitenciario de Madrid I Mujeres, Cánovas has, over thirty years, created a distinctive programme of prison theatre, performing plays that reflect or are adapted to reflect the women's concerns as well as developing their own texts. For Cánovas, her work as a prison officer developing a sustained and coherent programme of theatre practice is informed by her training in sociology, theatre and criminology and a commitment to penal reform from within the institution. She explicitly references Article 25 of the Spanish Constitution as the foundations for this work: 'Las penas privativas de libertad y las medidas

14   *Applied Theatre: Women and the Criminal Justice System*

de seguridad estarán orientadas hacia la reeducación y reinserción socialy no podrán consistir en trabajos forzados' ('Punishments involving deprivation of liberty and measures of security will be oriented towards re-education and social reintegration and may not consist of forced labour') (Con La A 2017). Over forty plays have been produced with casts of women and men, which include professional actors who rehearse inside the prison. The company has presented and toured work within Spain and to Germany and is recognized by both the theatre community and government departments including Consejeria de Servicios Sociales, Dirección General de la Mujer (Social Services within the remit of the Directorate of Women) and Ministerio del Interior (the government department responsible for public security including prisons). For Cánovas, 'each show serves as a window of communication between the women in prison and the people outside' (O'Connor 2006: 228).

The profile of the company in Madrid's theatre scene is reaffirmed through substantial documentation of Teatro Yeses in Spanish including *Quién Le Puso a Mi Vida Tanta Carcel* (*Who Put So Much Jail in My Life?*) (2001), *Teatro Yeses. Veinte años no es poco 1986–2006* (*Teatro Yeses: Twenty Years Is Not Little*) (2006), *Teatro Yeses: Conciencia, Voluntad y Coraje* (*Theatre Yeses: Consciousness, Will and Courage*) (2017) and Patricia O'Connor's book *Elena Cánovas y Las Yeses: Teatro Carcelario, Teatro Liberador* (2006). The story of Teatro Yeses also inspired Belém Macías' feature film, *Paptio de mi Cárceral* (*The Courtyard of My Prison*) (2008). This fictionalized account of the company, drawing heavily on stock characters of women-in-prison television series and films, focuses on 'un resquicio de libertad por medio del teatro' ('a loophole of freedom through theatre') (Macías 2008), presenting a more romantic or naive frame to the work and the relationships between the characters within it.

Some of the work, such as *Mal Bajío* (1989), has been explicit in critiquing the system from within, while other productions, including *La Balada de la Cárcel de Circe* (2000), have been reprised over the years, offering audience's insight into day-to-day life in prison while directly addressing their questions and assumptions. For Cánovas, Teatro Yeses' work engages with individuals and the circumstances of their lives: 'There are no opinions; the characters are shown exactly as they are. Unlike the disclaimer at the beginning of some films, similarity to real people and events in our work is openly sought' (Canova 2006: 227). Teatro Yeses is unique in being a programme initiated, developed and sustained by a prison officer who has negotiated and secured collaboration with prison authorities and cultural agencies to create an organizational structure that has endured despite political, institutional and social perceptions about the role and value of theatre with and about women in prison.

Introduction 15

Clean Break (UK)

Clean Break is a women-only theatre company that grew out of a prisoner-led drama workshop that took place between 1977 and 1979 in HMP Askham Grange, an open prison in the north-east of England. Over the past four decades it has evolved from a cooperative of women ex-prisoners into an internationally recognized theatre, education and advocacy organization that foregrounds narratives of women, crime and punishment for a wide range of audiences. The workshop regularly tours to theatres, prisons and voluntary-staff training events, as well as to audiences of policy-makers in criminal justice, arts and health. Since 1979, Clean Break has produced over seventy original plays written by women who have experience of prison or by professional writers, mentored by the company, who have undertaken research through residencies in prisons or as part of Clean Break's education programme in its women-only centre.

The conditions which supported the development of Clean Break in HMP Askham Grange are unusual. Like Teatro Yeses, Clean Break was developed from within a prison. However, unlike Teatro Yeses, this practice was organized by incarcerated women rather than prison staff. While HMP Askham Grange had, like many other prisons, a tradition of a Christmas pantomime with prisoners and staff performing ('Panto in a Prison' 1978), it had no formal arts activity programmed by the institution. Jennifer Hicks and Jacqueline Holborough were key to the development of the drama workshop. Prior to her sentence, Holborough had a successful career acting in theatre and television. She met Hicks in HMP Durham's H-wing, which was notorious for its inhumane conditions, having been condemned, a decade earlier, by two government enquiries (Mountbatten 1966; ACPS 1968). Much to the institution's ire, Hicks and Holborough attempted to stage *Trojan Women* and *Jesus Christ Superstar* in the prison yard. Holborough's transfer to Askham Grange ensured that the women's ambitions were foiled. But only temporarily. When Hicks and Holborough met again at HMP Askham Grange, they were supported by the progressive governor, Susan McCormick. After staging a number of productions, including Joe Orton's *Funeral Games* and Agatha Christie's *Black Coffee*, the drama workshop set about writing their own material. While prison regulations stipulated that they couldn't directly address their experiences of incarceration, the group developed a collection of scenes entitled *Efemera*, a play on the words 'feminism' and 'ephemera', staged at a local arts centre under the group title, ASK'EM OUT, a pun on both the prison's name and the social prejudice the women faced (*Efemera* 1980). Once released, Clean Break's work was an explicit indictment of the treatment of women at the hands of the state. Both

Killers (Holborough 1980) and *Decade* (Holborough 1984) expose the material conditions of incarceration at HMP Durham and the historical lack of consideration given to the needs of women in the criminal justice system (Kennedy 1993; McIvor 2004). *24%* (Randall 1991) examines the systemic racism that shapes the lives of young black women, within and beyond the criminal justice system. *Spent* (Chandler 2016) lays bare the implications of austerity and debt on women, crime and justice; and *Joanne* (Bruce, Ikoko, Lomas, Odimba and Sarma 2015) details the crises of care facing many women when released from prison, revealed through the testimony of five front-line workers from education, health, justice and social care. *Joanne* is a State of the Nation play, capturing the long moment of critical impact when the state refuses to attend to those who are most vulnerable within it. Each play exposes women's experiences of structural inequality and violence through criminalization and incarceration, revealing the personal, social, cultural and political implications of the incarceration of women in the UK across the late twentieth and early twenty-first centuries.

In addition to a catalogue of published plays, there are a number of documentaries featuring Clean Break's work during the 1980s and early 1990s – *Women of Durham Jail* (Dir. M. McDoughall 1984), *Sex and Violence in Women's Prisons* (Dir. B. Long 1984), *Killers* (Dir. B. Long 1984) and *Picking Oakum*, (Dir. B. Evans 1991). Clean Break's extensive education programme with women who have experience of the criminal justice system has been evaluated from economic and criminal justice policy perspectives (Abraham and Busby 2015; NCP 2011), trauma-informed practice (Herrmann 2009) and feminist criminology (Merrill and Frigon 2015). There is also growing academic consideration of Clean Break from performance studies, popular criminology and organizational management (Bartley 2019; McAvinchey 2020a, 2020b, 2020c; McPhee 2019, 2020; Walsh 2015, 2018).

International practices and perspectives

These three examples of sustained engagement with and about women's experience of the criminal justice system evidence a range of approaches – both aesthetic and pragmatic – that respond to local political, social and cultural contexts. Because prison theatres operate beyond economies of commercial theatre or theatre for general public audiences, it is almost impossible to undertake a comprehensive survey of international practice. Conversations and correspondence with artists and academics have revealed a more extensive range of international practice than is readily available in

Introduction

traces of work evidenced in leaflets and blogs, feature articles and reviews, evaluations, journal articles and books published by artists, companies, journalists or academics. The following section maps some areas of practice and the documentation of it.

Jean Trounstine's *Shakespeare Behind Bars: One Teacher's Story of the Power of Drama in Women's Prison* (2004) is an account of her ten years of experience of working with women in Framingham Women's Prison in Massachusetts. Trounstine's book focuses on the narratives of six women who participated in the programme, the ways in which they revealed themselves and their reconsideration of the world they lived in through their encounters with Shakespeare. Eve Ensler's work in Bedford Correctional Facility with women serving life sentences is documented in the film, *What I Want My Words to Do to You: Voices from Inside a Women's Maximum Security Prison* (Dir. J. Katz 2003), contributing to a wider body of community literacy practice and consideration of teaching artists working in prisons (Plemons 2013). Since 2005, Judy Dworin's Bridging Boundaries Arts Intervention Program has established cross-arts practice with incarcerated women and their families in York Correctional Institution, Connecticut (2010). Based in Seattle, Pat Graney is a choreographer with a professional dance company that works with women in prison. *Writings from Women on the Inside* (2003) is an edited collection of creative writing by women in prison who have participated in Graney's *Keeping the Faith* programme, which has also been documented by Jessica Berson (2008). *Razor Wire Women* (2011), edited by Ashley Lucas and Jodie Lawson, is a collection of articles, interview transcripts, sections of dramatic texts and visual arts practice written by academics, artists, activists and incarcerated women.

Since it was founded in 1987, Geese Theatre Company has developed interactive theatre and drama-based group work in prisons, community contexts and forensic mental health settings, working with over 250,000 individuals who have offended and those considered to be at risk of offending, and delivering training to over 20,000 professionals working in these environments. Based in Birmingham (England), the company has collaborated with arts and criminal justice agencies internationally, including those in Azerbaijan and Bulgaria. Geese Theatre practitioners are professional actors and group-work facilitators who undertake an intensive six-month training in the company's methodology. Geese are perhaps best known for their distinctive use of mask, engaging both full-face and half-mask, to explore the metaphor of the mask as 'front' or coping strategy. Their work explicitly invites participants and audiences to consider: What masks do we wear? What is revealed when we 'lift the mask'? Louise Heywood, Director of Programmes, talks about the company's purpose:

It might be best to start with our mission statement which is 'to use theatre and drama to enable choice, responsibility and change amongst individuals who have offended, other marginalised groups 'and those who work with them'. Our stance on responsibility is that there are many things in individuals' lives that they have no control over but we work with the bit they do have choices about. For example, a woman has no control over childhood experiences of abuse, but it may be beneficial for her to take steps towards taking control of her present aggressive behaviour which results in imprisonment. We're not about telling people what they need to do, but asking, 'What are the changes you would like to make? We want to know where you are now and where you would like to be and how we can help you with the journey between the two.'

Brown, Cifuentes-Poseck, Heywood and Smallman 2018

The company's work can be divided into three main categories: performances (often interactive, inviting audiences to discuss fictional dilemmas and advise characters), group work (ranging from stand-alone sessions to week-long prison projects, such as *Journey Woman*) and creative projects (in which a group are assisted to create a piece of theatre for an invited audience). The company works with women in four main contexts: women in prison, women on community orders, women in recovery and women who have been victims of domestic abuse. This work is delivered in close collaboration with the agencies who commission each project, whether that be a community organization, such as a women's support service, or a secure institution.

Other long-running programmes of theatre practice with women in prison beyond the UK and USA which will be attended to later in the book include Somebody's Daughter Theatre, an Australian company established in 1980 by Maud Clarke, working extensively with women in prison and post-release and with young women in secure welfare. In addition to developing a substantial and sustained prison partnership between theatre students at the University of Kwa-Zulu Natal, South Africa and Westfield Women's Correctional Facility, Miranda Young Janhangeer is committed to analysing the ongoing critical implications of this (2011, 2013, 2014).

There are also many other projects internationally with less available documentary evidence. In Jordan, Hakeem Harb, a director with a long-standing commitment to bringing theatre to diverse audiences, touring to remote towns and running a children's theatre festival, has developed a theatre workshop in Aljwaida women's prison, developing work that directly addresses patriarchal oppression and its manifestation in the social expectations of women's behaviours (Sheiker 2016). In Lebanon, Zeina Daccache's theatre practices intervene in prisoners' understandings of the

Introduction   19

limitations of the law in protecting their human rights and advocacy to enhance public and political understanding. *Scheherazade in Baabda,* informed by ten months of work with twenty women in Baabda prison, west Lebanon, highlighted the ways in which women are discriminated against through laws, attitudes and practices around divorce, domestic violence, enforced child marriage and custody of children (Stephenson 2014). This particular project was the subject of the film *Scheherazade's Diary* (Dir. Z. Daccache 2013), which exposed a criminal justice system that further punished prisoners beyond the removal of liberty through overcrowding, the inertia of judicial processes and inhuman prison conditions. Based in New York since 1986, Bond Street Theatre develops cross-arts community projects with international partners supporting cross-cultural understanding and humanitarian agendas. Between 2011 and 2014, Bond Street Theatre developed work in prisons in three Afghan provinces – Herat, Kabul and Jalalabad – addressing the ways in which the justice systems further punish incarcerated women (Bond Street 2011; Tjossen 2016). This work also involved training women who then took plays into local communities to stage work that directly engaged with women with issues that affected them. The Drug Treatment Unit of Arohata Prison in Wellington was the setting for *Come Listen to My Story of Wonderland* (2016), a performance devised and performed by women prisoners, actors and musicians, developed with the German director Uta Plate over a nine-day intensive process. The work, while situated in a therapeutic environment, was not explicitly therapeutic in its intentions but rather an exploration of addiction, trauma and barriers to rehabilitation (Arts Access Aotearoa 2016).

In Blantyre, Malawi, Nanzikambe Arts Development Organisation has addressed critical social issues including HIV in prison, access to justice and violence against women through capacity-building programmes. Between 2008 and 2012, Nanzikambe developed an artists' training programme with marginalized groups. Some of the women, trained by Nanzikambe facilitators Dipo Katimba and Effie Makepeace, went on to run regular workshops for women in Chichiri prison. Makepeace (2018) summarizes the rationale and impact of this work:

> We worked with four groups of marginalised people including prisoners and young women from two townships who were identified by the organisation as vulnerable. They were seventeen to twenty-five years old, most had children and were single mums, some were sex workers, all had dropped out of school. The groups would come to Nanzikambe and get a drink and a biscuit. The work was framed as actor training and the groups were thinking of learning, developing an awareness of process, an

20   *Applied Theatre: Women and the Criminal Justice System*

awareness of learning. We worked with them for over four years and many of the group are now employed by Nanzikambe.

Scope and structure

In identifying the work considered in the book, particular methodological considerations were in play. I was keen to attend to work that had limited documentation or academic engagement in order to extend the frames of reference for applied theatre, women and the criminal justice system. It was also important that the theatre practice was part of a sustained engagement with criminalized women rather than a one-off project. The academics and artists who have contributed to the collection have an established commitment to this field, developing partnerships with a specific institution or network of community-based organizations working with women in the criminal justice system.

As the previous section illustrates, there is a considerable range of theatre practice across the globe, taking place in different cultural contexts differently inscribed by politics, economics and faith. This work takes place in a range of languages other than English. The theatre practice addressed in this collection is facilitated and written about in English, and therefore reflects a partial picture of a rich tapestry of practice.

Each of the chapters and interviews contributes to new understandings about the intersectional injustices that shape women's experience of criminalization and the personal and political implications of this. They reveal a panoply of theatre practice – from cross-arts projects shaped by autobiographical narratives through to fantasy-informed cabaret; from process drama to radio plays; from popular participatory theatre to video-making. The examples of work addressed in the book raise critical questions about the audiences for prison theatre – which may include the participants, their families, the institutions, the general public, funding bodies and policy-makers – and the kinds of personal, social and political change that participation may encourage.

In 'Interplay: Tracing Personal and Political Transformation through Popular Participatory Theatre in Westville Female Correctional Centre, Durban South Africa', Miranda Young-Jahangeer examines the relationship between national and personal politics in post-apartheid South Africa and how this has been examined and articulated in a body of popular theatre, facilitated though a long-term prison–university partnership, for more than fifteen years. Ideas of story, storytelling and subjectivity inform Young-Jahangeer's consideration of three distinct, though at times interweaving,

Introduction 21

phases of work which she characterizes as the politics of the issue (2002–4), the politics of identity (2002–10) and the politics of Human Rights (2010–14). Young-Jahangeer considers how interpersonal exchange has enabled women to negotiate cultures of behaviour, develop a criticality and sense of self that has supported them in addressing injustices within the prison and debating the meaning of democracy in a 'new South Africa'.

In '"They Pink Dress Ain't Done Shit": Performing Black *Quare* Activism at a Women's Gulf Coast Prison', Lisa L. Biggs attends to the ways in which the prison's Drama Club members critiqued and contested repressive penal policies that punished women, particularly Black women and transmen, for 'disruptive' gender expression and the wearing of prison uniforms in 'too masculine' a fashion. Biggs frames the Drama Club's theatre practice as Black *quare* community praxis, creating a site of collective resistance and social justice activism that not only revealed the additional punishment of being forced to wear a pink caftan-esque dress but challenged institutional dogma. *Beauty Coming and Going*, devised by the Drama Club, was an explicit staging of alternative perspectives on sexuality, beauty and dress, reclaiming 'the criminalized, Black, queer body as an object of beauty'.

Sarah Woodland's 'Daughters of the Floating Brothel: Engaging Indigenous Australian Women Prisoners through Participatory Radio Drama' examines the historical and contemporary sociopolitical context of the 'crisis of Indigenous over-representation' in women's prisons in Australia. Engaging with trauma-trails, the transgenerational traumas experienced by Indigenous Australians since colonization, storytelling and culturally relevant materials and approaches, Woodland's project at Brisbane Women's Correctional Centre invited a critical consideration of racialized genealogies of punishment and the ways in which different theatrical forms, including radio drama, can support both personal and wider public understanding of them.

In 'What Works: The Affective and Gendered Performance of Prison', Aylwyn Walsh examines the ways in which political ideology writes narratives of reform into penal institutional structures which, in turn, prescribe expectations of gendered behaviours. Interweaving reflections on prison theatre practices in HMP Askham Grange (UK) with a consideration of stigma, shame, affective labour and institutional regimes, Walsh exposes the possibilities of arts practice to negotiate this penal framework, creating opportunities for collaborative resistance, support and the development of humane spaces within the carceral landscape.

Between 2001 and 2003, Lois Weaver and Peggy Shaw led a strand of People's Palace Project's *Staging Human Rights* with women in prison in England and Brazil. Shaw was very clear about the imperative for the work: 'We work with women. Prison is a place where women live' (2003). 'Possible

Fictions: Split Britches, Biography and Fantasy with Women in Prison' provides insight into Shaw's and Weaver's performance-making practices, characterized by a radical playfulness, engaging with biography and fantasy, carefully attending to power, identity and representation, optimistic for the possibilities of performance as a social and political practice.

In 'Theatre as Collective Casework: Clean Break Theatre Company's *Charged* (2010)', Molly McPhee considers Clean Break's production of *Charged*, six short plays staged across the different levels of Soho Theatre, London, and the ways in which this theatrical event demanded audiences' examination of their role in the social co-creation of criminal subjectivities. She engages case theory to explore how *Charged* recreated and challenged the carceral imagery of the criminal woman and how this, in turn, contributes to the material conditions for women to enter the criminal justice system. McPhee argues that, rather than being situated within dramaturgies of imprisonment, Clean Break's work negotiates paradigms of carcerality, carceral society and the carceral power of public perception, drawing audiences' attention to 'the machinations of social stigma at the heart of criminalization'.

Somebody's Daughter Theatre Company has, since 1980, developed an expansive body of theatre practice with women in prison and post-release in Australia. While working in collaboration with government agencies in criminal justice and social welfare, the company is adamant that its theatre practice is engaged with as art, not therapy or social engineering. In 'Somebody's Daughter Theatre Company: The Arts: Unapologetically Transcendent', Maud Clark offers a manifesto for art and makes a compelling case for the continued commitment to offer creative opportunities to those who experience exclusion.

Rachel Conlon's 'The Meeting Place: Collaborative Learning in a University–Prison Partnership' details a long-standing collaboration between York St John University, HMP Askham Grange and HMP New Hall (UK), and illuminates the opportunities and challenges of working across a range of partnerships and the possibilities for collaborative learning they engender. Conlon engages with four different programmes of work: sustained weekly drama practice in a unit that supports vulnerable women; a creative writing and song programme in an open prison; a film project, commissioned by a charity, that addresses the needs of children affected by parental imprisonment; and the collaboration with the team of the Donmar Warehouse's Shakespeare Trilogy (2012–16), staged in a prison, in theatres in London and New York and, through the *Shakespeare Trilogy on Screen* website, available to global audiences.

In 'Acting Out', Ashley Lucas invites Sherin Fitzer, Director of Women and Family Services at Logan Correctional Center who has extensive experience

Introduction 23

teaching and leading theatre projects with women in prison, to reflect on her work with Acting Out, a theatre troupe in a prison in the Midwestern United States. Since 2001, the troupe has performed plays by published playwrights and devised original work including a collaboration with Lucas, a creative response to her play, *Doin' Time: Through the Visiting Glass*, about the experience of people who have family members in prison. The interview attests to the extraordinary networks of professionals from theatre, education and the criminal justice system who, despite the challenges and obstacles of institutional regimes, navigate pathways to collaboration which, in turn, have a direct impact on the culture of a prison and a wider public understanding of the people who live and work within it.

In '"There is Still Life in Me, Despite What I Have Done": Assuaging Woundedness through Collective Creativity', Katharine Low and Clara Vaughan critically reflect on the cultural and historical constructions of well-being, and how these are exposed and negotiated in the context of a drama project in Johannesburg Correctional Centre. Low and Vaughan consider dignity, human interaction and witnessing as values and practices which contribute to well-being – values and practices which are antithetical in the context of a correctional centre, where individuality is erased in the service of managing a disciplined, homogenous group. Rather than argue for the long-term health impacts of arts interventions, Low and Vaughan attend to relational encounters which, though transient and temporary, have significant value in and of themselves, creating an expanded sense of self, witnessed by others.

The Stella Adler Studio is a centre for actor training that, since 1949, has been guided by the principle that growth as an actor and growth as a human being are synonymous. Since 2014, the Stella Adler Studio has run an outreach programme at Rose M. Singer Center for Women at Rikers Island Correctional Facility, a jail complex on the outskirts of New York City. In this interview, Tom Oppenheim, Artistic Director of The Stella Adler Studio, and Joanne Edelmann, Master Teacher of Movement who leads the women's work at Rikers, reflect on the institutional and political contexts which shape the material conditions of the work and how movement, poetry and performance practices have disrupted and critiqued the regime.

Open Clasp's work is informed by the lived experience of working-class girls and women in the north of England, developed in collaboration with professional theatre-makers, often in partnership with voluntary social and support organizations, and toured to community venues as well as regional, national and, at times, international theatres. The company's work is characterized by its commitment to fictionalized authenticity, working with testimony to inform carefully crafted narratives which foreground lives and stories that are too often marginalized from mainstream cultural

24   *Applied Theatre: Women and the Criminal Justice System*

representation or effective political intervention. In 'In Their Shoes: Participation, Social Change and Empathy in Open Clasp's *Key Change*', Kay Hepplewhite examines Open Clasp's first programme of work with women in prison, to consider how the company's approach was challenged and extended by the material and political contexts of its production within the criminal justice system.

I am keenly aware that the voices of the subjects of this book – women with experience of the criminal justice system – are carefully mediated through the accounts of artists and academics who work in solidarity alongside them. Between each chapter and interview, I have included an extract from a Clean Break performance text, written by a woman who has experience of the criminal justice system or who has been commissioned by the company. Each performance text is a critical consideration of women's experiences of structural inequality and violence through criminalization and incarceration. They are precise, visionary, poetic, angry, raw with hurt and, at times, full of humour. But most importantly, these words have been written for theatre, in anticipation of an audience who will bear witness to them, who will take action in response to them.

Notes from the field

By bringing together a range of theatre practices with and about women in criminal justice systems internationally, two thematic concerns are foregrounded.

The importance of research as well as evaluation in prison theatre practices with women

Internationally, over the past three decades, there has been growing recognition by government bodies and charitable foundations of the potential personal, social and economic benefits of the arts in criminal justice settings (Hughes 2005; Flemsburg 2005; Gardner et al. 2014; Caulfield 2018). This is often framed with specific questions: Does prison theatre contribute to criminal justice outcomes? If so, how? How do you prove this? This has led to the development of modes of monitoring and evaluation that attempt to map a causal or correlative link between participation in arts work and how this advances criminal justice outcomes including rehabilitation, desistence from crime, pathways to employment and a reduction in rates of recidivism. This important work has made a major contribution to the economy of credibility

Introduction   25

in the wider field of prison theatre. However, it is imperative that the terms of reference and language used for developing and analysing prison theatre are not limited to only consider the value of this work in relation to criminal justice outcomes. It is an urgent necessity that artists, academics and funders engage with the social, cultural and political implications of the intersectional oppressions reinscribed on criminalized bodies as they are processed within legal and penal frameworks. Evaluations of theatre practices with women in criminal justice systems cannot engage with a consideration of the complex relationships between individuals and the state – an examination of concepts of justice and the legal structures that affect them are beyond any evaluative remit, and they do not attend to the gap between the cultural representations of women who transgress legal and social norms and the lived experience of individuals masked by them. This book, while acknowledging the role of evaluation, prioritizes research, focusing on new understandings that unfold through theatre and performance practices with and about women in different criminal justice systems. This, in turn, highlights the contribution of universities in the development of prison theatre programmes and academic research in the field. Many of the projects addressed in this collection are the result of sustained relationships, fostered by academics who have negotiated and developed partnerships – often through teaching and community outreach programmes – which are, in some ways, protected from the shifting priorities of commissioning bodies, setting an agenda that responds to the needs of the women they work with.

The imperative for an expanded representational vocabulary of criminalised women's experience

Earlier in this Introduction, I referenced Jill Dolan's rallying call to those who make, consume and critique cultural work to attend to the choices we make in our practices, inviting us to interrogate who and what is made visible and who and what is invisible, 'to refocus the lens, to see from the side, as it were, where all the holes in the narrative are suddenly clear, and where all its presumptions and exclusions are most transparent' (2013: 9). The theatre practices engaged with in *Applied Theatre: Women and the Criminal Justice System* explode 'presumptions and exclusions' about criminalized women to reveal the material conditions and social implications of gendered experiences of poverty, racism and abuse. However, additionally, these practices offer an opportunity to address what the feminist philosopher Miranda Fricker has identified as 'epistemic injustices', identified specifically as testimonial injustice and hermeneutic injustice (2010: 1).

Fricker proposes that: 'Testimonial injustice occurs when prejudice causes a hearer to give a deflated level of credibility to a speaker's word [...]. An example [...] might be that the police do not believe you because you are black' (2010: 1). Hermeneutical injustice occurs, Fricker argues, 'when a gap in collective interpretative resources puts someone at an unfair disadvantage when it comes to making sense of their social experiences; [...] an example [...] might be that you suffer sexual harassment in a culture that still lacks that critical concept' (2010: 1). If cultural forms articulate ideological positions that negate the experience of criminalized women, or who are represented only as being other or socially deviant, then the kind of testimony offered through them is limited. This is epistemic injustice. I propose that the theatre and performance practices identified in this collection – their approaches, narratives and representations – act as testimony, offering new understandings and perspectives on the world. These practices attend to both the testimonial and hermeneutic injustice faced by women whose lives are shaped by the violence of societal structures of disadvantage. This theatre and performance practice expands the cultural vocabularies of representations of women, crime and justice, enhancing societies' collective interpretive resources; they attend to the lived experience of those who are too often invisible, on and off the cultural mainstage, and they contribute to understanding about the societal structural disadvantage that informs the lives of many women who offend. While all of these practices directly engage with the lived reality of women who are affected by the criminal justice system, the ways in which they do this are necessarily varied, using theatre and performance to reconfigure the representational landscape to see beyond facts, figures and statistics to the particularity of the individual lives blurred by them.

Theatre with criminalized women, framed as testimonial justice, has the potential to contribute to new understandings about the role of incarceration as a mechanism of state punishment, the impact of neoliberalism on ideologies of punishment and the intersectional inequality and violence on women's lives enmeshed in societal structures of disadvantage. In a context where women in the criminal justice system are too often dismissed as unreliable or untrustworthy, these theatre practices facilitate the creation of an economy of credibility where women are represented as expert witnesses.

Notes

1 https://www.artsincriminaljustice.org.uk/evidence-library/.
2 https://www.donmarwarehouse.com/production/10013/shakespeare-trilogy/.

References

Abraham, N. and S. Busby (2015), *Celebrating Success: How has Participation in Clean Break's Theatre Education Programme Contributed to Individuals' Involvement in Professional or Community Arts Practices?*, London: Central School of Speech and Drama.

Adams, K., Bennett, K. and T. Flanagan (1994), 'A Large-Scale Multidimensional Test of the Effect of Prison Education Programs on Offenders' Behaviour', *The Prison Journal* 74(4): 433–49.

Advisory Council on the Penal System (ACPS) (1968), 'The Regime for Long-Term Prisoners in Conditions of Maximum Security' (Radzinowicz Report), London: HMSO.

Agozino, B. (1997), *Black Women and the Criminal Justice System: Toward the Decolonisation of Victimisation*, Abingdon and New York: Routledge.

Ahmed, S. (2004), 'Affective Economies', *Social Text* 22(2): 117–39.

Annison, J., Brayford, J. and J. Deering (2015), *Women and Criminal Justice: From the Corston Report to Transforming Rehabilitation*, Bristol: Policy Press.

Arts Access Aotearoa (2016), 'Empowering Women in Arohata Prison through Theatre', 30 March. Available online: https://artsaccess.org.nz/Empowering+women+in+Arohata+Prison+through+theatre (accessed 1 June 2018).

Atwood, M. (2016), *Hag-Seed*, London: Vintage.

Baily, F. and D. Hale (eds) (1998), *Popular Culture, Crime and Justice*, Belmont CA: West/Wadsworth.

Baim, C., Brooks, S. and A. Mountford (2002), *The Geese Theatre Handbook: Drama with Offenders and People at Risk*, Hook, Hampshire: Waterside Press.

Balfour. M. (ed.) (2004), *Theatre in Prisons: Theory and Practice*, Bristol: Intellect.

Barnet, B. (2006), 'Medea in the Media: Narrative and Myth in Newspaper Coverage of Women Who Kill Their Children', *Journalism* 7(4): 411–32.

Bartley, S. (2019), 'Gendering Welfare Onstage: Acts of Reproductive Labour in Applied Theatre', *Contemporary Theatre Review* 29(3).

Berson, J. (2008), 'Baring and Bearing Life Behind Bars: Pat Graney's "Keeping the Faith" Prison Performance Project', *The Drama Review* 53(8): 79–93.

Bradshaw, S. (2002), *Gendered Poverties and Power Relations: Looking Inside Communities and Households*, Managua: ICD, Embajada de Holanda, Puntos de Encuentro.

Brewster, L. (1983), 'An Evaluation of the Arts-in-corrections Program of the California Department of Corrections California', California Department of Corrections.

Brown, L., Cifuentes-Poseck, A., Heywood, L. and E. Smallman (2017), Interview with the author, 31 March, Geese offices, Birmingham.

Brown, M. (2009), *The Culture of Punishment: Prison, Society, and Spectacle*, New York: New York University Press.

Bruce, D., Ikoko, T., Lomas, L., Odimba, C. and U. Sarma (2015), *Joanne*, London: Nick Hern Books.

28   *Applied Theatre: Women and the Criminal Justice System*

Cánovas, E., Talavera, J. and R. Cobos (2001), *Quién Le Puso a Mi Vida Tanta Carcel* (Who Put So Much Jail in My Life?), Madrid: Comunidad de Madrid, Consejeria de Servicios Sociales, Dirección General de la Mujer.

Cánovas, E. (2006), *Teatro Yeses. Veinte años no es poco 1986–2006*, Madrid: Ministerio del Interior.

Cánovas E. (2017), *Teatro Yeses: Conciencia, Voluntad y Coraje*, Madrid: Editorial Fundamentos.

Carlen, P. (2013), 'Against Rehabilitation: For Reparative Justice', *Criminal Justice Matters* 91(1): 32–3.

Caulfield, L. and E. Simpson (2018), 'Arts-based Interventions in the Justice System', in Ugwudike, P., Raynor, P., McNeill, F., Taxman, F., Trotter, C. and H. Graham (eds), *The Routledge Companion to Rehabilitative Work in Criminal Justice*, 396–408, Abingdon: Routledge.

Chelitois, L. (2016), *The Arts of Imprisonment: Control, Resistance and Empowerment*, Abingdon and New York: Routledge.

Christensen, K. (2018), 'Rhodessa Jones and The Medea Project: A Sisterhood of Healing', *Seismic Sisters*, 24 October. Available online: https://www. seismicsisters.com/newsletter/2018/9/6/medea-project (accessed 1 June 2018).

Clarke, M. (2004), 'Somebody's Daughter Theatre: Celebrating Difference with Women in Prison', in M. Balfour (ed.), *Theatre in Prisons: Theory and Practice,* 101–6, Bristol: Intellect.

Coady, C. A. J. (1995), *Testimony: A Philosophical Study*, Oxford and New York: Clarendon Press.

Con La A (2017), 'El Grupo de Teatro Yeses y Elena' in *Con La A*. Available online: https://conlaa.com/el-grupo-de-teatro-yeses-elena-canovas/ (accessed 1 August 2018).

Corston, J. (2007), *The Corston Report: A Report by Baroness Jean Corston of a Review of Women with Particular Vulnerabilities in the Criminal Justice System*, London: Crown Copyright.

Cox, M. (ed.) (1992), *Shakespeare Comes to Broadmoor: The Actors are Come Hither. The Performance of Tragedy in a Secure Psychiatric Hospital*, London: Jessica Kingsley.

Coyle, A. (2003), *Humanity in Prison: Questions of Definition and Audit*, London: International Centre for Prison Studies.

Coyle, A., Fair, H., Jacobson, J. and R. Walmsley (2016), *Imprisonment Worldwide: The Current Situation and an Alternative Future*, London: Policy Press.

Davis, A. (2003), *Are Prisons Obsolete?* New York: Seven Stories Press.

DfES & HM Prison Service (2003), 'Getting Our Act Together: Literacy through Drama in Prisons: A Manual for the Delivery of Basic Skills Communication through Drama', Canterbury: Unit for the Arts and Offenders.

Dolan, J. (2013), *The Feminist Spectator in Action: Feminist Criticism for the Stage and Screen*, Basingstoke: Palgrave Macmillan.

Dreisinger, B. (2017), *Incarceration Nations: A Journey to Justice in Prisons Around the World*, New York: Other Press.

Introduction 29

Dworin, J. (2010), 'Time In: Transforming Identity Inside and Out', in J. Shailor (ed.), *Performing New Lives: Prison Theatre*, 83–101, London: Jessica Kingsley.

Efemera (1978), Original programme for Ask'Em Out. Personal archive of J. Holborough.

Ensler, E. (2003), *What I Want My Words to Do to You: Voices from Inside a Women's Maximum Security Prison*. Dir. J. Katz. USA.

Fayad Skeiker, F. (2016), 'Prison Theatre in Jordan', *The Theatre Times*, 23 August. Available online: https://thetheatretimes.com/prison-theatre-jordan/ (accessed 12 June 2018).

Fitch, C., Hamilton, S., Bassett, P. and R. Davey (2011), 'The Relationship between Personal Debt and Mental Health: A Systematic Review', *Mental Health Review Journal* 16: 153–66.

Flensburg, M. (2005), 'Prison Theatre in Sweden – Report for the EU project "Teatro e Carcere in Europa"', translated by Clare James. Available online: http://www.teatroecarcere.net/download/46_SwedenResultsEn.pdf (accessed 1 June 2018).

Foss, K. (ed.) (2018), *Demystifying the Big House: Exploring Prison Experience and Media Representations*, Carbondale: Southern Illinois University Press.

Fraden, R. (1994), *Imagining Medea: Rhodessa Jones and Theatre for Incarcerated Women*, Chapel Hill: University of North Carolina.

Fricker, M. (2010), *Epistemic Injustice: Power and the Ethics of Knowing*, Oxford: University of Oxford Press.

Gardner, A., Hager, L. and G. Hillman (2014), 'Prison Arts Resource Project: An Annotated Bibliography', Washington: National Endowment of the Arts.

Garland, D. (1990), *Punishment and Modern Society: A Study of Social Theory*, New York: Oxford University Press.

Garland, D. (2018), *Punishment and Welfare: A History of Penal Strategies*, New Orleans: Quid Pro, LL.

Genders, E. and E. Player (2014), 'Rehabilitation, Risk Management and Prisoners' Rights', *Criminology and Criminal Justice* 14(4): 434–57.

Graney, P. (ed.) (2003), *Writings from Women on the Inside,* Seattle: Pat Graney Company.

Gunnison, E. and F. Bernat (2016), *Women, Crime and Justice: Balancing the Scales*, Chichester: Wiley-Blackwell.

Heritage, P. (2002), *Interim Report: Staging Human Rights Year 1*, London: People's Palace Projects, QMUL.

Heritage, P. (2002), 'Stealing Kisses', in M. Delgado and C. Svich (eds), *Theatre in Crises: Performance Manifestos for a New Century*, 166–78, Manchester: Manchester University Press.

Heritage, P. (2004), 'Taking Hostages', *The Drama Review* 48(3): 96–106.

Herold, N. (2014), *Prison Shakespeare and the Purpose of Performance: Repentance Rituals and the Early Modern*, Basingstoke: Palgrave Macmillan.

Herrmann, A. (2009), '"The Mothership": Sustainability and Transformation in the Work of Clean Break', in S. Preston and T. Prentki (eds), *The Applied Theatre Reader*, 328–35, Abingdon and New York: Routledge.

30   *Applied Theatre: Women and the Criminal Justice System*

Hewish, S. (2001), 'Interactive Intervention Programmes for Sex, Violent and Persistent Offenders: Final Report', Acting Out Company and Stoke-on-Trent Youth Offending Team.

Holborough, J. (1980), *Killers* (unpublished play text). Clean Break archives, Bishopsgate Institute, London.

Holborough, J. (1984), *Decade* (unpublished play text). Clean Break archives, Bishopsgate Institute, London.

Hughes, J. (1998), 'Resistance and Expression: Working with Women Prisoners and Drama', in J. Thompson (ed.), *Prison Theatre: Perspectives and Practices*, 231–8, London: Jessica Kingsley.

Hughes, J. (2005), *Doing the Arts Justice: A Review of Research Literature, Practice and Theory*, Canterbury: The Unit for The Arts and Offenders.

Joseph, J. (2019), *Inside Bitch*. Post-show discussion at the Royal Court Theatre, London. 12 March.

Kennedy, H. (1993), *Eve Was Framed: Women and British Justice*, London: Vintage.

Kennedy, H. (2018), *Eve was Shamed: How British Justice is Failing Women*, London: Chatto & Windus.

Lombrosco, C. and G. Ferrero (2004), *Criminal Woman, the Prostitute, and the Normal Woman*, translated with a new introduction by M. Gibson and N. Hahn Rafter, Durham, NC: Duke University Press.

Lucas, A. and J. Lawson (2011), *Razor Wire Women: Prisoners, Activists, Scholars and Artists*, New York: SUNY Press.

Lucas, A. (2020), *Prison Theatre and the Global Crisis of Incarceration*, London: Bloomsbury.

Machtinger, E., Lavin, M., Starr Hiliard, M., Jones, R., Haberer, J., Capito, K. and C. Dawson-Rose (2015), 'An Expressive Therapy Group Disclosure Intervention for Women Living with HIV Improves Social Support, Self-efficacy, and the Safety and Quality of Relationships: A Qualitative Analysis', *Journal of the Association of Nurses in AIDS Care* 26(2): 187–98.

Macias, B. (2008), 'The Courtyard of My Prison – Director's Notes', *La Higuera*. Available online: https://www.lahiguera.net/cinemania/pelicula/3604/comentario.php (accessed 1 August 2018).

Maguire, T. (2006), *Making Theatre in Northern Ireland: Through and Beyond the Troubles*, Exeter: University of Exeter Press.

Makepeace, E. (2018,) Interview with the author. 26 June. QMUL, London.

Mauer, M. (1999), *Race to Incarcerate*, New York: New Press.

Mauer, M. (2002), *Invisible Punishment: The Collateral Consequences of Mass Incarceration*, New York: New Press.

Mauer, M. (2016), 'Thinking about Prison and its Impact in the Twenty-first Century', *Ohio State Journal of Criminal Law* 2: 607–18.

Merrill, E. and S. Frigon (2015), 'Performative Criminology and the "State of Play" for Theatre with Criminalized Women', *Societies* 5(2): 1–19.

McAvinchey, C. (2007), *Possible Fictions: The Testimony of Applied Performance with Women in Prison in England and Brazil*. PhD Thesis, QMUL.

Introduction 31

McAvinchey, C. (2011), *Theatre & Prison*, Basingstoke: Palgrave Macmillan.

McAvinchey, C. (2017), 'The Performance of Prison Theatre Practices: Questions of Evidence', in M. Reason and N. Rowe (eds), *Evidence and Impact in Theatre, Music and Art*, 139–54, Basingstoke: Palgrave Macmillan.

McAvinchey, C. (2020a), 'Clean Break: A Practical Politics of Care', in A. Stuart Fisher and J. Thompson (eds), *Performing Care*, Manchester: Manchester University Press.

McAvinchey, C. (2020b), 'Bad Girls, Monsters and Chicks in Chains: Clean Break's Disruption of Representations of Women, Crime and Incarceration', in A. Lucas (ed.), *Prison Theatre and the Global Crisis of Incarceration*, London: Bloomsbury.

McAvinchey, C. (2020c), '"Something about Us": Clean Break's Theatre of Necessity', in M. Kelly and C. Weston (eds), *Prison Writing and the Literary World*, Oxford: Oxford University Press.

McCorkel, J. (2013), *Breaking Women: Gender, Race and the New Politics of Imprisonment*, New York: New York University Press.

McDonnell, B. (2008), *Theatre of the Troubles: Theatre, Resistance and Liberation in Ireland*, Exeter: Exeter University Press.

McIvor, G. (ed.) (2004), *Women Who Offend*, London and New York: Jessica Kingsley.

McPhee, M. (2019), 'Miasmatic Performance: Women and Resistance in Carceral Climates', *Performance Research* 23(3): 100–11.

McPhee, M. (2019), '"I don't know why she's crying": Contagion and Criminality in Clean Break's *Dream Pill* and *Little on the Inside*', in F. Walsh (ed.), *Theatres of Contagion: Transmitting Early Modern to Contemporary Performance*, 121–35, London: Bloomsbury.

Miles, A. (2004), 'What Works in Offender Rehabilitation: Revealing the Contribution of the Arts', in J. Cowling (ed.), *For Art's Sake? Society and the Arts in the 21st Century*, 107–19, London: Institute for Public Policy Research.

Moore, L. and P. Scranton (2014), *The Incarceration of Women: Punishing Bodies, Breaking Spirits*, Basingstoke: Palgrave Macmillan.

Moran, D. (2018), *Carceral Geography: Spaces and Practices of Incarceration*, Abingdon and New York: Routledge.

Mountbatten of Burma, Lord (1966), *Report of the Inquiry into Prison Escapes and Security*, London: HMSO.

NCP (2011), *Unlocking Value: The Economic Benefit of the Arts in Criminal Justice*, London: New Philanthropy Capital.

O'Connor, P. (2006), *Mujeres Sobre Mujeres en Los Albores del Siglo XXI: Teatro Breve Español / One Act Spanish Plays by Women About Women Written in the Early Years of the 21st Century* [Bilingual Edition], Madrid: Editorial Fundamentos.

O'Connor, P. (ed.) (2009), *Elena Canovas y Las Yeses: Teatro Carcelario, Teatro Liberador*, Madrid: Editorial Fundamentos.

32 *Applied Theatre: Women and the Criminal Justice System*

Palau, M. (2018), 'Colombia prisoners regain self-esteem through theatre', BBC News, 8 January. Available online: https://www.bbc.co.uk/news/world-latin-america-42493885 (accessed 8 January 2018).

'Panto in a prison' (1978), *Yorkshire Evening Post*, 1 February. Clean Break archives, Bishopsgate Institute, London.

Paptio de mi Cárceral (The Courtyard of my Prison) (2008), Dir. B. Macías. Spain: Deseo Productions.

Pappas, A. and R. Jones (2017), 'Not your Mother's Theater: Rhodessa Jones and the Medea Project', *Open Space*, 28 June. Available online: https://openspace.sfmoma.org/2017/06/not-your-mothers-theater-rhodessa-jones-and-the-medea-project/ (accessed 1 August 2018).

Pensalfini, R. (2016), *Prison Shakespeare: For These Deep Shames and Great Indignities*, Basingstoke: Palgrave Macmillan.

Phelan, P. (1993), *Unmarked: The Politics of Performance*, Abingdon and New York: Routledge.

Plemons, A. (2013), 'Literacy as an Act of Creative Resistance: Joining the Work of Incarcerated Teaching Artists at a Maximum-Security Prison', *Community Literacy Journal* 7(2): 39–52.

Punzo, A. (2013), *È ai vinti che va il suo amore. I primi venticinque anni di autoreclusione con la Compagnia della Fortezza di Volterra (His Love is for the Vanquished. The First Twenty-Five Years of Self-Closure with the Compagnia della Fortezza di Volterra)*, Beauberg.

Ramsbotham, D. (1997), *Women in Prison: A Thematic Review*, London: Home Office.

Randall, P. (1991), *24%*. Unpublished play text. Clean Break archives, Bishopsgate Institute, London.

Rafter, N. and M. Brown (2011), *Criminology Goes to the Movies: Crime Theory and Popular Culture,* New York: New York University Press.

Rickford, D. (2015), *Troubled Inside: Responding to the Mental Health Needs of Women in Prison*, London: Prison Reform Trust.

Rosen, M. (2015), 'The Medea Project's "Birthright"? A Powerful Voice for Women', *SFGate,* 13 April. Available online: https://www.sfgate.com/performance/article/The-Medea-Project-s-Birthright-a-powerful-6192061.php (accessed 12 October 2018).

Schenwar, M. (2014), *Locked Down, Locked Out: Why Prison Doesn't Work and How We Can Do Better*, Oakland, CA: Berrett-Koehler Publishers.

Schmeichen, B. (2017), *Birthright? Medea Project Women Speak Out: Reproductive Rights, Rape, HIV – Stories of Heartbreak and Healing.* Available online: https://www.filmmakerscollaborative.org/birthright (accessed 12 October 2018).

Schnaffer Goldberg, G. (2009), *Poor Women in Rich Countries: The Feminization of Poverty Over the Life Course*, New York: Oxford University Press.

Scott-Douglass, A. (2007), *Shakespeare Inside: The Bard Behind Bars*, London: Continuum.

Sewell, A. (2018), 'On A Theater's Stage, Inmates Get A Taste Of Freedom'. Available online: https://www.good.is/articles/lebanon-prison-therapy (accessed 12 October 2018).

Shailor, J. (ed.) (2010), *Performing New Lives: Prison Theatre*, London: Jessica Kingsley.

Sharpe, G. (2012), *Offending Girls: Young Women and Youth Justice*, Abingdon and New York: Routledge.

Stephenson, J. (2014), '"A peaceful, constructive riot": How prison theatre is changing policy in Lebanon', 8 May. Available online: https://newint.org/features/web-exclusive/2014/05/08/prison-theatre-lebanon (accessed 12 June 2018).

Stern, V. (1998), *A Sin Against the Future: Imprisonment in the World*, Boston, MA: Northeastern University.

Thompson, J. (ed.) (1998), *Prison Theatre: Perspectives and Practices*, London: Jessica Kingsley.

Tjossem, N. (2016), '"That Sh*t's Global" – Women Taking Theater Behind, and Beyond Bars', Extended Play. Available online: http://extendedplay.thecivilians.org/that-shits-global-theater-in-prisons-31616/ (accessed 12 October 2018).

Trounstine, J. (2004), *Shakespeare Behind Bars: One Teacher's Story of the Power of Drama in Women's Prison*, Ann Arbor: University of Michigan Press.

Wacquant, L. (2011), *Deadly Symbiosis: Race and the Rise of the Penal State*, Cambridge: Polity Press.

Walmsley, R. (2017a), 'World Female Imprisonment List. Fourth Edition. Women and Girls in Penal Institutions, Including Pre-trial Detainees/Remand Prisoners', London: Institute for Criminal Policy Research.

Walmsley, R. (2017b), 'World Prison Population List. Eleventh Edition', London: Institute for Criminal Policy Research.

Walsh, A. (2015), 'Staging Women in Prisons: Clean Break Theatre Company's Dramaturgy of the Cage', *Crime, Media, Culture: An International Journal* 12(3): 309–26.

Walsh, A. (2018), 'Performing Punishment, Transporting Audiences: Clean Break Theatre Company's Sweatbox', *Prison Service Journal*, 239: 22–6.

Ward, S. and R. Connolly (2018), 'The Play is a Prison: The Discourse of Prison Shakespeare', *Studies in Theatre and Performance*, 25 December.

Warner, S. (2004), 'Work in SA in Johannesburg Prison (2012). The Medea Project: Mythic Theater for Incarcerated Women', *Feminist Studies: The Prison Issue* 30(2): 483–509.

Weaver, L. (2009), 'Doing Time: A Personal and Practical Account of Performance Work in Prison', in S. Preston and T. Prentki (eds), *The Applied Theatre Reader*, 55–62, Abingdon and New York: Routledge.

Whitley, K. (2012), 'Monstrous, Demonic and Evil: Media Constructs of Women Who Kill' in D. Bissler and J. L. Conners (eds), *The Harms of Crime Media: Essays on Racism, Sexism and Class Stereotype*, 91–110, North Caroline: McFarland.

Women in Prison (2017), *The Corston Report 10 Years On: How Far Have We Come on the Road to Reform for Women Affected by the Criminal Justice System?* London: Women in Prison.

Young-Jahangeer, M. (2011), 'Acting out HIV/Aids Behind Bars: The Appropriation of Theatre for Social Change in the Renegotiation of Behaviours around HIV/Aids', in D. Francis (ed.), *Acting on HIV: Using Drama to Create Possibilities for Change*, 103–18, Rotterdam: Sense Publishers.

Young-Jahangeer, M. (2013), '"Less than a dog": Interrogating Theatre for Debate in Westville Female Correctional Centre, Durban South Africa', *Research in Drama Education. The Journal of Applied Theatre and Performance* 18(2): 96–200.

Young-Jahangeer, M. (2014), 'Panoptic Spaces, Democratic Places? Unlocking Culture and Sexuality through Popular Performance in Westville Female Correctional Centre, Durban, KwaZulu-Natal, South Africa', in H. Barnes and M. Coetzee (eds), *Applied Drama/Theatre as Social Intervention in Conflict and Post-Conflict Contexts*, 18–32, Cambridge: Cambridge Scholars Publishing.

Zhang, X. (2017), 'Prison Theatre as Method: Focused Ethnography and Auto-ethnography in a Chinese Prison', in S. Fletcher and H. White (eds), *Emerging Voices: Critical Social Research by European Group Postgraduate and Early Career Researchers*, 295–309, London: EG Press.

Wicked (1991)

Bryony Lavery

Rosie I thought about that place . . . Pompeii . . . where that volcano erupted and all the lava just covered everything and everybody was stuck doing what they was doing that day, and I thought, suppose that happened here, this prison suddenly gets swamped with lava and hundreds of years later somebody like me is digging and finds this prison and all these women stuck doing what they was doing that day, what would the person digging think? I tried to get my head around that. They'd find this building full, full of women. 'What this all about then?' That's what the archeologist would say. A building full of women. Why did these women live all together? Were they some sort of holy order? Was it . . . a brothel? Was it a place where women could go and enjoy each other's company? They all seem to be in together, in these small rooms. Then, when they swept away some of the dust, they'd find that some of these women wore the same clothes and had these belts with metal objects on them. Was that a type of jewellery, wonders the archeologist. And then the archeologist says, 'Wait a minute . . . this is a key!!!' All these women in the same clothes have got the same keys . . . and the women in the same clothes are all outside the rooms with the other women inside. And the archeologist suddenly puts it all together . . . 'Sussed it!' she says, 'The women in this place must be very, very important in some way, very, very special with very mighty powers because why else would they be so carefully watched over and kept safe?'

131–2

Bryony Lavery's *Wicked* (1991) was the first play Clean Break commissioned by a writer who didn't have personal experience of the criminal justice system. Three actors play twelve characters, including a trio of singing, dancing prison officers – the Screw Sisters – in a production that draws on vaudeville, cabaret, verse and farce to critique societal expectations of femininity, gender, crime and punishment. The character Baily, a reference to the Old Bailey, the Central Criminal Court in England and Wales, is a showman and wordsmith who represents the criminal justice system and his collection of 'freakiest', 'weirdest', 'shockingest' showgirls – Evvie, Banshee and Zombie (92) – are characters sculpted by institutional sexism which informs the criminal justice system's treatment of them.

1

Interplay: Tracing Personal and Political Transformation through Popular Participatory Theatre in Westville Female Correctional Centre, Durban, South Africa

Miranda Young-Jahangeer

Introduction: A transformational politics

My narrative of facilitating prison theatre in a South African women's correctional centre for the past nineteen years begins in a bedsit in West London in 1999. It was there, one chilly Sunday morning, that I came across a newspaper article on Geese Theatre Company. I had never heard of theatre being done inside a prison before. The idea was thrilling. South Africa was a fledgling democracy with crime on the increase. I was in London temping to fund travel. It was an incredible adventure, but it was the Mandela era and my Masters in Applied Theatre wasn't going to be of any use. This frustrated me. I began to cut out the article with a growing sense of purpose and by the time I had finished I had made the decision to return home and be part of the future of South Africa. After a series of uncannily synchronicitous experiences, within six months I was making plays with women in Westville Female Correctional Centre.[1]

I have chosen to open this chapter with this brief narrative for a number of reasons. First, this work since its inception has been about stories and storytelling as a form and strategy of transformation. Postcolonial feminists (Mohanty and Torres 1991) emphasize the necessity for women on the margins who have been 'written out' of history to use theatre, poetry and literature to sing, dance and act their way back into their own truths in order to manifest personal and political change.

Second, this narrative is my narrative. Although this chapter will focus on the narratives that the women have told, *I* am telling this story. I am a part of it, as is my subjectivity. Too often when writing up applied theatre work with communities, all the focus is on the impacts of the project/s on the participants

38   *Applied Theatre: Women and the Criminal Justice System*

(Guerra 2015). The facilitator remains a faceless catalyst. This, according to Tim Prentki, is dangerous: 'Facilitation requires a constant, dialectical flow between facilitator and participants … If only one party is open to the possibility of alteration, we are in the territory of the monolithic expert imparting higher level knowledge to those less intellectually gifted' (2015: 76). In light of South Africa's very recent political past, it was fundamental that the deconstruction of this binary was integral to the work.

With the theatre projects at WFCC, developing critical consciousness through dialogue (Freire 1970) has therefore been both the objective and an integral part of the pedagogical process of the theatre-making. This implies fostering both a political reading of the world and yourself in it. As a white, middle-class South African woman who grew up under apartheid and benefited from its racist advantages, this 'dialectical flow' has been essential not only in our respective transformation but in providing the proverbial 'jailer's key' which opened the gate to glimpses of freedom – alternative realities.

Lastly, this chapter is about tracing transformation and my observations around the interplay of national and personal politics as performed by the women of Westville. Democracy catapulted South Africa into rapid transformation. Although current debates centre on how little has changed for the economically marginalized (Mbembe 2014), the country has indeed seen profound change. Every conceivable landscape has been altered: physical, ideological and political.

The then head of education at Westville Correctional Facility, Pooben Pillay, who was employed during the political changeover of the mid-1990s, recounts an 'almost overnight transformation' (personal conversations 2003) from secrecy to an air of transparency. During apartheid, prisons had become closed institutions (Oppler 1998), which meant that all media and outside inspections were prohibited. Any inhumane and torturous activity could therefore go unchecked, and it did. Further, to add to the performance of power (Foucault 1977; Kershaw 1999) so evident in the prison system globally, the prisons were run on militaristic lines with staff ranked as paramilitary personnel although they were merely civil servants (Oppler 1998).

Without doubt, the prioritizing of the prison system as a focal point of transformation had much to do with the legacy of political prisoners (Nelson Mandela – the newly elected president – being the quintessential example). This brought to the new grand narrative of the country an understanding around the relativity of crime. Unfortunately, with the rise in crime post-democracy, this is now in constant contestation as many cry, 'Bring back the death penalty!'

Interplay 39

Nevertheless, the shift in policy from punitive to a rehabilitatory approach was profound. In the revised Correctional Services Act (1998: 16), it is stipulated that, in their aim of promoting a just, peaceful and safe society, the Department of Correctional Services (DCS) must protect and promote 'human dignity ... social responsibility and human development of all prisoners'. Prisons at this time were thus open to alternative approaches, which could assist them in fulfilling this mandate. Thus, in 1996, the DCS introduced recreational activities for the first time and, in 2000, the popular participatory theatre (PPT) programmes (Kerr 1995) began in WFCC.[2]

Popular participatory (prison) theatre

PPT is a form of applied theatre (AT) most akin to Theatre for Development (TfD) (Prentki 2015; Kerr 1995). As its name suggests, this form has as its objective the broad, problematic term 'development'. The community, with the guidance of a facilitator, devises the plays. They are typically never scripted or titled and remain fluid and improvisational. Popular theatrical forms of the participant community (in this instance, Zulu song, dance and games) infuse the performance.

Within TfD a range of theatre forms exist and, while current literature (Prentki 2015) emphasizes its roots in dialogic pedagogy (Freire 1970), its past and present manifestations still often display 'the anomaly of participation' (Kidd and Byram 1982; Mda 1993), a mere cliché to impress funders with no real substance. PPT is a form that aims to distinguish itself from these exhortatory examples. It is politically motivated and was conceived here with the intention to open up spaces of democratic debate inside the heart of the prison. In that respect, the work in the prison is perceived as neither rehabilitation nor therapy.

Although the programmes have yielded numerous pro-social impacts (Young-Jahangeer 2002), the focus has been concerned with collective and communal accountability. The old Zulu proverb, 'umunthu umunthu ngabanthu' ('a person is a person because of people'), sums up our philosophical base. This idea is well aligned with the Marxist–Socialist philosophy underpinning Freire's pedagogy, a seminal influence in this form, and emerges out of a politics that has noted the marginalization of African and female communities' 'ways of knowing' (Chilisa and Preece 2005: 33) and seeks to counter it.

Consequently, within less than a year, four powerful women inside had become my 'co-investigators' functioning as co-facilitators and partners in all aspects of the programmes. Thus the methodology in many respects freed me

40   *Applied Theatre: Women and the Criminal Justice System*

from being 'the white woman in the centre', as did the fact that, although the majority of women participating in the projects are fluent in English, the plays and much of the dialogue is in isiZulu, a language I am not fluent in. This allows me to experience the benefits of exclusion (Bharucha 2000).

The Prison Theatre projects operate as part of the Drama and Performance Studies curriculum at the University of KwaZulu-Natal.[3] Initially there was one undergraduate course, and Drama students and inmates worked separately (but with facilitation) over two months to devise plays on an issue. On a given Saturday, we bussed students into the Prison en masse to spend a morning of play-exchange.[4] Debate around these issues became complex and detailed. Part of the strategy was to upend conventional binaries of educated/ uneducated by repositioning the inmates as experts.

In 2002, we introduced a second programme involving postgraduate students in a course entitled Theatre for Debate. Here, students work in the prison intensely over a period of a month. Their role is to co-facilitate inmates in the creation of a participatory play that stimulates discussion for an audience of other female inmates.

There are a number of characteristics shared across this body of plays: they were devised and never scripted, without titles or even fixed character assignations, and actresses can switch roles that they have rehearsed for the final performance. Mostly their character names are their own names.

My analysis of the key concerns/issues articulated by the prison theatre at WFCC over the past fifteen years will be the focus for the second half of this chapter. If we understand that 'it is the social actors who use the conceptual systems of their culture [such as theatre] … to construct meaning, to make the world meaningful and to communicate about that world meaningfully to others' (Hall 1997a: 25), then such an inquiry can give invaluable insight into the 'conversation' that incarcerated women are having with the shifting landscapes of the not-so-new South Africa and with each other.

In my investigation, I identify three loosely overlapping phases: the politics of the issue (2000–4), the politics of identity (2002–10) and the politics of human rights (2010–14). These delineations are by no means discrete and do not presume to reflect trends in applied theatre in South Africa as a whole. However, what is significant is that this is a largely stable group of women (many have done the programmes more than five times) who have, through a process of discussion, collectively decided what debate the play will instigate. The plays respond directly to current areas of concern. Further, they understand and experience the multiple ways in which the prison theatre at WFCC can and has negotiated power at numerous levels.

Most typically, it has initiated interpersonal exchange, which has helped to renegotiate cultures of behaviour among the women inside, and to mobilize them around a common cause. However, it has also been a means through which the women have effectively spoken back to operations and policies within the prison system. This is expanded on later in the chapter.

The women of Westville

As this chapter focuses on the intersection of context and personal (embodied) politics, it would be amiss not to frame this example within the feminist politics of female incarceration in Africa as symptomatic of global hegemonies. South Africa as a society of cultural diversity is nevertheless bound by its relationship to patriarchy, which is entrenched in all the cultures of South Africa to varying degrees (Willemans 2013). Certainly, the use of critical pedagogies (Darder et al. 2009) to challenge patriarchy and create a female space of creative expression and societal critique was part of the ambition.

The subject of women and imprisonment in Africa directly engages the political–economic and spatial containment of women in terms of race/gender/class intersections (hooks 1989). In this way the imprisonment of economically marginalized women of colour, globally, I believe, can operate as a metaphor for, and is borne out by, the experiences of the majority of these women in their daily lives. This conclusion is based on fifteen years of plays which describe often with humour, grace and occasionally anger what it is to exist in a world where there are no 'systems' that operate to your advantage (Tatum 1997: 7). Yet, besides the obvious metaphoric associations, these systems of advantage have very real impact on how and why women get caught up in the criminal justice system.

The racism implicit in the global justice system is well documented as is the associated rise in female imprisonment globally (Agozino 1997; Parenti 2000; Alexander 2010). Interestingly, in South Africa since 2002, the female prison population, which had also increased significantly in the previous decade, began decreasing. According to Judge Van Zyl (JICS 2009/10: 13), this can be attributed to a 'current priority given to reducing the numbers of females in custody'.

Joanna Phoenix's (2002) UK study of women offenders showed that, the more economically disadvantaged women are, the more likely they are to land up in the criminal justice system. Poverty constrains the choices of women, which inevitably structures their involvement in sex work and other activity deemed 'criminal' (Phoenix 2002: 71). This has implications for black South African women, who are, despite political transformation, poorer than ever (Rogan 2014; Hassim 2006).

42   *Applied Theatre: Women and the Criminal Justice System*

Patriarchy is also implicated in female incarceration. Not just in terms of the patriarchal bias of courts (Agozino 1997; Parenti 2000), but global and local research has revealed an unfortunate parallel between gender-based abuse and female incarceration (Faith 2000; Hafferjee, Vetten and Greyling 2005). Statistics around the numbers of South African incarcerated women who have been abused differ. In one study (Artz, Hoffman-Wanderer and Moult 2012: 148) 67 per cent of their sample admitted to experiencing domestic violence, and in another (Hafferjee et al. 2005) it was as high as 78 per cent. It is certainly my experience that there are as many stories of abuse as there are women in prison.

Further, as abuse has become so 'normalized' in South Africa (Artz et al. 2012: 150), it is doubtful whether many women, let alone men, would even consider other more insidious forms of abuse, such as emotional or financial abuse,[5] abusive. However, as Hafferjee et al. (2005) have found, these delineations are significant in terms of the kinds of crime that women perpetrate. They found that not only is women's crime largely a consequence of patriarchal oppression but the type of crime that a woman commits is often directly related to the kind of abuse she has endured. In a random but proportional study of 569 female offenders in Gauteng province (Hafferjee et al. 2005: 42), they found 'women convicted of murder are much more likely to have experienced sexual violence in their previous relationship ... Women convicted of theft are considerably more likely to have experienced economic violence' (Hafferjee et al. 2005: 45).

Politics of the issue

Apartheid was an evil monolith – a common enemy as clearly defined as Nazi Germany during the Second World War. Within a Marxian dialectic, it was the thesis/status quo that revolutionary action must destabilize. The (critical) arts as a focused and motivated wing of this endeavour had their script written, and so protest theatre and other critical theatre such as workers' theatre and black consciousness theatre was born from the 1970s (Mda 1996; Solberg 1999).

Democracy, therefore, presented a problem for political theatre in South Africa: Should one use the arts to celebrate the new status quo? Should one/could one be critical of the new status quo? What was the role of the artist now that freedom had arrived? To support nation building? To be a watchdog?[6] Theatre had, in fact, through plays such as Mbongeni Ngema's *Woza Albert/Come Albert!* (referring to Albert Luthuli, past head of the ANC), elevated the liberation hero to the level of *morena* ('spirit'). At the end of the play, the main character invokes a second coming, in the form of the *morena* of the deceased struggle veterans, to save the country from its sins. It remains a powerful allegory, which nevertheless rendered any critique of the ANC and its leaders sacrilegious.

Socially engaged theatre thus turned its attention to 'the issue', and in many ways is still finding it hard to move on. Well-known South African playwright Mike Van Graan articulates his frustration in response, stating: 'It's getting rather tired, having our head stuffed with truisms' (2006: 278). Yet, this burgeoning of issue-based 'theatre for the theatre' may have had something to do with the growth of applied theatre in South Africa, which saw massive expansion as an area of study and activity post-apartheid.[7] Everything seemed to be about 'the issue' in the drive towards societal transformation.

Certainly, in the early years of the prison theatre at WFCC, the plays were overwhelmingly issue-based. This was partly my influence owing to the way that I explained the theatre in form and function; however, as Malawian academic Christopher Kamlongera (1988) argues, within an African paradigm, performance has always had a functional aspect to it. Socio-drama came very easily to the women.

In the first four years, fourteen plays were made inside the Female Centre. The issues that were engaged were HIV/AIDS, racism, class conflict, gender-based violence, substance abuse and crime. Of these, two stood out as the issues that the women most wanted to interrogate – these were HIV/AIDS and gender-based violence.

These issues, although major concerns of broader South African society, were particularly relevant for the women and are borne out by statistical evidence. While the high HIV/AIDS prevalence in South Africa is recognized as a major barrier to progress and transformation, the situation is worse for incarcerated women. An estimated 45.3 per cent of incarcerated women are infected with the virus (Goyer 2003: 30), with 'HIV prevalence in South African Correctional Centres ... expected to be twice that of the prevalence amongst the same age and gender in the general population' (Goyer 2003: 30).

The early plays around the illness sought to manage things like misinformation and stigma – a practical approach for curbing discriminatory behaviour in a closed community. In 2002, the women used the theatre to depict the then situation where deceased (from HIV/AIDS) prisoners were left in the infirmary overnight alongside other terminally ill patients. The play, which was performed to over 200 female inmates, caused a powerful reaction in the crowd to the point that I wondered if a prison riot would erupt. Fortunately, the energy was deflected by the following play, which was comic. News of this reached the Area Manager, and the policy regarding the treatment of deceased offenders was amended. I was also reprimanded.

44 *Applied Theatre: Women and the Criminal Justice System*

Previous research (Young-Jahangeer 2011) showed that the plays had a powerful impact in shifting perceptions around HIV/AIDS in the centre. One of my 'co-investigators' Lilly is openly HIV+ and has used the prison theatre as a way to conscientize inmates and members about the disease: 'Drama has given me the freedom of expressing my true feelings and emotions to people about HIV/AIDS. With drama I can tell and show people how I feel without offending anyone' (Interview 10 September 2005). Speaking to the effect of the programmes in the prison she explains: 'Before [the drama programmes] it was worse! Now there is [stigma] but it's not that much' (Interview 17 February 2012).

HIV/AIDS remains a daily struggle for incarcerated people. Many battles have been fought and won – through the efforts of the Treatment Action Campaign (TAC), antiretroviral drugs are now available to all inmates, as are special diets. This was not always the case. However, the most powerful battle is the one that infected women have with themselves. Of my four 'co-investigators' three were HIV+, yet despite our trusting and open relationship only one, Lilly, was comfortable to reveal her status. Joyce and Nomphumelelo – as 'elders', 'mothers' within their culture and the prison community, found it impossible to reveal their status. Further, their role as facilitators in the Drama programmes had given them a profile in the prison[8] among the management. Shamed by their incarceration, it seems they were determined to hang onto the status they had built up in the prison. They took their secret to their graves.

HIV/AIDS cannot be seen outside of gender power relations (Susser 2009), and it was the issue of gender-based violence that was also a priority for the women. As I have argued above, incarcerated women have invariably been in situations of abuse, and there is a causal link between the type of abuse and the type of crime (Hafferjee et al. 2005). In the years 2000–4, around half the group were imprisoned for murder, and half of those women were imprisoned for violent crimes against the claimed perpetrators of their abuse. In my team of 'co-investigators', two of the women were serving life sentences for murdering abusive husbands. On this issue, Nomphumelelo wrote: 'I am serving a 30-year sentence for my actions, substituting a prison of abuse for a prison of bricks' (Manyaapelo 2005: 110).

The plays revealed that the women are astutely aware of the affect that gender-based violence has had on their lives. In a post-performance discussion in September 2000, women commented:

> 90 per cent of female prisoners are here because they were abused by men, so if men did not abuse them, prisons would not be filled with women so much.

Interplay   45

[Without the experience of abuse] women would be more open, more honest, and more caring. Relationships would be more lasting and caring. Women would have high self-esteem and they would contribute more creatively in solving financial problems and all other problems.

The following section will engage how the plays shifted in their intention from an issue-based focus for the purpose of raising awareness to appropriating the theatre as a way to renegotiate individual and collective identity.

Politics of identity

During apartheid, the national culture of the prison system, as reflective of the dominant culture in the country, was Afrikaans. As a closed system, it had developed its own codes and practices, which all DCS members and inmates – irrespective of ethnic origin – were absorbed into. For example, when arriving at a locked unmanned gate, it was customary to shout, 'Dankie hek!' ('Thank you, gate!') to attract the attention of the guard, who, if male, was referred to as 'boetie' ('little brother'). For any local, entering the prison was a culture shock. KwaZulu-Natal, the region where I live and work, is an ex-British colony where Zulus are the majority. Afrikaans is rarely heard.

Consequently, post-apartheid, there was a need to dismantle the existing hegemony. While the policy was quick to change, the institutional culture took longer, and it was still in place in 2000 and for some time afterwards. The prison theatre plays at WFCC, which embrace African popular forms, became central in shifting the culture of the prison from Afrikaans to the majority culture – Zulu. As the prison theatre became more entrenched into the life of the Female Centre,[9] its ability to exorcize the old demons became apparent. Women's Day and other official ceremonies in the prison always included the drama group in the celebration. The response from the audience of 'members' and inmates was always powerfully jubilant.

In form, the prison plays were a celebration of Zulu culture; yet the dialogic element created a space for the women to debate aspects of the culture they wanted to interrogate. In this way, the plays (2002–10) became not only about transforming institutional culture but also how to renegotiate Zulu female identity in a democratic South Africa.

In 1996, Stuart Hall participated in a conference held by the Centre for Cultural and Media Studies (University of Natal), where I was doing my Masters. In reading the context of transformation in South Africa, his presentation cut right to this tension between 'roots and routes' (1997: 4). On the one hand, culture can be seen as that which 'embeds us in a place or in a context of recognition' and, on the other, 'as the different staging posts that we have been through in our lives, collectively and individually'.

The dialogic interaction, while being mindful of the physical context, both allowed for communication around those different 'staging posts' and generated them through the collective involvement in the project. Further, the plays themselves created a space for 'imaginative identification' (Hall 1997b: 13) – since, while identity is based on material conditions and personal and social relationships, it also depends on how we imagine ourselves (Hall 1997b: 13):

> We are the sum of the positions that we've assented to. We are the sum of the ways in which we've been willing to be recognized [...] We are the sum of where we hope we are going. What we are hoping to become. We are the sum of the subjects that we dream ourselves into.

In the project of reimagining the self/reimagining the collective, four key areas surfaced for the women: HIV/AIDS, abuse, motherhood and sexuality. Although HIV/AIDS and abuse emerged as primary 'issues', after the first few years it became apparent that the plays dealing with these topics were changing their focus and purpose. Instead of raising consciousness, the plays were more concerned with identity.

Intolerance of abuse and HIV/AIDS stigma became part of the way that women began to identify themselves in the group. It became commonplace for a woman to declare her status – either positive or negative – in a conversation, as a matter of course (which also makes Joyce and Nomphumelelo's non-disclosure more surprising). Further, HIV status became an aspect of identity that created a subcommunity of women who had solidarity around the disease. During a clash of opinions in a play on lesbianism, Lilly said: 'No matter if we disagree, she is my sister because we are both HIV+' (22 September 2004). The other woman concurred.

Gender-based violence was also rejected unequivocally within a renegotiation of Zulu female identity and culture in a democracy. The divide and rule manner in which patriarchy operates (as with all systems of inequality) facilitates the maintenance of the hegemony, which is then normalized (as argued above) and entrenched within the culture. In an all-female environment, conversations do not have to be tempered to accommodate male sensitivities, which we have been socialized to mitigate.

Findings of my research (Young-Jahangeer 2005) indicated that it was primarily through the common experience of abuse that women were able to surmount some of the isolating experience of the prison. It proved a potent rallying point for the unification of the women across race, class and ethnicity.

Interplay 47

As Joyce noted, 'the drama has created a sustainable bond between us – we are closer to each other now' (18 September 2002).

Being a mother was also a strong point of identification that the women wanted to incorporate into how they imagined themselves. The separation from children that incarceration brought was a deep and painful burden often discussed casually and in a theatrical context. A woman, Dianne, once declared in a performance in 2001 that the fifteen years of abuse was nothing compared to the pain of living without her children.

When students would come to the prison for the Saturday intervention, Joyce would invariably welcome them as her 'children', thereby invoking the role of 'mother'. In 2002, one of the groups chose to pose the problem of how, as mothers, relationships with children can be maintained while incarcerated. Discussion revolved around letters and phone calls. The women's main concern was that without them they might end up in the criminal justice system themselves.

Plays consistently represented mothers as supportive and nurturing (fathers typically drunk and abusive). The role of 'mother', with its positive associated qualities around caring – the antithesis of 'criminal' – was a very important part of how the majority of the women wished to imagine themselves.

The final aspect of identity that the plays engaged was that of sexuality, and it was here that the most conflict was generated. In August 2003, I was invited to a Women's Day event. Members of the drama group were making placards to attach to the bars that surrounded the staging area of the event. While couched in the logic of female pride, the slogans on the boards could only be read as homophobic and offensive. For example:

> There's no men behind bars in Female Prison, so if you are lost go to the male prison!
> If you have a confused or missed sexual identity in prison, what are you going to say to your children?
> Because we are women behind bars we don't stop being daughters, wives, mothers or human beings.

The issue being tackled here was lesbianism in the prison. Although constitutionally homosexuality is not a crime (and this links to the issue of human rights discussed below), in the prison it is not permitted. There are various reasons for this. Christianity has a powerful influence in the prison. Ministers of religion are ever-present with morning services daily, and twice on Sunday. Many 'members' and inmates identify as conservative Christians, who reject homosexuality.

48   *Applied Theatre: Women and the Criminal Justice System*

The rhetoric that homosexuality in 'un-African' is one well publicized by the likes of Robert Mugabe, who publicly stated that it 'degrades human dignity, it is unnatural and there is no question of allowing these people to behave worse than dogs and pigs' (Dunton and Palmberg 1996: 18). The public proclamation of such vitriol legitimates behaviours such as 'corrective rape' (the rape of a lesbian to 'make her straight'), common in South Africa (Wells and Polders 2006). The management of the prison (and thus 'good' inmates who must publically accept institutional values) therefore rejects lesbian activity as morally and culturally unacceptable. On an operational level, it is considered a security risk. Lesbian activity, which inevitably involves the power relations and emotional investment of any relationship, is said to increase the possibilities for conflict in the prison population.

In 2004, a year after 'the placards', the drama group decided to stage a play on lesbianism for the September programme. It was here that issues of identity came in direct conflict with the issue of human rights. The older women rejected lesbianism categorically. In a dialogue session, a women called lesbians 'less than dogs – even dogs know who to fuck'. The group consisted of many practising lesbians. It was clear that in the construction of Zulu female identity post-apartheid, a generational battle was being waged around the inclusion or exclusion of homosexuality. The play itself aptly depicted this. The character of the young lesbian (who *was* lesbian) was defiant and wore a smirk on her face while the disapproving characters in the play (who *were* disapproving) rebuked her for her behaviour. The older women closed down any post-performance discussion. This was non-negotiable.

Politics of human rights

South Africa is regarded for having one of the most progressive constitutions in the world, considered 'a beacon for emerging democracies' (Philp 2012). It is recognized and heralded for its explicit recognition of diverse groups and languages (Philp 2012). However, in the face of daily reportage of racism, homophobia and excessively high rates of gender-based violence in the country, it certainly appears that many seem unable to understand what the spirit of democracy truly is. And why should they be? At barely twenty-three years of age,[10] democracy in South Africa is a youngster.

Further, for democracy to be inculcated into a society, a constitution is a mere starting point. It is through the process of engagement, of dialogue and debate, that democracy begins to live. It is my contention that the popular participatory prison theatre facilitated an understanding of democracy for the female inmates, many of whom in the early years had never been free in a free South Africa. The form, with the posing of a problem that is then debated, enabled participants to enact a democratic process and, in so doing, become human for each other (Freire 1970).

As discussed, some debates were more impassioned and difficult; others created an opportunity for strong social bonds to form along identity formations. All were nevertheless healthy and vigorous. In fact, it was through the 'lesbianism play' that the very principles of democracy were on trial. The elders favouring collective before individual, where the older (wiser) members 'know best'; and the younger women favouring individual before collective: 'over [her]self, over [her] own body and mind the individual is sovereign' (Mill 1859/2001: 13).

Yet, although the older women did not accept the morality of homosexuality, their right to free speech entitles them to express their opinions. Further, their position that its practice in the prison caused collective harm, through creating a more stressful environment with the possibility of punitive outcomes for the group, is a fair one. To expand on J. S. Mill's proposition on liberty: 'The only purpose for which power can be rightfully exercised over any member of a civilized [sic] community, against his will, is to prevent harm to others' (Mill 1859/2001: 13). The irony that these issues can be teased out in a prison environment where many individual rights have been punitively suspended for inflicting harm is significant.

In discussing the work of Michael Etherton, Tim Prentki stresses the necessary shift in emphasis in 'development' from needs to rights: 'The words themselves are indicators of an attitude towards 'the other'. Needs have been determined, historically by those with the power to satisfy them ... Rights shift the emphasis ... to the participants' (2015: 47). The prison theatre in the female prison in the past four years (2010–14) shifted for a third time. While some 'issue' or 'identity' plays did emerge, for the first time a number of plays seemed to engage directly with the notion of rights: the right to equal treatment/equality, the right to equal education, the right to a fair trial.

The right to equal treatment was raised through plays about social status in prison (2012) and favouritism in the prison (2013). The issue of social status and unequal treatment is connected to various high-profile cases in the South African media where politically connected individuals were granted medical parole (Rossouw and Mataboge 2010). The debate was concerned with the fact that certain people with elevated status in prison get an easier ride: 'lowly' prisoners die of illnesses in prison while those with political currency serve their (foreshortened) sentences in private hospitals.

The following year, a similar topic was engaged but from a different angle. It concerned offenders who actively align themselves with power (members)

50 *Applied Theatre: Women and the Criminal Justice System*

by building relationships across the divide for benefits. This is part of an inherited situation of vassalage, which has remained in the prison after transition. It is a common sight for inmates to be doing the hair of members (braiding or extensions), polishing their shoes, fetching and carrying DCS members' personal objects, preparing food for them. Officers typically favour a particular inmate. In exchange for this service, women may occasionally get small gifts such as toiletries or takeaway food. Perhaps even a recommendation for early parole. They are 'connected'. The plays portrayed this scenario.

The resulting debate centres on the fact that this behaviour is essentially corrupt, unfair and sows dissent among the inmate population. The sentiment, to echo the previous year, was that all prisoners are equal – or at least they should be. Another more paranoid concern was that these 'favoured' women are recruited as 'spies' – selling out their cellmates for a KFC meal.

In the Youth Centre for young men, education is taken seriously. Their school is well run with classrooms, designated teachers and a headmaster. Not so in the Female Centre. The 'school', which is two designated rooms, was only opened in WFCC in 2003. Inmates with tertiary education comprise the teaching staff. There is now one volunteer. Women who succeed educationally do so based on their own determination rather than any real educational support. Thus a play in 2013 dealt with the issue of the right to quality education for women in the criminal justice system, marrying the right to education with the right to gender equality.

The volunteer educator was invited. She was a positive woman who took the opportunity to motivate the inmates to be more committed to schooling and push for resources. It was discussed that young women often lack the motivation to carry on with schooling in the prison. This attitude is used to justify the lack of commitment on the part of DCS to address the issue in the fact of financial constraints. Part of the aim of the performance was to motivate women to prioritize their education.

The final area of discussion on rights first reared its head in 2001 and has filtered into many plays since then. Its prolificacy is because all participants have experienced the criminal justice system and assessed its bias. The 2001 play was performed as part of 'The Justice for Women Campaign'[11] that was motivating to have women who had murdered abusive husbands released. Their long sentences, which disregard the history of abuse, were evidence of a patriarchal bias in the system. The women created a play in which the protagonist, a battered woman, turns to all sectors of society for help: family, church, social workers, police. Each has an entirely unsatisfactory response. The policeman, who knows her husband, tells the husband of the wife's attempt to lay a charge, and she is beaten. This drives her to orchestrate his

Interplay   51

murder for which she is caught and sentenced twenty-five years to life. It is her child, however, who ends up suffering most.

Thirteen years later, a different group of women devised an almost identical play, but with one difference. In the more recent play, the social worker who initially had good intentions is bribed by the husband's family to destroy the report. She does. Thus what is evident in the latest evolution of the plays is that, as much as they are dealing with issues of human rights, there is also a realization of democracy as a disappointment. In the face of a growing awareness of rights and democratic processes, there is a disjuncture. Freedom 'to' . . . (talk and laugh aloud) does not necessarily mean freedom 'from' (suffering).

South Africa the 'Rainbow Nation' was an illusion sold to the world and then sold back to us. When the southern sun dried it up, it revealed a stark reality of what it is to be an African country, post-independence, in a world of Western domination and capitalist imperative. An inmate once commented: 'When the rich steal from the poor it's business, when the poor steal from the rich it's crime.' As I have engaged in this chapter, for the women of Westville, the theatre has created a platform to discuss issues, to renegotiate identities and to debate democracy. How they have used the theatre, I have argued, has transitioned in response to the shifting political terrain. However, above all, the embodied experience of participating in these programmes has instilled a criticality and sense of self. This, I believe, has made the women – and I include myself – feel differently about themselves in the world, as they discover the world in themselves.

And that has made all the difference.

Notes

1   WFCC is located in Durban, South Africa. It houses approximately 400 women across age and sentence. It is part of the Westville Prison Complex which houses approximately 15,000 prisoners.

2   The theatre programmes initially ran in three Correctional Centres within the Westville Complex: Medium B (Maximum Security male); Youth Centre (young men between the ages of 18 and 23) and Female – which used to be the old 'white prison'. The team consisted of Chris Hurst, Beki Nkala, Dominic Zulu, Clement Ntuli and myself. I headed up the projects at the Female Centre.

3   In 2000 Chris Hurst was invited to assist in the staging on a play by offenders entitled *Shibobo 2000*. A member of the cast was an ex-student, Clement Ntuli. He approached Chris about continuing, and so the Prison Theatre programmes were conceived.

4 This would usually involve around three student plays and three 'offender' plays at each of the three sites, each group with around ten participants.
5 Financial abuse is the vindictive control of a woman by denying her access to financial resources in the family – even resources that she has earned.
6 Responses to this conundrum have been well articulated by André Brink (1997) and others (Mda 1996), but go beyond the scope of this chapter.
7 Most South African University Drama Departments offer Applied Theatre as part of basic undergraduate and postgraduate courses; see O'Toole et al. (2015: 117–22).
8 Subsequent to their involvement in the drama, the prison began to use them to MC prison events. They were recruited during their sentence as part of a schools' programme to speak about crime to learners. As Joyce and Nomphumelelo were also educated at tertiary level, they were recruited to start the school in the Female Centre.
9 In addition to the two projects annually in 2002, I conducted weekly sessions with the women. With the advent of the school, this no longer became possible.
10 The interim constitution came into effect in 1993, and was replaced by the current constitution in February 1997 (https://www.concourt.org.za).
11 The Justice for Women Campaign was launched in 2001 by the Centre for the Study of Violence and Reconciliation (CSVR) and partners National Network on Violence Against Women and the Commission on Gender Equity.

References

Agozino, B. (1997), *Black Women and the Criminal Justice System*, Aldershot, UK: Ashgate.

Alexander, M. (2010), *The New Jim Crow: Mass Incarceration in the Age of Colorblindness*, USA: The New Press.

Artz L., Hoffman-Wanderer, Y. and K. Moult (2012), *Hard Time(s): Women's Pathways to Crime and Incarceration*, Cape Town: Gender, Health and Justice Research Unit (UCT).

Bharucha, R. (2000), *The Politics of Cultural Practice: Thinking Through Theatre in An Age of Globalization*, Hanover, NH: University Press of New England.

Chilisa, B. and J. Preece (2005), *Research Methods for Adult Educators in Africa*, Cape Town, Bonn, Gaberone: UNESCO Institute for Education.

Correctional Services Act (1998), 27 November, Cape Town: Government Gazette.

Constitutional Court of South Africa (n.d.), Available online: www.constitutionalcourt.org.za (accessed 17 January 2016).

Darder, A. and R. Torres (2009), 'After Race: An Introduction', in A. Darder,

M. Baltodano and R. Torres (eds), *The Critical Pedagogy Reader*, 1–24, New York: Routledge.

Dunton, C. and M. Palmberg (1996), *Human Rights and Homosexuality in Southern Africa*, South Africa and Sweden: Nordiska Afrikainstitutet.

Faith, K. (2000), 'Reflections on Inside/Out Organising', *Social Justice: A Journal of Crime, Conflict and World Order* 27(3): 158–67.

Freire, P. (1970), *Pedagogy of the Oppressed*, London: Penguin.

Foucault, M. (1977), *Discipline and Punish: The Birth of the Prison*, London: Penguin.

Goyer, K. C. (2003), *HIV/AIDS in Prison: Problems, Policies and Potential*, Institute of Security Studies Monograph Series, 79 (February).

Guerra, R. (2015), 'The Game of Identities: Intercultural Theatre in the Peruvian Amazon', in T. Prentki (ed.), *Applied Theatre: Development*, 150–68, London: Bloomsbury Methuen Drama.

Hafferjee, S., Vetten, L. and M. Greyling (2005), 'Exploring Violence in the Lives of Women and Girls Incarcerated at Three Prisons in Gauteng Province, South Africa', *Agenda* 66(1.1): 40–7.

Hall, S. (1997a), *Representation: Cultural Representations and Signifying Practices*, London: Sage.

Hall, S. (1997b), 'Random Thoughts Provoked by the Conference: Identities, Democracy, Culture and Communication in Southern Africa', *Critical Arts* 11(1 and 2): 1–16.

Hassim, S. (2006), *Women's Organisations and Democracy in South Africa: Contesting Authority*, Madison: University of Wisconsin Press.

hooks, b. (1989), *Talking Back: Thinking Feminist Thinking Black*, London: Sheba Feminist.

Judicial Inspectorate for Correctional Services (2009), Annual Report for the period 01 April 2008–31 March 2009. Available online: https://acjr.org.za/resource-centre/InspectingJudgePrisonsAnnualRpt2008-2009.pdf (accessed 5 August 2019).

Kamlongera, C. (1988), *Theatre for Development in Africa with Case Studies from Malawi and Zambia*, Bonn and Zambia: German Foundation for International Development and Fine and Performing Arts Department.

Kerr, D. (1995), *African Popular Theatre*, Cape Town: David Phillip.

Kershaw, B. (1999), *The Radical in Performance: Between Brecht and Baudrillard*, London: Routledge.

Kidd, R. and M. Byram (1982), 'Popular Theatre and Non-Formal Education in Botswana: A Critique of Pseudo-Participatory Popular Education', Working Paper No. 5 (Revised), Toronto, Canada: Participatory Action Research Group.

Manyaapelo, N. (2005), 'Born to Suffer', in *Agenda: Empowering Women for Gender Equity* 66(1.1): 110–16.

Mbembe, A. (2014), 'Juju Prances into the Gaps Left by ANC', *Mail and Guardian*, 1 August. Available online: https://mg.co.za/article/2014-07-31-juju-prances-into-the-gaps-left-by-anc (accessed 5 August 2019).

Mda, Z. (1993), *When People Play People: Development Communication though Theatre*, London: Zed Books.

Mda, Z. (1996), 'Politics and the Theatre: Current Trends in South Africa', in G. V. Davis and A. Fuchs (eds), *Theatre and Change in South Africa. Contemporary Theatre Studies Vol 12*, 193–218, Amsterdam: Harwood Academic Publishers.

Mohanty, C. T., Russo, A. and L. Torres (eds) (1991), *Third World Feminism and the Politics of Feminism*, Bloomington and Indianapolis: Indiana University Press.

Mill, J. ([1859] 2001), *On Liberty*, Ontario, Canada: Batoche Books.

Ngema, M., Mtwa, P. and B. Simon (1983), *Woza Albert!* London: Methuen Drama.

Oppler, S. (1998), *Correcting Corrections: Prospects for South Africa's Prisons*, United Nations Development Programme in South Africa and Open Society Foundation. Available online: https://oldsite.issafrica.org/uploads/Mono29.pdf (accessed 5 August 2019).

O'Toole, J., Yi-Man, A., Baldwin, A., Cahill, H. and K. Chinyowa (2015), 'Capacity Building Theatre (and vice versa)', in T. Prentki (ed.) (2015) *Applied Theatre: Development*, 93–134, London: Bloomsbury Methuen Drama.

Parenti, C. (2000), *Lockdown America: Police and Prisons in the Age of Crisis*, London and New York: Verso.

Prendergast, M. and J. Saxton (2009), *Applied Theatre: International Case-studies and Challenges for Practice*, Bristol: Intellect.

Prentki, T. (2015), *Applied Theatre: Development*, London: Bloomsbury Methuen Drama.

Philp, R. (2012), 'In Love with South Africa's Constitution', *Mail and Guardian*, 24 February. Available online: https://mg.co.za/article/2012-02-24-in-love-with-sas-constitution (accessed 5 August 2019).

Phoenix, J. (2002), 'Youth Prostitution Policy Reform: New Discourse Same Old Story', in P. Carlen (ed.), *Women and Punishment: The Struggle for Justice*, 67–98, London: Willan Publishing.

Rogan, M. (2014), 'Poverty May have Declined, but Women and Female-headed Households Still Suffer Most.' Available online: www.econ3x3.org (accessed 2 September 2015).

Rossouw, M. and M. Mataboge (2010), 'Shaiks Medical Miracle', *Mail and Guardian*, 15 January. Available online: https://mg.co.za/article/2010-01-15-shaiks-medical-miracle (accessed 5 August 2019).

Solberg, R. (1993), *Alternative Theatre in South Africa: Talks with Prime Movers Since the 1970s*, Pietermaritzburg: Hadeda Books.

Susser, I. (2009), *AIDS, Sex, and Culture: Global Politics and Survival in Southern Africa*, Oxford: Wiley-Blackwell.

Tatum, B. (1997), *'Why Are All the Black Kids Sitting Together in the Cafeteria?' and Other Conversations about Race*, New York: Basic Books.

Thompson, J. (ed.) (1998), *Prison Theatre: Perspectives and Practices*, London: Jessica Kingsley.

Van Graan, M. (2006), 'From Protest Theatre to the Theatre of Conformity?', *South African Theatre Journal* 20(1): 276–88.

Wells, H. and L. Polders (2006), 'Anti-Gay Hate Crimes in South Africa: Prevalence, Reporting Practices, and Experiences of the Police', *Agenda* 20(67): 20–8.

Willemans, J. (2013), 'Patriarchy Reigns Supreme in SA', *Eyewitness News*, 8 August. Available online: https://www.ewn.co.za/2013/08/08/Patriarchy-reigns-supreme-in-SA (accessed 13 January 2015).

Young-Jahangeer, M. (2002), 'Theatre for a Developing Nation 2002: Exploring Sisterhood. An Evaluation Report for CHESP on the Service-Learning Module Course Run by the Drama and Performance Studies Programme at the University of Natal in Partnership with Westville Prison'. Unpublished report.

Young-Jahangeer, M. (2005), 'Bringing into Play: Investigating the Appropriation of Prison Theatre in Westville Female Prison, KwaZulu-Natal (2000–2004)', *South African Theatre Journal* 19(1): 130–43.

Young-Jahangeer, M. (2011), 'Acting out HIV/AIDS Behind Bars: The Appropriation of Theatre for Social Change in the Renegotiation of Behaviours around HIV/AIDS', in D. Francis (ed.), *Acting on HIV: Using Drama to Create Possibilities for Change*, 103–18, Rotterdam: Sense Publishers.

'Four Walls', *Voices from Prison* (1987)

Lynn, Clean Break

Four walls
Two long
Two short
One door
No handle
Stale air
Shit stains
Graffiti scrawl
Key rattle
Loud noises
Crying anguish
Mock sympathy
Lovers' faces
Hiding grief
Futile curses
Screw commiserate
Anger discussed
Washing teeth

Voices from Prison was a performance event produced by Clean Break theatre company in collaboration with the Royal Shakespeare Company (RSC) and staged at the Barbican, London on 2 February 1987. Each performance text was written by a woman with experience of incarceration. Some were Clean Break members, some were women who were still serving sentences, who had mailed their work to Clean Break. The pieces were performed by women from theatre companies including Clean Break, Asian Cooperative Theatre, Theatre of Black Women, Half Moon, the Royal Court and the Royal Shakespeare Company. The event was staged as part of the RSC's Early Stages programme, facilitated by Ann Mitchell who was, at the time, part of the RSC and had a strong affiliation with Clean Break, directing productions and running writing workshops.

Voices from Prison is an unpublished text, held in the Clean Break archive, Bishopsgate Institute, London.

2

'They Pink Dress Ain't Done Shit': Sex, Dress and *Quare* Activism in a Women's Gulf Coast Prison

Lisa L. Biggs

In the US, women are largely erased from contemporary discourses about prisons, crime and punishment despite being the fastest growing segment of the prison population. From 1980 to 2014, the total number of women in federal and state prisons and local county jails skyrocketed more than 700 per cent, from 26,378 to 215,332, a rate 50 per cent higher than the increase in men.[1] This change is not attributable to an increase in women's criminality. Stricter public policies now mandate incarceration for those offences women are most likely to commit – non-violent crimes of poverty (e.g. shoplifting, prostitution) and those related to problematic substance use and mental health disorders (e.g. drink driving, illegal drug possession). Poor and working-class women, especially women of colour, and members of the LGBTQ community are subjected to aggressive overpolicing and oversentencing, resulting in their disproportionately high numbers behind bars. These disparities in policing and sentencing are compounded by a lack of accountability within the criminal legal and penal systems. Inadequate vocational, educational, recreational and re-entry programmes for currently and formerly imprisoned women create still more barriers despite decades of protests and successful litigation. The inequalities persist in no small part because mainstream women's rights, racial justice, LGBTQ and prisoners' rights organizations have also largely failed to incorporate these community members within their campaigns for public safety and justice – this despite the fact that poor people, women of colour and LGBTQ folks are disproportionately the victims of crime.[2]

The Anahita[3] women's prison Drama Club offers an example of women's creative activism that puts the needs, experiences and knowledge of some of society's most vulnerable and stigmatized persons at the forefront of social justice organizing. With this chapter, I contribute a combined historiographic and ethnographic chronicle of imprisoned women's lives that reveals and

58   *Applied Theatre: Women and the Criminal Justice System*

illuminates the prison as a site for women's activism. Building on the work of E. Patrick Johnson (2006), I pay particular attention to the Black *quare* community praxis that undergirds the imprisoned women's efforts to organize at this site, including the use of dress and of performance to reveal, critique, challenge and transform repressive penal polices. Johnson coined the term *quare* to describe the previously ignored practices of community and coalition building between and among Black LGBTQ folks and their Black cisgender and/or heterosexual allies. In this chapter, I argue that, though little has been written about dress as a site for imprisoned women's activism, *quare* women prisoners and their allies use performance onstage in theatre productions at their facility, and in quotidian moments of masculine gender performance, to advance alternative, more inclusive modalities of community, sexuality, justice and belonging into the world.

The pink dress policy

In 2010, Anahita, a maximum security prison for women on the US Gulf Coast, imposed a new sartorial punishment to isolate and control women who did not conform to the prison administrator's expectations about appropriate female behaviour. The new warden ordered that prisoners who violated the facility's uniform dress code be identified, stripped of their clothing and forced to wear 'the pink dress'. The pink dress was a large, flowing, pink caftan, reminiscent of a muumuu or bed sheet with a hole cut out for the head. Its wearers stood out on a compound of over one thousand other women dressed in the decidedly un-masculine, regular uniform – baggy jeans, long- and short-sleeved white shirts and chambray, denim jackets.

The pink dress punishment did not redress any wrongdoing committed by the women outside the prison. During my two years of conducting ethnographic and historiographic research on Anahita, I was repeatedly told the pink dress was designed exclusively to discipline the too masculine prisoners, especially 'the homosexuals'. In keeping with several unfounded but still pervasive social science theories that criminals are the product of inherited degenerate biology and poor environment, prison administrators and a handful of influential volunteers framed Black women's homosexuality as the cause of all the problems at the prison – and by extension all criminal activity in the country.[4] The pink dress policy branded Black lesbians, their friends, lovers, families and allies at Anahita as exceptionally dangerous.

When members of the Drama Club learned of the change in uniform policy, they were outraged. Since 1995, Anahita's prisoners have brought their

Sex, Dress and Quare *Activism*   59

most pressing issues to the Drama Club for creative, collective analysis. A group of lifers (women serving life sentences) anchor the ensemble, complemented by another fifteen to twenty women serving shorter sentences. They are led by two women volunteers – Jodie and Ngozi – who each direct their own professional performing arts companies in a nearby metropolitan area. Drama Club has met almost every Saturday since 1996 for a two-hour performance workshop in which Jodie and Ngozi share performance-making techniques from their respective backgrounds; Jodie from an imagistic, movement-infused, Western theatre-making tradition, and Ngozi from her expertise with West African and Circum-Atlantic 'Mardi Gras' Black Indian story, song and dance. Drama Club members quickly realized that the pink dress would not only punish 'the homosexuals' targeted by prison officials, but potentially could leave many people open to harm. The public shaming threatened to interrupt the vital social networks they relied upon to survive behind bars.

In the early twentieth century, social scientists first noted that incarcerated women organized 'kinship' networks to provide themselves with much-needed social and economic support behind bars. According to Regina Kunzel (2008: 19), new arrivals learned proper decorum from their adopted 'family' members, including how to navigate the hierarchies of guards and prisoners, what behaviour was expected of them by corrections staff and other inmates and their responsibilities to their fellow prisoners. Today, such affiliations further enable them to gain institutional privileges, enjoy prison social events and access the essential, if illicit, underground economies that circulate goods and services (e.g. so many packages of ramen noodles in exchange for a book or laundry done in a certain way). Without these invisible networks, the women would be more vulnerable to psychological and physical harm, including sexual violence.

The Drama Club's response to the pink dress policy unfolded over a series of weeks and months, as the ensemble worked to process the policy and its implications. Ultimately, they chose to embed five short scenes into *Beauty Coming and Going,* a play they already had in development about women's social value. The scenes about a returned citizen's (i.e. formerly incarcerated woman's) efforts to get a job at a women's clothing boutique that exclusively sold pink dresses would serve, in the words of D. Soyini Madison, as an 'act of activism' (2010: 12). Through their one and only performance before an audience of other women imprisoned at Anahita, a crew of officers and a handful of volunteers (including me), the prisoners would express their collective discontent with the pink dress policy and their dissent from the underlying homophobic logic that animated it. More than merely criticizing the policy, through performance the prisoners were able to articulate their

60   *Applied Theatre: Women and the Criminal Justice System*

desires for an alternative, 'more humane and democratic social order to emerge' (Madison 2010: 1). Because they are artists committed to social change, the Drama Club appropriated the opportunity to perform in order to constitute momentarily on the prison stage the more fair and just world they desired.

Because of their relatively small numbers and propensity for non-violent acts of defiance (instead of rioting), imprisoned women's experiences, as well as their efforts to contest and transform the conditions of confinement, have been historically under-reported. Victoria Law, Beth Richie, Cheryl D. Hicks, Talitha L. LeFlouria, Regina Kunzel and Sarah Haley among other scholars have recently published histories about the gendered nature of crime, justice and punishment in the US. Their intersectional approaches expose how race, gender, class and sexuality have been used to produce the contemporary penal system. Critical analysis of a diverse array of archival materials, including convict leasing, whipping reports, prison matron journals, newspaper articles, court filings and incarcerated women's blues has revealed a rich, if hidden, history of women's lives behind bars. In this chapter, I hope to expand current understanding of the practices of punishment, correction and rehabilitation, and the role of the arts in women prisoners' efforts to contest and transform the conditions of their confinement. The experiences and insights offered by the women artists at this site – both free and incarcerated – reimagine what a safe and just society might look and feel like, and offer an example of inclusive social justice organizing in one of the least free spaces in the world.

Drama Club herstory

The Anahita women's prison Drama Club began in 1996 soon after Jodie, then a young white American actress and playwright, volunteered to perform for prisoners at the facility a solo piece she had devised about women's murderous rage. *Fury* shared oral histories and life stories of women convicted of killing their abusive partners in the years prior to the passage of the 1994 Violence Against Women Act (VAWA), which for the first time criminalized domestic violence, including spousal rape, and allocated funding for survivor services nationwide.[5] At the end of the show, the prisoners praised Jodie's performance and told her that she 'couldn't leave'. Though at first taken aback by their pronouncement, Jodie soon realized the women needed her to return to teach them how to make performances based on their own ideas.

With the support of a small grant and the permission of the warden, Jodie returned to offer a weekly drama workshop and has continued to do so almost every Saturday morning since for the past twenty years. The

Sex, Dress and Quare *Activism*   61

programme is co-directed today by Jodie and Ngozi, an African-American woman with deep ties to local Black communities. Jodie asked Ngozi to join her in 2001. Sceptical as to why she should participate, it was during her first trip to Drama Club that Ngozi realized there was much she could contribute and much she could learn. A small, rotating cast of one or two other women performing artists now round out the leadership team.

The women inmates also organized themselves to sustain the programme. Core members from the very first Drama Club workshops now recruit and screen potential participants. Ensemble members observe the temperament and artistic skills of potential performers in the open spaces of the prison compound, such as the yard or dining hall, before talking to them individually about the commitment. It is important that potential members take the programme seriously. They must pledge to regularly attend the workshops, respect the ideas of the other women in Drama Club and contribute to the artistic process. Most importantly, they must uphold the Drama Club's responsibility to serve their community as artists and activists. Once a potential candidate completes the audition process, participation is voluntary and flexible. Every woman who meets the inmates' criteria and wants to be in a show is cast.[6] Once a woman is part of Drama Club, they are always part of Drama Club, even if at times they need to opt out of a production to pursue other needs or interests. Jodie, Ngozi and the rest of the ensemble are always ready to welcome inactive cast members back.

Jodie and Ngozi begin each week with a check-in. Sitting in chairs in a large circle in one of the reformatory's windowless programme rooms, everyone shares how they are feeling and what is going on in their lives. Check-in is followed by a short physical warm-up. From there, they might transition into acting games inspired by Viola Spolin, or opportunities to tell stories, do scenes and write short stories or poetry in response to a prompt Jodie or Ngozi brings in. Depending on the mood and needs of the group, song and dance may be incorporated as well. These training sessions build the participant's artistic skill base and establish trust. Each week Ngozi and Jodie reflect upon what they learn during the ninety-minute drive back home and brainstorm next steps. Creative prompts encourage the women to delve deeper into emerging themes. In the past, these have included prompts such as 'What part of your body do you love and why' or 'Relay a memory of a moment where your breath was taken away'. Because many of the women prefer to improvise rather than write down their responses, Jodie and Ngozi often facilitate what they call 'popcorns', a physical theatre 'brainstorming' exercise in which the women share ideas in rapid succession spontaneously on their feet. Performance pieces are developed over the course of a year, and emerge out of the rich, imaginative mix of stories that the prisoners share.

62   *Applied Theatre: Women and the Criminal Justice System*

In 1996, the Drama Club staged their first play, inspired by *The Oprah Winfrey Show*. Since then they have done adaptations of the Nativity, devised original poetic choral pieces about losing loved ones that reframe the prison walls into a kind of Wailing Wall and, under Ngozi's expert direction, incorporated West African and Circum-Atlantic ritual dance. Audiences of other imprisoned women at Anahita get to see Drama Club shows at least once a year, often at the holidays – Christmas, Mother's Day or for Black History Month. The first production I attended in 2010, *Life Is,* expressed the lifers' perspectives on living behind bars. Its rousing chorus, 'Life is what you make it / Life is happiness / Life is where you're going / Life is where you've been,' has become a kind of anthem for the ensemble and for a small group of returned women citizens who perform with Ngozi and Jodie on the outside, called The Graduates.

Ngozi and Jodie reject the popular, agonistic model of prisoner 'correction' and 'rehabilitation', which values the arts as little more than a 'less explicitly punitive' aspect of the regular prison regime (Thompson 2004: 57). They recognize theatre and dance can do far more than train prisoners to comply with orders or, more narrowly, to confess, express remorse and seek forgiveness in a convincing manner (Lucas 2013: 135). What sustains Drama Club week after week, year after year, is the facilitators' refusal to impose limits upon the women's creativity, actions, emotions and desires. Prisoners and facilitators instead describe Drama Club as 'freeing' and 'healing', for the process of art-making allows the women to 'leave' the facility 'physically, mentally, emotionally and spiritually' (Drama Club Members 2011). Ngozi explains:

> When you lend yourself, your energy, your thoughts, your persona, your presence ... when you allow that to be used in a more sincere and honest way then the work becomes healing ... They know we are there because it is just love. It's none of these things other than love, and wanting to see them be better, grow better, even if they never leave [Anahita]. Still manifest your destiny. You are still obligated. Your destiny does not stop because you are incarcerated.

Drama Club is undergirded by the belief that despite past misdeeds and harm done, the women are not their mistakes; as human beings, they can – do – have lives of value and meaning. Jodie's and Ngozi's artistry and teaching praxis emerged from a feminist or womanist pedagogy of caring that encouraged the women to learn to do more for themselves and for each other. The women at Anahita spent most of their time together. The facility was under-resourced and often understaffed. Prisoners' family members and other supporters were far away, if they were in contact at all, and American society as a whole had abandoned them. When crises arose, the women had to be able to respond and help each other. The Drama Club offered its members a network of supportive care when there was no one else upon whom to rely. From the outset, however, Drama Club members also recognized that, under the guise of doing theatre, they could challenge institutional norms and impact the conditions of their confinement. When the ensemble heard about the pink dress policy, the women committed to addressing the issue in a new theatre work already under construction, *Beauty Coming and Going.*

Beauty Coming and Going

Kalenda, one of the Drama Club co-facilitators, an African American lesbian known for her vibrant singing voice, related to me some of the steps taken to break down the impact of the pink dress policy and begin exploring it with the inmates:

> We talked about ... dressing butch, dressing femme, transgender, and why certain women prefer to dress that way ... At the root of it for many women is having been abused or having been attacked. Wearing clothes that identify them as having a typically feminine shape or body [was uncomfortable] ... After that experience, they moved ... on to clothes that don't accentuate their figure, because it makes them feel less vulnerable ... [The pink dress was] like adding to the trauma ... To say to a woman, 'Oh you're trying to dress like a man, you're wearing your pants baggy so we're going to put you in a dress' – a *pink* dress no less?! This symbol of what you're supposed to be as a woman, or what a girl is supposed to dress like and look like.
>
> Kalenda 2011

Little has been published about the impact of clothing on the American legal system, yet there is little doubt that attire plays an important role in our understanding of crime. As I. Bennett Capers writes, 'from the bank robber who is identified by his ski mask or balaclava in summer, to the teenager who raises reasonable suspicion, and thus becomes suspect, because of his baggy jeans and hooded sweatshirt, to the rape victim who is doubted, and thus somehow raises reasonable doubt, because of how she was dressed' (2008: 3), dress influences the performance of law enforcement. Prison administrators have long valued uniforms for their perceived ability to discipline inmates to comply with prison rules and, by extension, with hegemonic expectations about appropriate behaviour. Contrary to the Anahita administration's position that the 'homosexuals' were wearing baggy clothes to instigate disorder, in Drama Club, the women revealed they deployed loose-fitting uniforms for self-defence.

Historically, Black women in the US have been the object, not the subject or authors, of laws. To protect white oppressors, laws were written from the earliest colonial era forward that enshrined the notion that Black women had no selves worth defending. It was not until the mid-1970s that a legal precedent was established that recognized Black women had the right to use lethal force to defend themselves against white male attackers, including police.[7] Legal systems around the world largely fail to protect women and girls from abuse. In 2014, just over one third of women behind bars in the US had been convicted of a violent crime (37 per cent),[8] but in numerous studies scholars have found that the majority of incarcerated women have survived at least one traumatic instance of interpersonal violence prior to their incarceration, most often in childhood (Wolff et al. 2009: 469–70). For many women inmates, experiences of interpersonal violence continue behind bars. Knowing they were vulnerable, at Anahita, women dressed in oversized clothing for self-defence. Visibly fashioning their uniforms in a 'masculine' style enabled some to establish and preserve their bodily integrity and, I would argue, their identities. Within the political sign system of clothing, people use attire to communicate 'externally' what is sensed 'inside', thus fulfilling the human 'desire to be self-present' (Holliday 1999: 481). But, as Ruth Holliday has argued, individual identities are always constituted in relation to others. She finds that comfort and belonging within LGBTQ communities (as in others) in part 'derives from being recognizably queer', or out to self and to others (1999: 481). More than announcing the presence of individual Black lesbians, Anahita's women prisoners used loose-fitting uniforms to collectively constitute and signal the presence of active and engaged *quare* communities.

According to E. Patrick Johnson, *quare* communities emerge from and value 'Black culture and community'; as such, they are 'committed to struggle against all forms of oppression – racial, sexual, gender, class, religious' – and more (2006: 125). The *quare* community embedded at Anahita first raised the alarm about the pink dress policy. To discuss violence behind bars, gender and homosexuality in a climate of racist, sexist and homophobic hostility was to risk much. Nonetheless, Drama Club members set out to establish and hold a community space in which beauty, self-worth, violence against women and homosexuality could be investigated. They initiated discussions within the Drama Club about homosexuality and dress out of a deep-seated concern for their personal welfare and for the well-being of other women

Sex, Dress and Quare *Activism* 65

who might be impacted by the change. An alliance of Drama Club ensemble members, including some folks who were part of the *quare* community networks, would work for nearly a year on a performance piece that could communicate their collective dissent from the pink dress policy, and enact or model for the world the more fair, just and equitable world they desired.

Pinky's Boutique

A four-phase creative process emerged that began with 'popcorn' sessions and in-depth discussions about Black women, beauty and attire. This transitioned into the writing and devising process, followed by rehearsals, during which time the piece continued to be refined. Finally, after many delays due to staffing shortages, bad weather and a medical emergency that locked down the entire facility, the Drama Club performed. I was allowed to attend the one (and only) performance in the prison's combined auditorium-gymnasium in September 2011 with a handful of other invited guests.

That Saturday afternoon I climbed into Ngozi's car for the ninety-minute ride. Like many places in the Gulf Coast, tall oaks and magnolia trees lined the highways and sheltered squat, single-family homes embedded in verdant, green terrain. When we finally pulled off the highway, I did not realize we had arrived until bright lights illuminated a tall, barbed-wire fence. After a brisk pat-down, we followed a Black woman officer across the yard. I was struck by the multitude of fresh flowers planted across the compound and the arrangement of the squat, two-storey, cell blocks in formations reminiscent of a small women's college. In sharp contrast to the quiet outdoors, the auditorium was filled with a thunderous cacophony of voices, feet stomping and metal folding chairs scraping the linoleum floor as some 300 women prisoners, and a handful of officers and invited guests like myself, took our seats.

Almost as soon as we are ushered into the front row, Ngozi took the stage to welcome everyone. As she returned to the audience, two women pulled aside a makeshift front curtain of blue bed sheets strung on a white clothes line. The ninety-minute performance interwove individual monologues with choral poems that challenged listeners to reflect upon our society's preoccupation with outward, physical appearance. Five short, scenes in the middle – performed as structured improvizations – specifically addressed the pink dress policy.[9]

The blue bed-sheet curtains pulled back to reveal Rae, a soft-spoken, middle-aged, Black woman and long-time Drama Club member who was known on the

66   *Applied Theatre: Women and the Criminal Justice System*

compound as 'The Mack'. Rae was a smooth talker much admired for her ability to enact a confident, self-controlled style of working-class Black masculinity. Onstage, she wore her Afro cut into a short fade and a baggy, white, long-sleeve shirt over loose-fitting white cargo pants and white tennis shoes. Rae's character – Starkey – was a serious uniform code violator. Her clothing and hairstyle enlarged her body and made her appear masculine. Rae/Starkey's masculine appearance was heightened by the immediate arrival of a highly feminine Black woman who sat, ankles crossed, at a small desk down centre-stage, wearing a 1980s-style, light grey, women's suit with knee-length skirt and expansive epaulettes. In this, the first of the five 'pink dress' scenarios, they established the conflict. Starkey was a recently returned citizen looking for work:

Scene One

Parole Officer   Now, what skills do you possess?

Starkey   Well, I can do just about anything. I can lift, and stock shelves, what do you need?

Parole Officer   I do not have anything for stocking at this time. I do have something in sales –

Starkey   Sales, what would I have to do?

Parole Officer   It is a lady's boutique and there is one stipulation. You have to wear a pink dress.

Starkey   Pink dress?! . . .

Parole Officer (*aside to audience*)   The nerve of her, coming in here, demanding assistance. I guess she doesn't realize that I am her Parole Officer and I hold the keys to her freedom. She can either accept this job or . . .

Starkey (*interrupting*)   At this point, I have to do what I have to do.

Parole Officer   Very good, here's the address to Pinky's Boutique. Good luck.

Having introduced Starkey and her search for employment the cast transitioned into the next scene at Pinky's Boutique by replacing the Parole Officer with a Receptionist at the desk. To establish the boutique, the Receptionist wore a loose-fitting, 1980s-style, business suit with enlarged shoulder pads in a bright shade of pink. Behind her, three women in elaborate pink ball gowns froze as store mannequins. The Receptionist greeted Starkey:

Sex, Dress and Quare *Activism* 67

Scene Two

Receptionist   Welcome to Pinky's Boutique!

Starkey   Hello, mama! I came for the job, but I sure would like to work on you.

Receptionist   Let me get the manager. (*Exits*)

Starkey (*looking closely at the mannequins*)   Even the dummies look good up in here.

Starkey's bold flirtation with the Receptionist and open admiration of the mannequins produced an avalanche of audience laughter. The sound seemed to me to affirm a surprised, collective recognition that these scenes would address the prison's ban on baggy uniforms, masculine gender performance and homoerotic desire. My quick glance around the room – repeated by many others – revealed the corrections officers were also having a good laugh from their stations on the perimeter. This content had been approved.

Black folks in the US and throughout the Circum-Atlantic are known for 'signifyin'', using a clever and funny turn of phrase to slyly point out incongruities or faults in another person (Smitherman 1977: 58). As Esther Newton (1979) found in her research on gay drag-queen performers in 1970s and 1980s New York City, for oppressed communities humour is often the only available mechanism through which to voice otherwise inexpressible experiences or emotions. Within LGBTQ and other marginalized groups, humour articulates the incongruous juxtapositions and challenges of life that result from being the object of hegemonic social contempt (Newton 1979: 104–5). Donna Goldstein concurs that jokes between members of a marginalized group often get their 'punch' by revealing the shared, devalued perspectives and experiences of the tellers and the told (2003: 129). In one of the only scholarly treatments on humour behind bars, Charles M. Terry further finds that jokes interrupt and reveal the everyday routines of confinement and punishment (1997: 30). Through humour, inmates instruct newcomers on how to behave behind bars, build a sense of solidarity between the prisoners and 'help [them] maintain their dignity' in the face of the demeaning practices of the state (Terry 1997: 32).

In *Beauty Coming and Going,* Rae presents a familiar expression of urban, working-class, Black masculinity that invokes laughter for its bold, flirtatious style. Her portrayal, however, resists the trap of equating this type of flirtation with predation – what Estelle Freedom, Don Sabo and others have characterized as the most prevalent representation of 'prison masculinity'

68   *Applied Theatre: Women and the Criminal Justice System*

(Sabo et al. 2001). Instead of fearing her, Starkey's struggle to reintegrate into the free world and find work seemed realistic. The dilemma made her highly sympathetic and relatable. In the next scene, the store Manager met Starkey:

Scene Three

Manager   May I help you?

Starkey   They sent me here for the job and I can't wait to start working up in here.

(*Starkey glances longingly at the saleswomen and mannequins*)

Manager   First of all, here is a copy of our sexual harassment policy (*hands her the paper*). Here is a copy of our rules and regulations (*hands her another piece of paper*). And one other thing; you must wear a pink dress and stilettos. Here is the application, fill it out and meet me back here at 1 p.m.

Starkey's exaggerated ogling of the saleswomen and mannequins clarified for all her sexuality. But the Manager chose not to explicitly or directly rebuke her desire. Rather than reprimanding Starkey for her homosexuality, the Manager offered her their employee handbook and sexual harassment policy. This gesture demonstrated that she attributed Starkey's behaviour to a lack of knowledge of proper workplace decorum, not to her sexuality, and sought to educate her. Most importantly, she demonstrated that she had faith Starkey could master these skills. As audience members, we realize Starkey may have a future that includes working at Pinky's if she can learn the rules and modulate her behaviour accordingly. However, as Starkey stepped away, the other boutique employees challenged the Manager's decision:

Worker One (*turning to the Manager*)   You cannot possibly hire her!

Worker Two   She act like something is wrong with her, like she just came out of rehab! She look gay!

Manager   Some of y'all just came out of rehab ... Let's go to lunch.

In judging Starkey so harshly, the Workers restage the homophobic logic of the prison's pink dress policy. The Manager responds by using her knowledge of the Workers' own pasts to check their fears, and express her distaste at their assumption that Starkey is a threat. Whether or not Starkey has actually 'just come out of rehab' (i.e. prison) or is 'gay', we learn that the Workers have been in 'rehab'. The Manager's humorous, but pointed critique, interrupts

Sex, Dress and Quare *Activism*   69

their speech by challenging the reliability of their interpretation of Starkey's 'look'. Instead of reading Starkey's clothes and mannerisms as evidence of perversion, the Manager undercuts the Workers' reliance upon the visual as an arbitrator of human value. By implication, in critiquing the Workers, her words further rebuke the prison administration.

The challenge to the pink dress policy continues when the Workers and Manager exit and, through the magic of theatre, the Mannequins came to life to discuss the employees' concerns, until they, too, are interrupted by Starkey, who performs a short monologue:

Scene Four

Mannequin One (*gesturing to one of the exiting sales women*)   She needs a perm!

Mannequin Two   I cannot believe the other one is talking about how somebody look, she too old to be working anyway. Why do they have to judge people all the time?

Mannequin Three   Where do they get these clothes from? They are really horrible.

(*They freeze as Starkey suddenly returns*)

Starkey (*entering*)   Hello? Hello? I guess I'm early . . . I really need this job. I'm tired of being what everyone else wants me to be. I am good just as I am.

Lord why can't they just accept me for who I am?
Just as I am cause I'm proud of who I be
Cause God created perfection, when He created me.
They say beauty's only skin deep, I say that's a lie –
I feel, Beauty is Love, and it comes from the inside.
So what my stomach isn't flat, I'm still a lady.
The reason for that is because I carried not one, not two, but three babies.
My hair is mine, it's natural and I like it like that.
Does that mean I'm not a woman, cause it's not down my back?
My breast used to be firm, it sags now, not a perfect pick,
That's alright with me, it's nothing a support bra can't fix.
I've put on a few pounds, so when I walk I wobble;
I guess I'll never be a contestant on *America's Next Top Model*.
Society tells me, I should look better, because I have cellulite.
When I walk my thighs rub together.
My eyes are not blue, hazel, green or grey,

70   *Applied Theatre: Women and the Criminal Justice System*

[But] I don't need to buy contacts to see a mile away.
God made my nose the way he wanted it to be,
That's why I'm not self-conscious and can smell insecurities.
I am a Phenomenal Woman, God's work at his best –
Holding my head up high and wearing beauty around my neck.
When I look at myself in a mirror, I can't help but to grin
Because God made me perfect, He made me
Just as I am.

Here, the show explores most explicitly the potential for alternative perspectives on the issue of sexuality, beauty and dress. The Mannequins coming to life as not only experts on fashion, but on beauty, offers one take. But the notion that there are alternative frameworks or standards through which to evaluate human life most fully comes to fruition in Starkey's monologue. Its tone and content, including the repeated references to divine intervention, reflect an ongoing interest among Drama Club members in spirituality. Local clergy offer multiple religious services at Anahita on a weekly or daily basis, which the women attend. The monologue also hints at the specific influence of Maya Angelou's (1978) signature poem, *Phenomenal Woman*, on their creative process. Jodie introduced *Phenomenal Woman* in the Drama Club's early years. Angelou's work reclaims the Black female body as a source of pride, power and wonder. Starkey's monologue echoes Angelou's poem in its alliterative rhyme structure and praise of the Black female body. Starkey's words extend Angelou's framework to symbolically reclaim the criminalized, Black, queer body as an object of beauty and product of divine design.

In response, the Mannequins voiced words of encouragement that Starkey was surprised to overhear:

Mannequins   You can do it . . . Believe in yourself!

With the Mannequin's words echoing in the space, the Manager returned for the final scene. After dealing with several disruptive customers, she pulled Starkey aside:

Scene Five

Manager   Fifteen year ago I was imprisoned . . . And somebody gave me a chance. I know what it is like to be judged before you even open your mouth; folks stopping being your friend when you tell them that you've been incarcerated, and even having your family not trusting you because they still don't see you as a family member – they see you as a criminal, a

Sex, Dress and Quare Activism

convicted felon. My God is a god of second chances, and I am willing to give you a chance, but I expect great things from you!! Can you lift boxes and maybe stock the shipments when they come in?

Starkey Yes, I can do that.

Manager I've been thinking about our dress code. Do you have a pink T-shirt and some pink pants?

Starkey Yes I do, thank you, thank you so much!

(*They exit together*)

With this final scene, the workplace itself changes to accommodate Starkey's needs. Rigidly gendered employment guidelines are revealed to be negotiable as long as they adhere to the pink colour requirement. This change is possible because the woman – Manager – in charge is able to access her own personal story, express empathy for Starkey and apply the knowledge gained from her own experience in prison to the workplace.

Moments later, as the curtain closed at the end of the show, every member of the Drama Club reappeared on stage wearing a pink costume and an avalanche of applause erupted. The audience of three hundred rose to their feet in an expression of spontaneous joy; but, before the celebration could draw down, we were surprised by the arrival of two final characters – the Mardi Gras Indian Queen (Ngozi) and her Chief, resplendent in pink feathers and detailed beadwork. Entering from the back of the auditorium, their steady parade to the stage respatialized the room, extending the performance to the ground where we audience members stood. In response, we were moved to action and collectively began to sing and dance the Indians' signature incantation: 'Won't bow down! Don't know how!'

At any other time, this robust display would have been considered a riot, but in the afterglow of the show it was allowed. Our spontaneous response declared a collective rebuke of the reductive notions of Black, queer identity and the repressive power relations that the prison, and the nation that created and sustained it, produced. Like the Drama Club, through performance we demonstrated our desire and determination to (re) occupy this prison/nation space that has been marked for exclusion for the embodied expression of a Black and queer belonging. The masculine-attired, African American, lesbian catalyst that ignited this action by daring to fashion herself in a flamboyant style of working-class Black masculinity (onstage or off) was met at the end of the night by a moving sea of white and blue denim uniforms dancing a welcome and affirmation of her presence now, and in the future.

72 *Applied Theatre: Women and the Criminal Justice System*

The response and the trajectory

This practice of performance with women behind bars is dangerous for it 'proclaims a making and remaking of selves despite state attempts to confine, fix and stabilize identities as inmates ... it is also dangerous because it proclaims a "we" within the confines of the razor wire and disrupts the individualistic discourse and practice on which any system of oppression is dependent' (Stanford 2004: 277–8). The women inmates along with their directors commit to this work because social justice and public safety ought not to be left to a handful of elite or influential stakeholders; instead, for public policies to be truly effective, all members of the public ought to be included in the decision-making processes. Unlike other programmes for incarcerated populations that seek to 'rehabilitate' or 'correct' the imprisoned, that measure their success only by their ability to get already immobilized prisoners to comply with orders or pronounce conservative Christian values, the Anahita Drama Club strives to 'correct' systemic injustices perpetrated by the penal system writ large. By recognizing the women to be the subjects or agents of their own lives, rather than the objects of someone else's (white supremacist misogynist) agenda, Drama Club creates a space in which women prisoners can affirm connections between themselves and with others. Together, they chose to use performance to redress wrongs committed against them – in this case by the state. The practice of doing so produced powerful and long-lasting feelings of healing and wholeness among ensemble members.

In the act of reappropriating the sign of the pink dress, *Beauty Coming and Going* challenged prison policy and the prevailing, societal myths associated with queer people of colour behind bars. Through performance, the ensemble turned the stereotypes on their heads and repositioned their own stories, their experiences, their questions and fears centre-stage. The pink dress in their hands encouraged audience members to look beyond the reductive representations. Women attire their bodies in various styles for a variety of reasons. Whether representing dress as a method of self-defence or as sign of *quare* community belonging, the production at its root emphasized that, far from being frivolous, dress is essential to the process of constituting, ordering, interpreting and navigating human social relations. Rather than repeat the most repressive social practices, however, in Pinky's Boutique dress operated as a vernacular sign system to produce a larger community of belonging.

Misogyny authorizes violence against women and girls in the US and abroad, as but one of many attributes or privileges of masculinity. However, at Anahita, the practice of Black (female) masculinity upends the notion

Sex, Dress and Quare *Activism* 73

that gender expression as a whole is biologically determined and that masculinity is always already predicated upon violence against women. Closer examination of the prison's assertion that 'the homosexuals' were the source of all the troubles at Anahita reveals their complaint to be an ill-conceived response to the inmates' determination to assert their self-worth and defend themselves from harm. Despite the administration's efforts to penalize the women with the pink dress policy, the Drama Club demonstrates that dressing in pink will not destroy their belief in themselves nor in each other. In the hands of the *quare* community, the pink dress helps constitute the more fair, equitable and inclusive world that they desire.

Kalenda (2011) perhaps summed it up best. In an interview a couple months after the production, I asked her about the show's impact:

LB Are they [the imprisoned women] wearing fewer baggy clothes?

Kalenda They pink dress ain't done shit.

Acknowledgements

I wish to express my sincere thanks to the *Beauty Coming and Going* cast and crew, Caoimhe McAvinchey, E. Patrick Johnson, D. Soyini Madison, Ramon Rivera-Servera, Austin Jackson, Ruth Ann Jones, Munjulika Rahman and the corrections officers who helped make this research possible.

Notes

1. See the U.S. Bureau of Justice Statistics publications, *Historical Corrections Statistics in the United States, 1850–1984* (1986); *Prison and Jail Inmates* Series (1997–2014); *Prisoners in 2014* (2015a). These materials are nicely summarized in the Sentencing Project's 'Fact Sheet: Incarcerated Women and Girls' (http://www.sentencingproject.org/publications/incarcerated-women-and-girls/).
2. U.S. Bureau of Justice Statistics (2015b). For information about crime victimization among queer folks, see Mogul, Richie and Whitlock (2011).
3. To protect the identities in this article of the incarcerated women at this centre, I use pseudonyms when referring to them, the facility where they are held, the officers and administrators who run the prison and the volunteer artists who direct the Drama Club.
4. According to Estelle Freedman, popular discourse and medical science have historically represented incarcerated Black women as inherently

74   *Applied Theatre: Women and the Criminal Justice System*

biologically deformed, aggressive and predacious. Early-twentieth-century sociological theories about the impact of environment and biology on sexuality determined Black women were more male than white American women. Harlem, the South Side of Chicago, Detroit, and other African American urban enclaves were understood to encourage homosexuality and the 'masculine' qualities of 'aggression' and 'violence', making it impossible for African American women to be law-abiding and to 'accept the "feminine role"' (1996: 401). Prison administrators asserted Black women behind bars who engaged in same-sex sex were therefore the only real lesbians. It was feared they would lure susceptible white women into sexual relationships and cause them to reject both heterosexuality and their duty to reproduce the white race. Prison administrators condemned same-sex couplings and attributed every kind of problem that arose at the reformatories to them to justify racial segregation and differential treatment.

5   The Violence Against Women Act (VAWA) for the first time provided permanent, coordinated community care at the federal level among police and other first responders, emergency shelters, health care providers and attorneys. For a history of VAWA, see Banguid (2002).

6   There may be times when officers and administrators prevent the women from participating. All programmes get cancelled when the facility goes on lockdown. Individuals who break prison rules may be prohibited from participating as well.

7   For treatments of the Joan Little rape-murder trial which set the new precedent, see McNeil (2008); McIntyre (2010); Greene (2015).

8   For information about women offenders, see Carson (2015: 16).

9   The scene is taken from the final script provided to me by Jodie and Ngozi. During rehearsals, Ngozi takes detailed notes on what the women say, but in performance they are allowed to improvise around the agreed upon content. As such, this dialogue does not represent exactly what was said onstage, but it is the only archival record available of the show at the time of this publication.

References

Banguid, M. B. (2002), 'The Violence Against Women Act', *Georgetown Journal of Gender and the Law* 4(1): 489–501.

Capers, I. B. (2008), 'Cross Dressing and the Criminal', *Yale Journal of Law and Humanities* 20(1): 1–30.

Carson, E. A. (2015), *Prisoners in 2014* (Sept 2015), Washington DC: Bureau of Justice Statistics.

Drama Club Members (2011), Interview with the author in December, New Orleans LA.

Freedman, E. (1996), 'The Prison Lesbian: Race, Class and the Construction of the Aggressive Female Homosexual, 1915–1965', *Feminist Studies* 22(2): 397–423.

Goldstein, D. (2003), *Laughter Out of Place: Race, Class, Violence and Sexuality in a Rio Shantytown*, Berkeley, Los Angeles, London: University of California Press.

Greene, C. (2015), '"She Ain't No Rosa Parks": The Joan Little Rape-Murder Case and Jim Crow Justice in the Post-Civil Rights South', *Journal of African American History* 100(3): 428–47.

Holliday, R. (1999), 'The Comfort of Identity', *Sexualities* 2(4): 481.

Johnson, E. P. (2006), '"Quare Studies," Or (Almost) Everything I Know About Queer Studies I Learned from My Grandmother', in E. P. Johnson and M. G. Henderson (eds), *Black Queer Studies: A Critical Anthology,* 124–60, Durham NC: Duke University Press.

Kalenda (Drama Club co-facilitator) (2011), Interview with the author in December, New Orleans LA.

Kunzel, R. (2008), *Criminal Intimacy: Prison and the Uneven History of Modern American Sexuality*, Chicago: University of Chicago Press.

Lucas, A. (2013), 'When I Run in My Bare Feet: Music, Writing and Theatre in a North Carolina Women's Prison', *American Music* 31(2): 134–62.

Madison, D. Soyini (2010), *Acts of Activism: Human Rights as Radical Performance*, Cambridge: Cambridge University Press.

McIntyre, D. L. (2010), *At the Dark End of the Street: Black Women, Rape and Resistance – A New History of the Civil Rights Movement from Rosa Parks to the Rise of Black Power*, New York: Knopf.

McNeil, G. R. (2008), 'The Body, Sexuality and Self-Defense in *State vs. Joan Little*, 1974–75', *Journal of African American History* 93(2): 235–61.

Mogul, J., Richie A. J. and K. Whitlock (2011), *Queer (In)Justice: The Criminalization of LGBTQ People in the United States*, Boston: Beacon Press.

Newton, E. (1979), *Mother Camp: Female Impersonators in America*, Chicago: University of Chicago Press.

Sabo, D. with Kuppers, T. A. and W. London (eds) (2001), *Prison Masculinities,* Philadelphia: Temple University Press.

Smitherman, G. (1977), *Talkin and Testifyin: The Language of Black America*. Boston: Houghton Mifflin Company.

Stanford, A. F. (2004), 'More Than Just Words: Women's Poetry and Resistance at Cook County Jail', *Feminist Studies* 30(2): 277–8.

Terry, C. M. (1997), 'The Function of Humor for Prison Inmates', *Journal of Contemporary Criminal Justice* 13(1): 23–40.

Thompson, J. (2004), 'From the Stocks to the Stage: Prison Theatre and the Theatre of Prison', in M. Balfour (ed.), *Theatre in Prison: Theory and Practice,* 57–76, Bristol: Intellect.

U.S. Bureau of Justice Statistics (1986), *Historical Corrections Statistics in the United States, 1850–1984,* Washington DC: Bureau of Justice Statistics.

U.S. Bureau of Justice Statistics (1997–2014), *Prison and Jail Inmates*, Washington DC: Bureau of Justice Statistics.

U.S. Bureau of Justice Statistics (2015a), *Prisoners in 2014*, Washington DC: Bureau of Justice Statistics.

U.S. Bureau of Justice Statistics (2015b), 'Rate of Violent Victimization, by Victim Demographic Characteristics, 2005, 2013, and 2014', in *Crime Victimization 2014* (August 2015), Bureau of Justice Statistics, Washington DC: 9.

Wolff, N., Shi, J. and J. A. Siegel (2009), 'Patterns of Victimization Among Male and Female Inmates: Evidence of an Enduring Legacy', *Violence and Victims* 24(4): 469–70.

Decade (1984)

Jacqueline Holborough

Jane The whole thing is designed to keep us gagged and in our place. We're all like that here, statutory rights don't matter. We're only women. We don't riot because then they'd set the men on us – and the dogs [...] They fill the place with such a mixture it would be impossible. Middle class book-cookers, foreign drug dealers, nutters throwing stones at aeroplanes [...] I could start a revolution in the bog but mention solidarity and the subject is changed to parole dates. They've got too much to lose [...] Put in your two or three Category A women, add a sprinkling of lifers and fill up with day trippers [...]

Me and a few other Category A women, your so-called terrorists. Rushed through our trials like a dose of Epsoms to keep the public confident. Without us this wing would have no reason to exist, it would be seen for what it is, a control unit with nothing to control [...] If I were a man there'd be a dozen dispersal units to shunt me around but as a woman I'm just a token. A freak. Caged up in this tiny space in the middle of a man's prison because I'm all there is [...] Which is greater punishment, death or endless rot in this vile box? [...]

I'm like a sin eater. Forced to swallow all the filth in society so it can sleep peaceful in its cosy bed. That's what we all are here, sin eaters.

Decade is set in HMP Durham's H-Wing, between 1977 and 1987. Written by Jacqueline Holborough and originally performed by Holborough and Hicks, Clean Break's founder members, it is directly informed by their experiences of incarceration in the Category A, high security wing, referred to in the tabloid newspapers as 'She Wing'. There are two characters, Mo, a prison maintenance worker, and Jane Wood, a prisoner sentenced to 298 years' imprisonment for multiple murders. The character of Jane is based on Judith Ward, convicted in 1974 for IRA terrorism acts and released in 1992 when the government acknowledged that she had been wrongfully convicted.

Decade is an unpublished play text, held in the Clean Break archive, Bishopsgate Institute, London.

3

Daughters of the Floating Brothel: Engaging Indigenous Australian Women Prisoners through Participatory Radio Drama

Sarah Woodland

Introduction

Daughters of the Floating Brothel was a drama project that I delivered with women in prison over 2014–15 which focused on creating work based on historical stories of criminality and sites of incarceration. The project represents my early experimentation with audio recording and radio drama as an approach to engaging the participants. I piloted the project in 2012 at Brisbane Women's Correctional Centre (BWCC), at the time, a maximum security prison on the outskirts of the city that held up to 300 inmates. I then continued through two iterations of the work in 2014 and 2015 at the same facility, with support from performance practitioner Daniele Constance, writer/director Shaun Charles and a small group of Applied Theatre undergraduate students from Griffith University Australia. The federal and state government arts bodies provided some funding for the project. The focus of the work was to explore moments in Australia's penal history from the convict arrival to the present, including the women's contemporary experiences of incarceration. Over 2014 and 2015, we worked with two different groups of women in sixteen two-hour sessions, each using improvised performance, image, writing, soundscape and audio recording. The outcome was a polished creative development version of the radio drama that incorporated documentary narration, dramatic scenes, soundscapes, personal stories, diary entries and poetic monologues created with the women, which were edited and produced by the artistic team. This version of the drama was played in a series of listening events: one for the public in the Griffith University theatre and three at the women's prisons in the region. The work was designed to function in a number of intersecting ways: engaging women in positive, empowering creative practice within the prison; inviting them to explore and interpret their contemporary experiences of incarceration

80   *Applied Theatre: Women and the Criminal Justice System*

through a fictional and historical frame; bringing the voices and experiences of women outside the prison walls to a wider audience; and creating a piece that would critically trace what Baldry, Carlton and Cunneen (2015: 175) describe as the 'colonial and racialized genealogy of punishment' in Australia.

The Floating Brothel was the nickname given to the *Lady Juliana* (also *Lady Julian*), a ship that sailed from Portsmouth in 1789 to transport 226 female convicts from the overcrowded jails of England to the new penal colony in Australia. It was given its nickname because the sex trade that many of its passengers had practised in London prior to being transported, and reputedly in ports as the ship made its way to Australia.[1] In conceiving this project, I saw this ship arriving on Australian shores as a potentially rich starting point for creative work with the women. The story represents a troubled and controversial beginning, signifying the beginning of Australia's master narrative of incarceration. It, therefore, represented a marker in time from which to investigate the experience of all women who have since been imprisoned in this country, and to explore some of the different versions of institutional confinement that were enforced by the colonists. The ship was also a recurring metaphor for the isolation, banishment and containment of incarceration in all its forms. The most recent (2015) version of *Daughters of the Floating Brothel* mixed fact and fiction in an episodic structure that moved through three historical spaces of incarceration that evoke key phases of Australia's penal history:

1. The ship itself, including fictional diary entries from women convicts, as well as the sighting of the ship and its passengers by the traditional Aboriginal landowners – the Eora people – as it arrived in what is now Port Jackson.
2. The Barambah Aboriginal Mission in 1901, established under the government's moves to 'protect' and segregate Aboriginal peoples. In this episode, Dorothy – a young Bidjara woman – becomes pregnant out of wedlock and decides to run away from the mission. This is now the site of Cherbourg, a local Aboriginal community where many of the women in the group had ties.
3. Brisbane's historic Old Boggo Road Gaol, an imposing neoclassical structure that was built in 1883 and decommissioned in the early 1990s. In this episode, a young woman, Mary, is arrested for vagrancy, locked in jail and sent to the punishment cell for allegedly inciting violence among the other incarcerated women.

Each of these episodes is framed by factual historical narration and spliced with moments of contemporary storytelling set in the modern prison, BWCC.

Daughters of the Floating Brothel   81

In this chapter, I will reflect upon how the groups of predominantly Aboriginal women engaged with the project. The work became a vessel to contain poetic conversations between the personal and the political, and the contemporary and the historical. Within the process the women expressed their own experiences of imprisonment through fictional and factual interpretations of penal history. The process and the developing artistic product reflected the politics of a colonial and (post)colonial[2] patriarchy that continues to imprison Indigenous Australian women at an alarming and disproportionate rate. This chapter, therefore, interrogates the project as a response to Indigenous women's over-representation in the prison system in Australia.

Background

The idea for a historical radio drama came from two particular strands in my previous work with women at BWCC. In my first drama project in 2010, the women were reluctant to create performance based on their own stories (see Woodland 2016b), but many seemed to value the drama space as a place where they could safely narrate their own experiences and lives, and experiment with new roles and ways of being themselves. Inspired by Annie McKean's (2006) description of a project in HM Prison Winchester, I subsequently decided to experiment with Australia's penal history as a dramatic frame through which women might explore their contemporary experiences of imprisonment. I piloted this approach in 2012, where a group of six women engaged enthusiastically with the history of Old Boggo Road Gaol, and observed that it allowed them to safely express their own emotions and experiences. The decision to produce a radio drama came about when I began to consider the representation of voice, and how a wider audience than just their peers might experience the women's performances. I also thought it might be a useful way to capture performances from a highly mobile group, whose attendance was regularly interrupted by medication calls, drug testing, legal visits and work programmes. Having experienced Pan Pan's production of the Samuel Beckett radio play *All That Fall* (Quinn 2014), Daniele and I were also excited about the contemporary possibilities of a historical form of storytelling that has all but disappeared from Australian radio.

In 2014, the General Manager of the prison requested that we target our programme to what she described as the most 'intractable prisoners', who were known to have continued drug dependency and behavioural problems inside, and who had not enrolled themselves in other programmes on offer in the centre. Initially, we did not include the Aboriginal Missions into our historical frame, focusing only on the Floating Brothel and Boggo Road Gaol stories in the posters that advertised the programme to women at BWCC. Enrolment in the project was voluntary and, given that there was no specific focus on the Indigenous history and culture, we were somewhat surprised to find that around ten out of the fifteen women who signed up at the start were Aboriginal. While any story about the convict arrival and the early days of Australian colonization would certainly include the Indigenous experience, this balance in our group caused us to shift the focus of the project much more towards the treatment of Indigenous Australians within the colonial penal system. Although this was tense territory for a team of non-Indigenous practitioners, we embraced it as a learning experience, and in 2015 enlisted the help of local Elder and memoirist Aunty Ruth Hegarty, who had written extensively about her own experiences of Cherbourg (Barambah) Aboriginal Mission in the 1930s and 1940s (Hegarty 1999). While there was a small number of non-Indigenous women in both groups whose engagement was equally important and interesting, I have chosen to foreground in this chapter the participation of Aboriginal women in the project, their artistic interpretations of Indigenous history and the personal stories and experiences that they shared. I am choosing this focus in response to the crisis of Indigenous over-representation that is currently occurring in Australian prisons (Bartels 2010; Baldry and Cunneen 2014; Cunneen 2009, 2011; McEntyre 2015; Stubbs 2011), the need for culturally relevant and engaging programmes for Indigenous women in prison (Biddle and Swee 2012; Dockery 2010; Jones, Masters, Griffiths and Moulday 2002) and the need to respond aesthetically and critically to the wider systemic drivers of this inequality. I, therefore, consulted Aunty Ruth on the development of this chapter in order to ensure a level of integrity in terms of ethically representing her story, and those of the Aboriginal women participants.

Daughters of the Floating Brothel was a collaborative work between the artistic team and the women at BWCC. It was a performance in prison, by imprisoned women, about incarceration. As such, it reflects the multiple performative layers that are at play in the field of prison theatre as described by authors such as Balfour (2004), McAvinchey (2011) and Thompson (1998, 2000). Discussing the project as an artistic response to the over-representation of Indigenous women in Australian prisons, therefore, involves interrogating the creative processes that we undertook in terms of how the Aboriginal women participants engaged with them, as well as the artistic product that was the radio drama in terms of how it depicts their stories and experiences. Although we did not set out at the beginning of the project to explore Indigenous incarceration as a formal line of enquiry, the practice led us there. Alongside the intrinsic generation of knowledge through the applied theatre

Daughters of the Floating Brothel

process, we also conducted more formalized interviews with participants during and after the project, as well as focus group feedback sessions with audience members at performances both inside and outside the prison, and these also informed our understanding.

The trauma trails of indigenous female incarceration

McEntyre (2015) draws on recent figures from the Australian Bureau of Statistics to report that Aboriginal and Torres Strait Islander women are now the fastest growing population in Australian prisons. Representing only 2 to 3 per cent of the female population of Australia, they are currently 21.2 times more likely to be imprisoned than non-indigenous women Australian (Law Reform Commission 2017). This over-representation is seen to be driven by systemic discrimination that includes the overpolicing and arrest of young Indigenous women for minor offences (Bartels 2010; Stubbs 2011), as well as the high rates of poverty, homelessness, low educational attainment, drug and alcohol abuse, violence, sexual abuse, disability, trauma and mental ill health among Indigenous women (Bartels 2010; Baldry and Cunneen 2014; Stubbs 2011; Victorian Equal Opportunity and Human Rights Commission 2013).

Atkinson (2002) coined the term 'trauma trails' to describe the transgenerational traumas experienced by Indigenous Australians since colonization. Drawing on her Jiman and Bundjalung heritage, she uses this term as a deliberate reimagining of the 'song lines' that integrate the spiritual, geographical and cultural in the tracing of pathways through the Aboriginal landscape, as handed down in traditional songs, stories, dances and paintings. Atkinson sees 'trauma trails' as the physical, spiritual and emotional pathways that run across the land and across generations, as people moved away from the many sites of pain, violence and the forced removal of children from their families. There is now acknowledgement that Indigenous Australians experience significant levels of mental ill health caused by inter- or transgenerational trauma (see Atkinson 2002; Cunneen 2009; Maddison 2011; Sherwood and Kendall 2013). Trauma is particularly prevalent in prison, where there are high levels of PTSD, depression, anxiety, self-harm and suicidal ideation among Indigenous women (Heffernan, Anderson, Davidson and Kinner 2015; Heffernan, Anderson, Dev and Kinner 2012). Recent studies into the epigenetic transmission of trauma offer a scientific interpretation of how 'trauma trails' can be imprinted on the DNA (Franklin et al. 2010; Gapp et al. 2014). Some scholars are now using these discoveries to examine major cultural traumas such as the Jewish Holocaust (Kellermann 2013), the Tutsi genocide in Rwanda (Perroud et al. 2014), and the postcolonial

84   *Applied Theatre: Women and the Criminal Justice System*

subjugation of Canadian Aboriginal peoples (Aguiar and Halseth 2015). In Australia in 1987, the pivotal enquiry into Aboriginal Deaths in Custody (Johnston 1991) outlined major changes that needed to be made to reduce the mortality and disadvantage of Indigenous peoples being dealt with by the criminal justice system. Similarly, 'Bringing them home: The Report of the National Inquiry into the Separation of Aboriginal and Torres Strait Islander Children from Their Families' (Wilson 1997) officially documented the extent and impacts on what are now called the Stolen Generations, precipitating a national apology by the then Prime Minister Kevin Rudd in 2008. Yet despite these developments, Weatherburn (2014) suggests that Australians are still indifferent to the staggering scale of the problem of Indigenous incarceration. 'Trauma trails' are leading many Indigenous young women to prison, which then becomes another potentially traumatic site where the pain, violence and separation continue.

The cultural balance of our 2014 group, therefore, led to us conceiving the history of incarceration in Australia in much wider terms than the convict arrival and the nineteenth-century jail building. Through the nineteenth and early part of the twentieth centuries, Aboriginal and Torres Strait Islander women were unlikely to be housed in these buildings, but as Cassella and Fredericksen (2004: 108) assert, 'For Aboriginal Australians, their sense of "being Australian" can often involve shared experiences of missions, residential schools, hospitals, police lock-ups and prisons – places that commemorate particularly institutional forms of confinement.' Cunneen (2009: 211) suggests: 'The historical memory of massacres, containment on reserves, the forced removal of children and a discriminatory criminal justice system is very much alive in Indigenous histories.' Baldry, Carlton and Cunneen (2015: 177) refer to the 'protection' legislation that was brought in at the end of the nineteenth century, which segregated individuals in reserves and missions under strict curfews and penal regimes that paralleled the existing criminal justice system. This meant that despite not being interred in the official prison system, Indigenous Australians were 'as imprisoned as if they had been locked in a proper jail' (see also Hogg 2001). The following excerpts from the radio drama reflect this history by describing the origins of Cherbourg Community when it was known as Barambah Mission:

> **Narrator**   Cherbourg Community began as Barambah Mission. It was
> started in 1901 by a Salvation Army missionary who camped with a
> small number of Wakka Wakka people on the banks of Barambah
> Creek. The Queensland Government took control of the settlement in
> March, 1904. Residents were known as 'inmates' and they were put to

Daughters of the Floating Brothel

work – clearing land for farming, raising animals and erecting buildings. From 1910 to 1919, men, women and children from over fifty clans across Australia were forcibly removed to Barambah Mission. The system split up families – children were taken away from their parents to live in dormitories and adults were sent to work.[3]

After some establishing soundscape, this narration leads into a speech by the white Superintendent of the mission, which describes the prison-like restrictions:

Superintendent *(authoritative)* Everyone line up! Line up and be quiet! Alright, now that you are here in Barambah there are rules to how things are done. You must obey the rules. First, you are not permitted to leave the settlement without my permission. Also, you will not speak your language. If you use your own language you will be punished. To leave the settlement, you need a permit – even for fishing or hunting. Obey these rules and you will be alright. If anyone is thinking of running off – of *absconding* – then know we have a black tracker, yes one of your own, who will go out, track you down and bring you back, whereupon you will be punished.

The map that Aunty Ruth Hegarty drew for us of the mission in the 1940s included a prison cell for such punishment to occur. She told us that for more serious crimes such as adultery, the woman concerned may be sent to Palm Island – a remote Aboriginal mission off the coast of North Queensland that was used as a penal colony by the white administrators (Watson 2010). The adulterous man in this scenario would likely be allowed to remain at Barambah. The story of the Stolen Generations, therefore, is a story not only of intergenerational trauma resulting from the removal of children and the displacement of families, but also of 'the unbroken chain from 1788 to the twenty-first century, of discriminatory institutional methods of control of Indigenous Australians' (Baldry and Cunneen 2014: 291).

Blessing and releasing the past

In another volume in this series, I have described the tensions of navigating this territory as a practitioner-researcher from a position of white privilege, and the need to work critically and reflexively in viewing the workshop space as a potential site for reconciliation (Woodland 2016a). We had to acknowledge that our arts 'intervention' could be seen as another form of

86   *Applied Theatre: Women and the Criminal Justice System*

recolonization, replicating the traumatizing effects of other government-sanctioned interventions in the lives of these women and their communities (see Altman 2007; Maddison 2011). There was also a need for criticality around the representation of Aboriginal peoples within both the workshop space and the finished radio drama (see Langton 1993b; Hodge and Mishra 1991; Preston 2009). Maddison (2011: 67) cites Cowlishaw (2004) in suggesting, 'We must remain alert to our tendency to limit our recognition of past injustices to a "sanitised, romanticised, or victimised Aboriginality".' Further, Maddison (2011: 155) warns that memory and commemoration of the Stolen Generations can have a 'dark side': 'An endless fixation on trauma can also prolong the pain of those who have suffered.' Scholars such as Balfour (2009), Cox (2008), Jeffers (2008), Salverson (2009) and Thompson (2009) question the uncritical perpetuation of an 'aesthetics of injury' (Salverson 2009: 254) through the personal narratives of trauma and victimhood that characterize much applied theatre practice. However, there exists a strong presence of personal story and testimony within contemporary Indigenous performance. Plays such as *The Cherry Pickers* (Gilbert 1988), *Whispers of this Wik Woman* (Doyle 2004), *The 7 Stages of Grieving* (Enoch, Mailman and Beaton 2002), *Oodgeroo – Bloodline to Country* (Watson 2009) and *The Story of the Miracles at Cookie's Table* (Enoch 2014) all depict biography and autobiography in the context of a geographical, spiritual and cultural lifeworld that spans all of history, foregrounding the shattering traumas of colonialism.

Once we began working with the historical material, we discovered that there was a strong thread of intergenerational incarceration running through the personal histories of the women in our group, and that many of them already knew or were related to each other, coming from the same neighbourhoods and moving through the systems of state care and incarceration together since childhood. Seven of the sixteen women that we worked with over 2014 and 2015 had direct connections to Barambah Mission via grandparents and great grandparents who had been born there, or removed there as children. One young woman, Jade,[4] told the story of how her great-grandfather had been taken there as an infant in a shoebox, and then reminisced about her own happy childhood growing up with her grandparents in what is now Cherbourg Community. At the end of her story, she cried as she observed that she would probably have been better off if she had stayed there with them, rather than moving to the city. She described how they were quite strict to live with, because 'My grandparents were frightened of us growing up to how I am now.' Her story describes the transition of Cherbourg Community from a place of confinement during its early days to an open community in which people now choose to live, in

Daughters of the Floating Brothel

many cases due to the family ties that bind them there. Ironically, Jade was pregnant during our project and spoke about her fears that the child would be taken from her and put into state care. This directly echoed the fictional story that the women created in 2014 and formed the centrepiece of our Barambah Mission episode in the radio drama. The character Dorothy, a young Bidjara woman, falls pregnant and decides to run away from the mission to prevent the *wadigan* (white woman) from taking her baby. Jade never verbalized a connection to this part of the drama, but the two stories – fictional and real, historical and contemporary – illustrated the same cycle of forced separation and induction into state systems of 'care' that Aunty Ruth Hegarty (1999: 126) describes in her memoir: 'I was painfully aware that our lives were beginning to mirror those of our mothers ... This pattern had begun when we were babies, and it looked like it was continuing on through our children.' Elsewhere, she describes this as a 'victim trap' (128). These connections were not limited to the Barambah Mission story. Two of the women in the project said that their mothers had been imprisoned in Old Boggo Road Gaol in the 1980s and 1990s, and many others said that they knew older family members, male and female, who had been there. Another participant, Tayla, had both Aboriginal and Vanuatuan heritage. She described seeing a picture of her 'kanaka' ancestor with shackle marks on his ankles and railway bolts in his ears where he had been chained up and forced to work in the cane fields of North Queensland, a situation of so-called indentured servitude that was supposed to have replaced slavery (see Hogg 2001). Another participant, Jasmine, recorded a contemporary diary entry for the piece in which she described her feelings of sadness and isolation when she was told that her uncle had become 'a victim of black death in custody'. Her personal story alerts the listener to a wider controversy that has continued to plague the Australian criminal justice system since the Commission of Inquiry twenty-five years ago (Johnston 1991). The piece, therefore, became a vehicle through which the Aboriginal women participants might poetically follow the 'trauma trails' of incarceration leading from convict settlement to now. We began with some trepidation about whether digging into this troubling history might result in retraumatization, as well as the perpetuation of the trauma aesthetic that I have described above. However, when I brought my concerns to the late Aunty Anne Leisha, an Aboriginal Elder-in-Residence at Griffith University, she explained to me that, in her opinion, it was imperative to address this difficult history in order to 'bless it, release it and move on' (see also Woodland 2016a). It soon became apparent that the women were engaging deeply and positively with the process and that, despite the sadness contained in the stories, their connection to culture was important. After Jade shared the emotional story of her connection to

88   *Applied Theatre: Women and the Criminal Justice System*

Cherbourg, she said it had been a relief to be able to speak about these issues openly in a safe environment. At another point Jasmine said:

> I love hearing about my culture, yeah. I get a real happy feeling in me when I hear about it ... But it's sad at the same time if you know what I mean, because of what they had done to them – to Aboriginals back in the past.

The participants Lara, Carly and Nicole all expressed similar feelings about the sense of pride they felt in their own culture. Another layer to this sense of pride seemed to stem from the women having an opportunity to educate themselves and others about their culture and history – particularly the Stolen Generations. Jasmine talked about how little Aboriginal history and culture were taught in mainstream Australian schools, and Tayla also highlighted how little she had known previously about this aspect of history. In one workshop after a group discussion about how Aboriginals had been forced into servitude during the early days of white settlement, Carly was genuinely shocked: 'Did they treat us like slaves?' she asked. All of these women said that they valued the opportunity to learn more about their cultural history, and to pass it on to their own children. Once the women considered a wider audience would be hearing the work, they saw this as a source of pride as well. Tayla, Nicole and Jasmine all discussed how important it was to educate a wider audience about Aboriginal history.

Representing intergenerational incarceration

Through the previous sections I have given some background into the *Daughters of the Floating Brothel* project and into the 'trauma trails' of Indigenous female incarceration. I have also begun to discuss how the Aboriginal women participants in our group engaged with the notion of exploring and representing the history of the Stolen Generations, and the feelings of pride in their culture that this process seemed to bring about. I will now delve more deeply into the creative process and the radio drama as an artistic product, exploring how the group poetically represented Aboriginal culture and history within each episode, and how it was positioned within an artistic rendering of Australia's genealogy of punishment. The premise of the project – of imprisoned women representing themselves within a wider critique of imprisonment – is inherently both risky and promising, particularly within the context of Indigenous incarceration. As leading Indigenous Australian scholar Marcia Langton (2008: 145) asserts:

The crisis in Aboriginal society is now a public spectacle, played out in a vast 'reality show' through the media, parliaments, public service and the Aboriginal world. This obscene and pornographic spectacle shifts attention away from the everyday lived crisis that many Aboriginal people endure – or do not, dying as they do at excessive rates.

Imprisonment is a key aspect of this crisis, and as such *Daughters of the Floating Brothel* could run the risk of contributing to the spectacle. Yet our hope was that, although the project may have reinforced the *fact* of Aboriginal imprisonment, criminality and victimhood, it employed a self-conscious criticality in representing these differently from the usual mainstream media depictions of violence, verbal abuse, drunkenness and abject poverty. In *Daughters*, the imprisoned women were recast as artists, actors, narrators and critical commentators, interpreting the (post)colonial legacy of incarceration. However, in 2014 and 2015, the women were interacting with and responding to the historical Aboriginal experience as mediated and presented by white facilitators, albeit with some guidance from an Aboriginal Elder (Aunty Ruth) whom they never met in person. The facilitator team was using many historical documents and images that were themselves authored by whites. There existed the ever-present power relationship of facilitator–participant; and, due to the constraints of time and access that I have discussed earlier, we had most of the control in terms of script editing and post-production.

Episode one: The ship and its arrival

The radio drama begins with the *Lady Juliana* en route to Australia, with the voices of English women convicts reading diary entries that describe their fears and hopes for the future. Members of the 2014 group generated these texts, imagining what it would be like to make this perilous journey. Sheree, an Aboriginal woman who was released about halfway through the 2014 project, wrote one of these:

> Dear Diary, March 23, 1789. We've been at sea for two months now. Sarah is terribly ill with the scurvy. She lies in her hammock most days. The boat creaks and moans as if it is in pain. Who knows how much longer we will have to endure this. This boat, and this ocean, is our prison.

In 2015, the entries were minimally edited and recorded with a group of women from HMP Styal in the UK with the help of the Prison Radio Association, London. Several audience members felt that this lent the piece a sense of authenticity in performance; but it also served to unequivocally position the story of institutional confinement for women in Australia as beginning with the European colonial – and by extension patriarchal – project of convict transportation. The stories of the female convicts were a kind of hook for both Indigenous and non-Indigenous group members alike, who were amused and fascinated by the idea of the Floating Brothel. The women created fictional backstories for some of the real women whose names and convictions had appeared on the original ship's manifest. The costume drama romanticism of the stories and scenes that the women created demonstrated a strong frame of reference from film and television – for example, several of the women were familiar with the story of Mary Bryant, who made a daring escape from the colony by boat to Timor (see Cook 2004; Hughes 1987). It seemed that this more distant history allowed the women to see whether or not they enjoyed our approach and, for those who did, to develop some trust in the group before moving into stories of Old Boggo Road Gaol and Barambah Mission that were closer to their personal experiences.

For the workshops, we introduced each historical moment with some contextual storytelling and the passing around of printed images – for example, early colonial paintings of the settlement, photographs from the turn of the last century – of Old Boggo Road Gaol and Barambah Mission when they were first established. Our early sessions included introductory drama exercises to warm up and engage the group, including tableaux. After the convict women's diary entries, the radio drama shifts perspective onto the shoreline of southern Australia, where a group of Eora people observe its passage along the coast towards what is now New South Wales. We touched on this moment several times during the creative process, not only to create content for the radio drama but also to establish the context of the piece in the minds of the group early on. In the beginning, we invited the women to create tableaux of the ship approaching Australia with the convict women watching the shore and a group of Eora people on the shore watching the ship. While we did not prescribe the casting of this image, the group nevertheless instinctively divided along racial lines, and the Aboriginal women enthusiastically created a depiction of the Eora people looking on with surprise, concern and curiosity as the ship arrived. Some of the women playfully imitated the early colonial depictions of the Eora people, holding spears and standing on one leg. In order to move past this stereotypical colonial imagery of the 'noble savage', we invited the women to consider the emotions that they would be feeling as they watched the ship approaching. This appeared to be a moment of deep engagement for the women, when they committed fully to the physical and emotional qualities of the scene.

Several sessions later, we invited the whole group to collaborate on a poetic monologue for the piece built around how the Eora people might describe an approaching ship if they had never seen one before. Several ideas were offered during this discussion, which we noted down and edited into the final monologue which Jasmine performed with a beautiful sense of wonder and curiosity:

From afar I see wavy sheets that almost look like giant seagulls flying in the distance. As they come closer, I see dark brown floating wood, like one of our canoes but much bigger, with holes cut into the side. It roars through the water, cutting the waves in two. There are pretty women, standing on the top. They wear cloaks of flowing paperbark, as white as sand. They stare towards the shore. Are they spirits?

This passage certainly contains elements of the romanticism I have discussed earlier; but there was a high level of focus and reflection in the group during its creation, and it stood out as one of the most enduring images from the piece in the minds of several of our audience focus groups afterwards. In the context of the radio drama, Jasmine's vocal performance conveyed a sense of innocence and wonder, presaging the inevitable disaster that would follow for Indigenous people in the larger story of Australia's colonization and settlement.

Once we began thinking more widely about the notion of incarceration, I considered just which mechanisms of containment and control would have been entirely new to the Indigenous Australians, and incorporated this into the narration that introduces the Aboriginal sighting of the ship above:

Narrator The Europeans brought many things to Australia, including their own ideas of punishment and control. They brought fences, gates, doors, locks, keys. They brought prisoners, and built prisons. They built prisons that were cleverly disguised as factories, orphanages, hospitals, schools, farms and missions.

Alongside this, we had been creating soundscapes with the group that included doors slamming, jangling keys, creaking hinges and echoing footsteps. These were recurring motifs throughout the piece, with the loud slam of a prison door signifying each change of scene. Once we moved into the Barambah Mission scene, we added the sounds of creaky gates and the mission bell to signify the institutionalization that marked this place, juxtaposed against the other atmospheric sounds of frogs, birds and children laughing and playing that might otherwise signify freedom.

Episode two: Barambah Mission

The episode of the radio drama that is set in Barambah Mission at the turn of last century is arguably the most accomplished aesthetically, narratively and in terms of the women's performances. There are several possible reasons for this. First, in both 2014 and 2015 we worked on the content for this scene last, reasoning that we needed to build sufficient trust and safety in the group before tackling such culturally sensitive material. In terms of Bolton's (1984) notion of distancing and 'protecting into emotion' in drama education, it could be suggested that the convict stories provided sufficient distancing from the women's real lives and experiences, enabling them to gradually move closer to the material to which they had a much stronger personal and emotional connection. By the time we began working with the Barambah Mission material, the group had become more stable and was working well together, and, therefore, the quality of the material that they were creating had improved significantly. The Aboriginal women participants in both years also stated that this was the episode with which they most identified, and which they wanted to be carried forward into future iterations of the project. Both Tayla and Jasmine described the episode as 'real', implying that it was culturally relevant and connected directly to their own experiences and family history. This may have impacted on how the women engaged during the creation of scenes for this episode, and the evident sensitivity and care with which the women approached the work. The episode begins with Jasmine narrating the passage I have included in the previous section, describing how the mission was established and how people from all over the state of Queensland were forcibly removed there from their traditional homelands. As we rehearsed for her recording session, I encouraged her to bring some feeling into the words.

She asked, 'What feeling? Should it be sad?'

I said, 'How does it make you feel?'

'Angry,' she said.

'Well maybe use that feeling of anger then?' I suggested.

'It makes me feel angry and sad.'

And then she read the piece. Her reading of this narration was in stark contrast to her sense of wonder and curiosity in voicing the Eora woman sighting the ship. Here Jasmine was not simply just imparting historical facts in an educational sense, she was also able to imbue them with her own emotional response within a developing understanding of that painful history.

After the narration and the introductory speech by the Superintendent, the episode moves into the story of Dorothy, the young pregnant Bidjara

Daughters of the Floating Brothel

woman. As I have mentioned, the character of Dorothy and the scenes within her story were created with the first group in 2014. This was done through a 'role on the wall' (Neelands and Goode 2015: 27) style of exercise in which the group collaboratively created the young woman and her backstory:

Dorothy   My name is Dorothy, I am 19 years old. I am Bidjara tribe, from out Charleville way. They brought my family to Barambah Mission when I was four. We were removed and 'escorted'. This Wakka Wakka land, but we here now, too. I do cleaning in the hospital. I have a man. His name Dennis. He looks after the yarraman – the horses. We're not allowed to see each other ... but we do.

The group was very quick to build her storyline, drawing in part from the popular film *Rabbit-Proof Fence* (Noyce 2002), whose storyline also dealt with the Stolen Generations in the early part of the twentieth century. Dorothy's tribal group – Bidjara – was chosen entirely arbitrarily after I had found a Bidjara language dictionary online and brought it to the group (Crump n.d.). Not only did the women seem really interested in the language – reading the dictionary avidly and playing around with the pronunciation of the words – but I was also aware that it would make the piece sound more culturally accurate if we could include some words from an Aboriginal language group who would have been present in Barambah. This would also represent the speaking of language in secret or private as an important act of rebellion against the rules of the mission. After the monologue from Dorothy above, the episode moves into the following scene inside the mission:

The sound of a girl crying.

Aunty   Come here bub, talk to Aunty. What's wrong?

Dorothy   Aunty, I had a dream. I seen the kookaburra in the bluegum tree.

Aunty   *Gagubara* up in the *dangun*, that is a good sign. That means you pregnant. You're having a gandu, a baby!

Dorothy   I know. I wanna run away back home out west. I don't want white woman taking my baby.

Aunty   Yeah, *wadigan* take your baby you stay here. No good running home but – nobody there anymore. All our mob here now girl.

94   *Applied Theatre: Women and the Criminal Justice System*

> **Dorothy** (*crying*)   Help me Aunty, what I'm gunna do? Where I'm gunna go?

> **Aunty**   Wait for another dream. *Birrangulu* will tell you. God will tell you what to do.

Here, Aunty is portrayed as the Elder who still retains some of the traditional language phrased in such a way as to educate the listener about the meaning of certain words. In this, I was inspired by Big Hart's production *Ngapartji Ngapartji* (Rankin 2005), an Aboriginal theatre and language project that aims to keep alive the traditional languages that are under threat of extinction. Yet there appeared to be another important element of language at play in the creation of this scene, which was the use of what Jade and Nicole referred to as 'mission talk' – the specific grammar and syntax that is still used in the more remote Aboriginal settlements that were once missions. The two women, who were from the city, enjoyed playing with this in their rehearsals for the scene, and Nicole was very detailed in amending and editing the script that had been brought forward from the previous year so that it would contain the correct expressions and phrasings of mission talk. I have since heard from Aunty Ruth that mission talk was an important language that Indigenous peoples developed in order to communicate in secret without having to use their prohibited traditional languages. This has parallels in today's prison culture, where people develop their own ways of communicating that can operate on the margins and under the radar of perpetual listening and surveillance by the authorities. Jade and Nicole appeared to be treating mission talk as an important aspect of Aboriginal language and culture from the past that could be represented in the radio drama.

Lara, one of the 2014 participants, contributed the idea of the dream to the story, and another participant, Tanya, wrote a poem that was adapted to become the narration that underscores the end of the scene:

> But the dream is more a nightmare. The girl is running. She's with child. She's running through the bush. The grass is frosty. She's surrounded by clouds and bush, and the kookaburra is still laughing. Her heart is beating so fast. Whispers in the night. Campfires hidden. She's finally free from something. Run, girl, run! But the tracker is following her, chasing her. He's a clever one. He follows her in darkness. He can hear whispers. He can read the movements of birds. She needs to get away. She needs to be free.

In both years, the groups were highly involved in the creation of soundscapes for the dream sequences, and most of the participants later reported that this had been the most engaging aspect of the process. We built these soundscapes using a combination of human voice and body, and whatever objects we could find in the spare space of the prison classroom. They functioned not only as integral aspects of the radio drama as a product, but also became exciting collaborative group performances in the moment, as we played with the sequencing and building of the soundscape for each scene. At these moments, the room was abuzz with the women rushing around, grabbing a piece of paper that could be scrunched up to create a crackling fire or a plastic bag that could be waved around to create a breeze in the leaves or two cups of water that could be poured into each other to create a running creek. At one point, Lani experimented with a rotating magazine rack that Carly and Nicole said sounded like a rusty old windmill – its metallic screech becoming a key sound underscoring the nightmare above.

At the end of the Barambah Mission episode, Dorothy makes her escape at night as we hear the gate creaking shut and her bare footsteps running away. The draft script that was brought forward from 2014 did not contain an ending beyond this for Dorothy. In consultation, Aunty Ruth speculated on three possible endings to her story, which I noted down and brought to the group. After some discussion, I suggested that we could present all three to the audience and allow them to speculate also. Jasmine liked this idea, and so in her role as Dorothy's younger sister, she voiced the final monologue of the scene:

> **Gladys** I walked out into the cold dawn after Dorothy had gone.
> The first birds were singing her away. I thought about where she
> would go. Would she find another mob to camp with down south?
> Or would the tracker catch her and bring her back here? Or maybe
> she would make her own little campfire for her new family –
> somewhere nearby, close to me and Dennis [*her boyfriend*]. I saw
> a white flicker on the fence. A hanky that she sewed for the
> Wadigan [*white woman*], left behind, caught on the wire and
> waving goodbye in the morning breeze.

Several audience members in the prison listening events did not like the uncertainty of this story – they wanted to *know* what happened to Dorothy, and they wanted a happy ending for her and her baby. But the unanswered question of this passage forces the listener to contemplate the all too familiar reality of Dorothy's dilemma: imprisonment and separation from her unborn child, or separation from her existing family and a life (or more likely death) on the margins away from her Country.

Episode three: Old Boggo Road Gaol

The final episode of *Daughters of the Floating Brothel* takes place in Old Boggo Road Gaol. It centres on the character Mary, a white woman who is arrested for vagrancy on the streets of Brisbane, taken to the jail and then locked in the 'black hole' – the jail's notorious solitary punishment cell – for inciting violence among the other women. As with the other episodes in the drama, the protagonist Mary and her story were created over the two years, using old black-and-white images and factual stories from Boggo Road Gaol as stimulus. Again, we created improvised scenes, poetic monologues and soundscapes, and the episode was spliced with contemporary narration from one of the white women participants who described her experience in the contemporary equivalent of the black hole. Creating this episode appeared again to be a highly engaging process for many of the participants. As I have mentioned earlier, Aboriginal women would not have been held in Boggo Road Gaol during its early days, most having been removed to missions and reserves that sat outside, but strongly paralleled, the official penal system. Yet through the 1970s to the 1990s, Boggo Road Gaol became home to many Aboriginal men and women, some known to our group of participants.

The episode contains a scene in which two male police officers are walking their beat through the streets of Brisbane in 1912 and they discover Mary sleeping rough. This scene was devised through a group discussion and then improvisation with contributions from a number of different participants over the course of its development. Ultimately though, the police officers were played by two Aboriginal women – Nicole and Debora – which was an entirely arbitrary decision based on who was available and who was not already playing another role in the episode. What occurs is, therefore, an unintentional, yet powerful example of 'whitefacing' (see Gilbert 2003; Gubar 2000), where the two women invert the usual racial- and gender-based power relationship to play the role of white male law enforcement. An excerpt from the script also demonstrates the somewhat playful and ironic approach that the team took with the dialogue:

Sergeant   . . . Well well well, what have we here?

Constable   Hmmm. Another tart no doubt.

Sergeant (*chuckles*)   This is no place for a woman to sleep. Not even a tart!

Constable (*leans in towards Mary*)   Ma'am . . . ?

Sergeant   Excuse me, Miss . . . ?

Mary (*wakes up with a start*)   Oh goodness. Oh dear . . .

Constable   What is your name please, Miss?

Mary   Mary . . .

Constable   Mary who?

Sergeant (*smug*)   Oh yes . . . this is Mary Taylor, I know her well. (*Pause*) Mary Taylor, you know that vagrancy is on offence.

Mary   Is it?

Sergeant   Yes, you *know* it is. You may not sleep on the streets of Brisbane.

Bartels (2010) refers to the prevalence of arrests among young Indigenous women for public order offences, and, in a direct parallel, the two officers are arresting Mary for vagrancy. This brought about a unique kind of engagement for Nicole and Debora, who had been on the receiving end of this kind of police intervention many times in their lives. Both women played the scene for humour, appearing to relish the opportunity to be playful with the roles of police officers and to co-opt the voices of white male authority. Nicole observed that the police would never get away with calling her a 'tart' if the situation were to happen now. There was much hilarity during the rehearsals of the scene, and, afterwards, Nicole said that she had enjoyed using her voice to characterize the role of Sergeant, consciously differentiating it from her vocalizing of Dorothy's mission talk.

In her pivotal work on representations of Aboriginality in film, television and radio, Langton (1993b: 37–8) suggests that many Australian film-makers (up to the point of writing) 'want to see "Europeans" portrayed only as oppressors and all the complexities eliminated. They fail to admit the intersubjectivity of black/white relations.' In Langton's terms, *Daughters of the Floating Brothel* might be seen in terms of her third category of intersubjectivity in representing Aboriginal culture in the arts: where 'Aboriginal and non-Aboriginal people engage in actual dialogue, where the individuals test and adapt imagined models of each other to find satisfactory forms of mutual comprehension' (81). In addressing our traumatic colonial legacy, Maddison (2011) similarly suggests that there must be room for meaningful dialogue that comes from both sides of the conflict. In this sense the project, therefore, became a conversation between Indigenous and non-Indigenous Australian perspectives on incarceration. Yet it must be acknowledged that the complexity that Langton is suggesting within this approach did not necessarily translate to the first and second creative developments of the radio drama.

98   *Applied Theatre: Women and the Criminal Justice System*

Although much more polished, the 2015 version is somewhat simplistic in the portrayal of Europeans as oppressors and incarcerated women as victims of a (post)colonial patriarchy. This resulted, in part, from the problems of access and attendance that we experienced as I have described earlier. The actual face-to-face time that we had with each group only amounted to a total of around thirty hours, with a great deal of fluctuation in terms of personnel and regular attendance. This meant that it was difficult to engage deeply in developing the themes and narratives within the final piece. Some audience focus groups also felt that the piece lacked meaningful character development, humour and hope, which potentially perpetuated the aesthetics of injury or victimhood that I have described earlier. Instead, the intersubjective complexity existed in the creative process and the workshop space, where there were many different discussions and interpretations of the historical material and the contemporary situation, and where knowledge was exchanged between non-Indigenous and Indigenous group members that was informed by their own cultural experiences and views. Similarly, the workshop space was where most of the humour, hope and positive collaboration were experienced, with these not necessarily being represented in the final piece.

Conclusion

After two iterations of the project, it has become clear that the approaches that we used in *Daughters of the Floating Brothel* have potential in terms of addressing Indigenous women's over-representation, and contributing to the limited number of culturally relevant and engaging programmes, within the prison system in Australia. The project responds as both process and product, where the participants might make sense of the 'trauma trails' of incarceration, and experience a sense of enhanced well-being by engaging in aspects of their cultural history and language (see Biddle and Swee 2012; Dockery 2010) and a sense of pride and achievement in educating themselves and others about this culture. The project also has the potential to engage the wider community in critical debate over the (post)colonial legacy of incarceration in Australia. Yet the project certainly has room to evolve ethically and aesthetically. As I have suggested, the latest version of the product is somewhat lacking in the more complex portrayal of Aboriginal/ white intersubjectivity (Langton 1993b), and the portrayal of hope and positivity that we experienced through the process. The project invited Indigenous women inside the system to learn and teach others about their culture, but there are inherent ethical problems with a team of white

Australian facilitators 'educating' a group of Aboriginal women in prison about their own cultural heritage. This is why we engaged the services of Aunty Ruth Hegarty in script development once we saw the mix of our group, and in my projects since *Daughters*, I have worked much more closely alongside Aboriginal artists and researchers from the outset. A significant goal of the radio drama was also to reach a wider audience outside the prison walls and invite them to consider the genealogy of punishment in Australia that can be traced back to colonization. This poetic, narrative approach might also have brought some depth and dimension to the statistics surrounding Indigenous incarceration: several public audience members reported that the voicing of the work by incarcerated women lent the piece a sense of authenticity and poignancy. But this goal was largely unmet in terms of reaching the broader public. Management at BWCC initially approved the recording and broadcast elements of the project as described in the arts funding application for 2015, and continued to allow the project to unfold as planned throughout the course of the workshop programme for that year. In the end, however, Queensland Corrective Services refused permission at the executive level to broadcast the piece on community radio and internet podcast. It seems that there had been some kind of error or miscommunication within their bureaucratic processes that led to this occurring. After I sent a letter appealing the decision, they replied that the decision would be upheld, stating that the content of the piece did not 'meet community expectations' for Queensland Corrective Services and could potentially be 'confrontational for listeners'. They did not elucidate how and why this might have been the case, but unfortunately the decision resulted in the continued marginalization of the group by denying them a wider public voice.

Through this chapter, I have described the process in terms of how it engaged the Aboriginal women participants in the group, and how their stories and histories were represented within the drama. I would suggest that a key aspect of addressing the crisis of Indiengous over-representation must be to engage this particular group, and to create safe spaces for frank and meaningful dialogue around their imprisonment using culturally relevant materials and approaches. This investigation, therefore, does not measure the success of the piece in changing the attitudes of audiences who heard the piece, or impacting on the culture of the criminal justice system as a whole, but rather places the emphasis on the participants in terms of how they interpreted and represented the intergenerational legacy of incarceration in Australia. The geographical and emotional journeys embodied in the piece represent 'trauma trails' that the group could follow in perhaps beginning to make some sense of their current situation. Yet there is a sense that each trail is not linear, but rather a continuous cycle, that somehow must be broken. In working with the supposedly most 'intractable prisoners', we discovered that the form of radio drama and the theme of institutional confinement were highly engaging, and the work that the women produced became for them a source of pride and cultural connection (which was then unfortunately censored by the system). The participatory approaches that were used allowed space to explore this history and culture poetically and perhaps safely, and also became a form of education for both the participants themselves and the wider prison audiences.

Acknowledgements

The research discussed in this chapter was completed with support from Queensland Corrective Services. The views expressed herein are solely those of the author and in no way reflect the views or policies of Queensland Corrective Services.

Notes

1 Our understanding of the Floating Brothel story came predominantly from a historical novel by Sian Rees (2001), a personal account by one of the crewmen John Nicol and Tim Flannery (1997) and the brief description in Robert Hughes' *The Fatal Shore* (1987).
2 Naming the world as 'post-colonial' is, from Indigenous perspectives, to name colonialism as finished business (Smith 1999).
3 The factual information in the Barambah episode was taken from the website The Cherbourg Memory: http://cherbourgmemory.org/ (Williams and Besley n.d.).
4 The names of the women prisoners have been changed to protect their privacy.

References

Aguiar, W. and R. Halseth (2015), 'Aboriginal Peoples and Historic Trauma: The Processes of Intergenerational Transmission', Prince George BC: National Collaborating Centre for Aboriginal Health.

Altman, J. C. (2007), *The Howard Government's Northern Territory I ntervention: Are Neo-Paternalism and Indigenous Development Compatible*, Australian National University, Centre for Aboriginal Economic Policy Research.

Atkinson, J. (2002), *Trauma Trails, Recreating Song Lines: The Transgenerational Effects of Trauma in Indigenous Australia*. Vol. 1. North Melbourne: Spinifex Press.

Australian Law Reform Commission. (2017) *Pathways to Justice—Inquiry into the Incarceration Rate of Aboriginal and Torres Strait Islander Peoples*, Final Report No 133. Sydney: Australian Law Reform Commission. https://www.alrc.gov.au/publications/indigenous-incarceration-report133

Baldry, E. (2009), 'Prisons and Vulnerable Persons: Institutions and Patriarchy'. Proceedings from the Australia & New Zealand Critical Criminology Conference 2009 (18–30). Available online: https://www.researchgate.net/profile/Alex_Steel/publication/43128227_Bail_in_Australia_legislative_introduction_and_amendment_since_1970/links/0deec5267bca9afa80000000.pdf#page=18 (accessed 1 August 2019).

Baldry, E. and C. Cunneeb (2014), 'Imprisoned Indigenous Women and the Shadow of Colonial Patriarchy', *Australian & New Zealand Journal of Criminology* 47(2): 276–98.

Baldry, E. and R. McCausland (2009), 'Mother Seeking Safe Home: Aboriginal Women Post-Release', *Current Issues in Criminal Justice* 21(2): 288–301.

Baldry, E., Carlton, B. and C. Cunneen (2015), 'Abolitionism and the Paradox of Penal Reform in Australia: Indigenous Women, Colonial Patriarchy, and Co-option', *Social Justice* 41(3): 168–89.

Balfour, M. (2004), *Theatre in Prison: Theory and Practice*, Bristol: Intellect.

Balfour, M. (2009), 'The Politics of Intention: Looking for a Theatre of Little Changes', *Research in Drama Education: The Journal of Applied Theatre and Performance* 14(3): 347–59.

Bartels, L. (2010), *Indigenous Women's Offending Patterns: A Literature Review*. Vol. 107. Canberra: Australian Institute of Criminology.

Biddle, N. and H. Swee (2012), 'The Relationship between Wellbeing and Indigenous Land, Language and Culture in Australia', *Australian Geographer* 43(3): 215–32.

Bolton, G. M. (1984), *Drama as Education: An Argument for Placing Drama at the Centre of the Curriculum*, Harlow: Longman.

Casella, E. C. and C. Fredericksen (2004), 'Legacy of the "Fatal Shore": The Heritage and Archaeology of Confinement in Post-Colonial Australia', *Journal of Social Archaeology* 4(1): 99–125.

Cook, J. (2004), *Mary Bryant*, Oxford: Oxford University Press.

Cox, E. (2008), 'The Intersubjective Witness: Trauma Testimony in Towfiq Al-Qady's "Nothing But Nothing: One Refugee's Story"', *Research in Drama Education: The Journal of Applied Theatre and Performance* 13(2): 193–8.

Crump, D. (n.d.), *Bidjara Lexicon* (Draft), Beenleigh: Yugambeh Museum.

Cunneen, C. (2009), 'Indigenous Incarceration: The Violence of Colonial Law and Justice', in P. Scraton and J. McCulloch (eds), *The Violence of Incarceration*, 209–24, New York and Abingdon: Routledge.

102   *Applied Theatre: Women and the Criminal Justice System*

Cunneen, C. (2011), 'Punishment: Two Decades of Penal Expansionism and its Effects on Indigenous Imprisonment', *Australian Indigenous Law Review* 15(1): 8–17.

Dockery, A. M. (2010), 'Culture and Wellbeing: The Case of Indigenous Australians', *Social Indicators Research* 99(2): 315–32.

Doyle, F. (2004), *Whispers of this Wik Woman*, Brisbane: University of Queensland Press.

Enoch, W. (2014), *The Story of the Miracles at Cookie's Table*, Strawberry Hills: Currency Press, in association with Griffin Theatre Company, Sydney.

Enoch, W., Mailman, D. and H. Beaton (2002), *The 7 Stages of Grieving*. Vol. 3, rev. Brisbane: Playlab Press.

Foucault, M. (1991), *Discipline and Punish: The Birth of the Prison* (trans. Alan Sheridan), London: Penguin.

Franklin, T. B., Russig, H., Weiss, I. C., Gräff, J., Linder, N., Michalon, A., Vizi, S. and I. M. Mansuy (2010), 'Epigenetic Transmission of the Impact of Early Stress Across Generations', *Biological Psychiatry* 68(5): 408–15.

Gapp, K., von Ziegler, L., Tweedie-Cullen, R. Y. and I. M. Mansuy (2014), 'Early Life Epigenetic Programming and Transmission of Stress-Induced Traits in Mammals: How and When Can Environmental Factors Influence Traits and Their Transgenerational Inheritance?', *Bioessays: News and Reviews in Molecular, Cellular and Developmental Biology* 36(5): 491–502.

Gilbert, H. (2003), 'Black and White and Re(a)d all Over Again: Indigenous Minstrelsy in Contemporary Canadian and Australian Theatre', *Theatre Journal* 55(4): 679–98.

Gilbert, H. and J. Tompkins (2002), *Post-colonial Drama: Theory, Practice, Politics*, London: Routledge.

Gilbert, K. (1988), *The Cherry Pickers*, Canberra: Burrambinga Books.

Gubar, S. (2000), *Racechanges: White Skin, Black Face in American Culture*, Oxford: Oxford University Press.

Hassall, L. (2012), 'Evoking and Excavating Representations of Landscape: How Are Experiences of Landscape Explored in the Creation and Development of a New Play: Dawn's Faded Rose'. Unpublished thesis, Griffith University: Brisbane.

Heffernan, E., Andersen, K. C., Dev, A. and S. Kinner (2012), 'Prevalence of Mental Illness Among Aboriginal and Torres Strait Islander People in Queensland Prisons', *Medical Journal of Australia* 197(1): 37–41.

Heffernan, E., Andersen, K., Davidson, F. and S. A. Kinner (2015), 'PTSD Among Aboriginal and Torres Strait Islander People in Custody in Australia: Prevalence and Correlates', *Journal of Traumatic Stress* 28(6): 523–30.

Hegarty, R. (1999) *Is that you, Ruthie?* Brisbane: University of Queensland Press.

Hodge, B. and V. Mishra (1991), *Dark Side of the Dream: Australian Literature and the Post Colonial Mind*, Sydney: Allen & Unwin.

Hogg, R. (2001), 'Penality and Modes of Regulating Indigenous Peoples in Australia', *Punishment & Society* 3(3): 355–79.

Hughes, R. (1987), *The Fatal Shore*, London: Collins.

Jeffers, A. (2008), 'Dirty Truth: Personal Narrative, Victimhood and Participatory Theatre Work with People Seeking Asylum', *Research in Drama Education: The Journal of Applied Theatre and Performance* 13(2): 217–21.

Johnston, E. (1991), *Final report of the Royal Commission into Aboriginal Deaths in Custody*, Canberra: Australian Government Publishing Service.

Jones, R., Masters, M., Griffiths, A. and N. Moulday (2002), 'Culturally Relevant Assessment of Indigenous Offenders [Series of two parts]: Part 1: A Literature Review', *Australian Psychologist* 37(3): 187–97.

Kellermann, N. P. F. (2013), 'Epigenetic Transmission of Holocaust Trauma: Can Nightmares be Inherited?', *Israel Journal of Psychiatry and Related Sciences* 50(1): 33–9.

Langton, M. (1993a), 'Rum, Seduction and Death: "Aboriginality" and Alcohol', *Oceania* 63(3): 195–206.

Langton, M. (1993b), *Well, I Heard it on The Radio and I Saw it on the Television: An Essay for the Australian Film Commission on the Politics and Aesthetics of Filmmaking by and about Aboriginal People and Things*, Sydney: Australian Film Commission.

Langton, M. (2008), 'Trapped in the Aboriginal Reality Show [The Howard Government Intervention in Northern Territory Aboriginal Communities]', in 'Re-imagining Australia', J. Schultz (ed.), *Griffith REVIEW* (19): 143–62.

McAvinchey, C. (2011), *Theatre & Prison*, Basingstoke: Palgrave Macmillan.

McEntyre, E. (2015), 'How Aboriginal Women with Disabilities are Set on a Path into the Criminal Justice System', *The Conversation*, Melbourne, 03/11/2015.

McKean, A. (2006), 'Playing for Time in "The Dolls' House".' Issues of Community and Collaboration in the Devising of Theatre in a Women's Prison', *Research in Drama Education: The Journal of Applied Theatre and Performance* 11(3): 313–27.

Maddison, S. (2011), *Beyond White Guilt: The Real Challenge for Black–White Relations in Australia*, Sydney: Allen & Unwin.

Neelands, J. and T. Goode (2015), *Structuring Drama Work*. Vol. 3: Cambridge: Cambridge University Press.

Nellis, M. (2009), 'The Aesthetics of Redemption: Released Prisoners in American Film and Literature', *Theoretical Criminology* 13(1): 129–46.

Nicol, J., and T. Flannery (1997), *The Life and Adventures of John Nicol, Mariner: 1776–1801*, Melbourne: Text Publishing.

Noyce, P. (2002), *Rabbit-Proof Fence*, Becker Entertainment.

Perroud, N., Rutembesa, E., Paoloni-Giacobino, A., Mutabaruka, J., Mutesa, L., Stenz, L., Malafosse, A. and F. Karege (2014), 'The Tutsi Genocide and Transgenerational Transmission of Maternal Stress: Epigenetics and Biology of the HPA Axis', *The World Journal of Biological Psychiatry* 15(4): 334–45.

Preston, S. (2009), 'Introduction to Ethics of Representation', in S. Preston and T. Prentki (eds), *The Applied Theatre Reader*, 65–9, Abingdon and New York: Routledge.

Rankin, S. (2005), *Ngapartji Ngapartji*, Australia: Unpublished Performance.

Rees, S. (2002), *The Floating Brothel: The Extraordinary True Story of an Eighteenth-Century Ship and Its Cargo of Female Convicts*, Bath UK: Chivers Press.

Salverson, J. (2009), 'Clown, Opera, the Atomic Bomb and the Classroom', in S. Preston and T. Prentki (eds), *The Applied Theatre Reader*, 33–40, Abingdon and New York: Routledge.

Sherwood, J. and S. Kendall (2013), 'Reframing Spaces by Building Relationships: Community Collaborative Participatory Action Research with Aboriginal Mothers in Prison', *Contemporary Nurse: A Journal for the Australian Nursing Profession* 46(1): 83–94.

Smith, L. T. (1999), *Decolonizing Methodologies: Research and Indigenous Peoples*, London: Zed Books.

Stubbs, J. (2011), 'Indigenous Women in Australian Criminal Justice: Over-Represented but Rarely Acknowledged', *Australian Indigenous Law Review* 15(1): 47–63.

Thompson, J. (1998), *Prison Theatre: Perspectives and Practices*, London: Jessica Kingsley.

Thompson, J. (2000), 'Theatre and Punish/Discipline and Display', *Research in Drama Education: The Journal of Applied Theatre and Performance* 5(2): 272–5.

Thompson, J. (2009), *Performance Affects: Applied Theatre and the End of Effect*, Basingstoke: Palgrave Macmillan.

Watson, J. (2010), *Palm Island: Through a Long Lens*, Canberra: Aboriginal Studies Press.

Watson, S. (2009), *Oodgeroo: Bloodline to Country*, Brisbane: Playlab Press.

Weatherburn, D. J. (2014), *Arresting Incarceration: Pathways Out of Indigenous Imprisonment*, Canberra: Aboriginal Studies Press.

Williams, L. and J. Besley (eds) (n.d.), *The Cherbourg Memory*. The Ration Shed Museum: Cherbourg. Available online: http://cherbourgmemory.org/ (accessed 1 August 2019).

Wilson, M., Jones, J. and M. Gilles (2014), 'The Aboriginal Mothers in Prison Project: An Example of How Consultation Can Inform Research Practice', *Australian Aboriginal Studies* 2014(2): 28–39.

Wilson, R. (1997), *Bringing Them Home: Report of the National Inquiry into the Separation of Aboriginal and Torres Strait Islander Children from their Families*, Sydney: Human Rights and Equal Opportunity Commission.

Woodland, S. (2016a), '"All our Stress Goes in the River": The Drama Workshop as a (Playful) Space for Reconciliation', in S. Preston (ed.), *Applied Theatre: Facilitation*, 107–30, London: Bloomsbury.

Woodland, S. (2016b), 'The Art of Living in Prison: A Pragmatist Aesthetic Approach to Participatory Drama with Women Prisoners', *Applied Theatre Research* 4(3): 223–36.

'I am a theatre', *Voices from Prison* (1987)

Abigail, Clean Break

I am a theatre. Sometimes I turn myself inside out. I am a very flexible theatre ... a world within a building within a world. I do not begin or end.

Allow me to introduce myself.

I am deep red curtains and I divide in order to create life.

I am a sexual being.

I am standing alone onstage.

The spotlight and the audience are objective.

This way I may appear as a sexual object.

I turn myself inside out.

I am an audience watching itself.

For information on *Voices from Prison,* please see p. 56.

4

What Works: The Affective and Gendered Performance of Prison

Aylwyn Walsh

This chapter examines a particular example of applied theatre practice from HMP Drake Hall in the UK to theorize prison's performance as affective and gendered. Attending to the work of applied theatre within the wider institutional frame allows critical considerations on the risks, benefits and implications of women's participation. This approach draws on the critical ethnographic approach of feminist criminologist Lynne Haney (2010). This contribution asserts the need for practices to shift beyond the predominant paradigms in applied theatre research, namely studies of behavioural change-focused programmes. I suggest that these often replicate prison's disciplinary function as arts interventions that rehearse scripts related to women's strength, future success and resilience. Drawing on research journals and field notes, I develop a critical analysis of the institutional framing, its correlative power and its implications for practice. The focus of this chapter is thus not a case study of the applied theatre project itself but rather what it allows me to access about prison, gender and affective labour.

My work is theoretically framed by James Thompson's and Sara Ahmed's approaches to affect. James Thompson proposes attention to both effect and affect in applied theatre scholarship (2009), requiring a critique of languages of impact and 'effect', in which he 'proposes new models of theoretical engagement which reframe the political and aesthetic possibilities of affect' (McAvinchey 2011: 233). I take forward Thompson's (2009) discussion, attending to aesthetics and emotion in addition to merely instrumental evaluative narratives that are necessary for funded applied theatre practice. I use 'affect' in the sense that emotions are generated and circulate through the body, as discussed by feminist critical theorist Sara Ahmed (2004; 2014). This is particularly productive for applied theatre analysis in order to consider how affect is produced, contained and also disseminated by its context, in this case, prison. As I demonstrate in the chapter, this is necessary and important because arts practices in prison operate within a wider social context that

108   *Applied Theatre: Women and the Criminal Justice System*

generates and orchestrates the terms of crime and punishment. Applied theatre practice is not just practised *within*, but evaluated *on*, these terms and values.[1] As such, attending to the implications of social, political and economic values is necessary to avoid the charge of projects replicating the values of the institution by seemingly doing its work without any explicit recognition (see Biggs 2016: 13–14; Thompson 2004). The contrasting view is that theatre practice is ineffectual in light of the overwhelming residue or, in sociologist Erving Goffman's (1963) terms, stigma of the institution. In order to move beyond these simplistic either/or formulations, and from an approach informed by feminist criminology, I begin by thinking through how gender and affect work in the context of prison. This sets the ground for thinking about the place of applied theatre's work within the criminal justice system in the UK.

Affect and stigma

My practice draws on the work of Ahmed's feminist affect theory (2004; 2014) in which she writes about the need to consider how emotions circulate. She is particularly interested in how emotions and their objects produce rhetorics of self/other that become a way of justifying marginalization, hate speech and social divisions. This is because, rather than 'hate', or 'shame', residing in the subject itself, affects work on and between bodies – developing feeling in common that moves beyond an individual subject but that constitutes a group. In relation to women in prison, this works in a general way whereby the group 'women in prison' is formulated from outside, but also within the everyday life of the prison where women are labelled and form in-group hierarchies according to their crimes, sentences or 'types'. Further, Goffman's formulation of stigma as a residue from what he calls a 'spoiled identity' (1963) relates to how behaviours, self-beliefs and performances of everyday life present the effects of institutionalization. In his original study, this understanding of the impacts of the institution presupposes that prison (and other institutions) produces a spectacle of punishment that results in the stigma. To put these concepts in relation to gender, the stigmatization of women prisoners highlights the ways normative formulations of women (as non-violent and nurturing, for example) attempt to contain and limit their performances. When women are unruly, they are offensive, and thus stigmatized (Chesney-Lind and Pasko 2004). To attend to affect, according to Ahmed, allows for a critical reading of institutions, discourses and collectivities that can help to unpick the often exclusionary, binary, gendered thinking that sticks to figures such as women in prison.

The Affective and Gendered Performance of Prison 109

Putting Goffman's thinking in relation to Ahmed's, it is not necessarily an emotion of shame at *being* a prisoner that sticks, but that the regime of the institution effects a sticky stigma related to, for example, producing compliant bodies for a security count, or developing hunger according to the regime timetable. In other words, the stigma is not an affect *of* the prisoner, but one that is produced by the relation of the prisoners and the institution, or, in other words, how the prison works *on* and *through* affect.[2] Part of the paradox that arises in this understanding is that prisons focus on reducing stigma through programmes (or, in the UK terminology, 'interventions', such as drug and alcohol awareness, or assertiveness training) that seek to produce people capable of contributing to society. Yet, by promoting the need for productive, economically independent citizens, the criminal justice system does not recognize the stickiness of the stigma and its particularities for women. So while interventions ostensibly work to make women less 'offensive', their very effect is to circulate the stigmatizing affect of offence, and the binaries of inside and outside.

'What works?' Applied theatre as intervention

This section examines the idea of 'what works' in the UK government framework of prisons and then considers how applied theatre practices negotiate or serve this political narrative. I offer a brief introduction of my specific applied practice before approaching workplaces in prisons as a cogent example of how different interventions in prisons operate in relation to gender. This is within the remit of prison abolitionist Angela Davis' critique (2003) of the prison industrial complex, in which she demonstrates the conflation of private business, investment in building prisons and the exploitation of prison labour. She draws on the genealogy of prison labour through slavery, and makes the explicit concern about the racialized and gendered bodies of prisoners whose labour is put in service of the profit of big corporations. While the UK context of criminal justice is not yet all privatized, there is a great deal of private contracting for prison workplaces. Davis' approach aims for a 'humane, habitable environment' for prisoners 'without bolstering the permanence of the prison system' (2003: 103). We might see Davis' activism as a confluence with the potential for arts interventions (including applied theatre) to contribute towards the project of developing humane spaces for communication, connection, cooperation and enjoyment that are otherwise anathema to the largely punitive regimes of the US and UK.[3]

Yet, in his criminological literature survey of Anglo-American twenty-first-century arts interventions, criminologist Leonidas Cheliotis (2012b;

110   *Applied Theatre: Women and the Criminal Justice System*

2014) points out that there is also the tendency for arts projects in prisons to be put in service of the institution's aims. He posits that, while ostensibly benevolent in aim, the claimed results of compliant prisoners and convincing stories of change and transformation can be used to bolster the prison's – and by extension, the state's – image as rehabilitative, as working to keep citizens secure. As such, it is necessary to develop critical considerations of how theatre practices and other arts institutions 'work' within the context of criminal justice institutions. The 'what works' agenda relates to UK policy-makers seeking evidence-based outcomes.[4] In criminal justice contexts, this is largely interpreted as reducing reoffending. Though I refer specifically to the criminal justice system in the UK, it is worth thinking about the resonances beyond that context that indicate how the state operates through institutions and, by extension, through the interventions hosted within them.

My own project was conceived as a co-investigation into how prison works, and was conducted in HMP Drake Hall over the course of two months in 2012. I had previously worked in ten of the female prisons in the UK as a freelance artist with Clean Break theatre company and as a writer-in-residence in two male prisons for three years, as well as in South African male prisons for six years. HMP Drake Hall closed prison houses around 320 women, and I worked with a fairly consistent number of thirteen women who volunteered for the duration of the project, as well as joining other activities with my collaborator, writer-in-residence, Mary Fox. The consistent presence of the writer-in-residence meant that the prison had a range of arts projects underway, including a thriving prison magazine, a pantomime group and a mature women's group that was structured around leisure games and debate. What I aimed to do during my residency was to deploy a range of applied theatre strategies including improvisation and devising materials that we ultimately shared with other women and select staff in order to understand the work of performance to cope with imprisonment. 'Coping' is characterized differently from resilience, which I see as having co-opted the values of neoliberalism requiring subjects to develop strength to prevail in a hostile environment, as discussed by Imogen Tyler in *Revolting Subjects* (2013). By contrast, 'coping' suggests a residual autonomy in the subject to respond to the environment and its interventions.

HMP Drake Hall operates several workplaces for women including a DHL (*Deutsche Heitwasslabungden Luffposte*) contract for packaging items for deliveries and a large laundry which has a contract to clean all uniforms, bedding and towels for several other (male) prisons in the region. In addition, workplaces that service the prison domestic sphere include the kitchens and the impressive gardens. Women may engage in education activities as well as courses relating to 'offender management', including enhanced thinking skills and drug and alcohol awareness that are run by the 'interventions' team – a

The Affective and Gendered Performance of Prison 111

term that signals the operationalization of learning and labour. There are accredited vocational courses in hair and beauty, catering, horticulture and laundry. Criminologist and pedagogue Amanda Davis says that many prisons

> continue to offer vocational programs informed by gendered assumptions about female behaviour and workplace potential. Although women who enter prison are normally among the most disadvantaged in terms of educational and vocational training, they seldom learn skills that will aid them in being self-supporting. Instead, they are often trained to focus on traditional, low-paying 'feminine' skills such as food services, sewing, laundry, and sometimes, clerical work.
>
> 2004: 262

While this feminist critique rightly observes that traditionally 'feminine' skills are overexploited, it also neglects the fact that cooking and laundry are activities that must be done in the context of institutional living, regardless of gender. However, what is important is the need for vocational qualifications in activities that broaden the potential for future employment upon release (Prison Reform Trust 2015). The workplaces in prison are by and large gendered (seen in the popularity of hair and beauty courses), and this places certain restrictions upon what skills women in prison are able to develop. Criminologists Ferraro and Moe (2003: 80) demonstrate that women's work in prison is often still limited, despite the need for a range of choices for training and vocational development (Britton 2003; Simon 1999).[5] The UN Convention on the Elimination of All Forms of Discrimination Against Women (CEDAW) indicates there needs to be the right to work, and the convention on rights for prisoners indicates that prison work needs to be vocational in nature and needs to be 'appropriate' for female prisoners (UNODC 2014: 48–9). Yet, despite these provisions, there is often a lack of appropriate work and vocational training in prisons internationally (UNODC 2014: 50–1). Assumptions about the women's likely limited socio-economic capacity after release are reflected in the bias towards gendered labour that centres on the domestic sphere. The result is that women may leave prison without ever having gained marketable skills (including low attainment of additional education qualifications), or have a partial understanding about how a criminal record may affect their future employability. This can lead to unrealistic expectations on the part of women, and accounts for many of the women's (anecdotal) examples of reoffending, whereby women feel trapped in an inevitable cycle of offending because they do not have experience of surviving or managing in the world of 'legitimate' work, without the chaos and accessibility of crime. In addition, Haney's

112 *Applied Theatre: Women and the Criminal Justice System*

(2010) important work on 'offending women' in US community settings explores how narratives of 'dependency' and 'recovery' are out of touch with the social realities of the women's lives, serving to flatten and eliminate the multiple ways women experience incarceration, as well as the multiple contingencies they face when imagining a life after incarceration, including lack of education, few job opportunities and limited social support.

The logic of prison is such that, if women are judged to have 'worked on' themselves, they will be expected to undertake 'outwork' – placements in local shops and businesses – to prove they are fit and able to join society as productive citizens. In these instances, women's labour in the community replicates a model of value that is explicitly related to normative earning power. Although I am critiquing this model of value, it is not only because of its ties with capital. It is also because the mechanics of outwork do not adequately challenge the ways prison and its affects stick. As I analysed women's reflections and improvisations about undertaking outwork, what was evident was the unintended but ubiquitous ways the prison regime reinforces the labelling of women as 'offenders' and marks them as distinct from the general public. This happens through naming, as well as the regime extending its effects beyond the walls when a count delays women from leaving in good time for work, for example. A repeated example was of being called 'the prisoner' in the workplace by colleagues, or being asked to work in 'the back' because of workers assuming 'the public' would not want to associate with a prisoner. These assumptions are predicated on a visible, or affective, stigma that would be perceived by the public.

One problematic claim that is put forward is that applied theatre projects can interrupt these sticky residues of stigmatizing labels (Goffman 1963, 2007). These claims of transformation are well meaning but often uncritical in replicating neat narratives (Cheliotis 2012a; Bilby, Caulfied and Ridley 2013; Herrmann 2009). In my own practice in this prison, I attempted to get women to engage with building alternatives to these stigmatizing labels, fully aware that its short-term nature was unlikely to fundamentally challenge stigmas that are generated over time, often years of institutionalization and lives of crime. There are, however, examples of arts organizations whose long-term (and often qualification-aligned) interventions are ideally positioned to serve as building alternative repertoires of behaviour.[6]

Affect and aesthetics: HMP Drake Hall

In our improvisation sessions, women were engaged with identifying issues relating to their tactics of coping within the institution, or how they work

The Affective and Gendered Performance of Prison 113

within the prison. This was intended to articulate vocabularies and performances that are adopted in relation to incarceration – rather than in relation to crime. Their scenes would demonstrate concerns about institutional living, about assumptions and threats to their person, about vulnerabilities in relation to the regime and the sense of a lack of agency. In part, what emerged from the scenes was the sense that women felt restricted in their capacity to challenge or throw off the stigma of being in prison. This was explored directly, in scenes where women tried to confront stigmatizing labels (in retelling stories about outwork, for example), and indirectly, in aesthetic choices that returned to tropes and recognizable prison motifs despite claiming to set the scenes outside the prison context. While I was not explicit about deploying Ahmed's thinking about the stickiness of affect in sessions, her formulation of proximity and the other (2014: 63) becomes productive to think through how different emotions perform with(in) and against the body in prison. My short-term project was not intended to develop resilience as such, nor to work towards the often therapeutic aims that longer-term funded projects can offer. Rather, it was positioned as a sharing of women's existing feelings and experiences about how prison works.

The background for the labour of applied theatre practices in prisons necessitates a critical focus on the issues raised by the power differentials, and the potential for the arts being co-opted by the institution (Cheliotis 2012b, 2014). Nevertheless, there are some compelling examples of the women asserting their own positions outside the routinized and flattening operations of the prison. This vignette from one of the focus groups attends to assumptions about what connects women in prison, and, in particular, attends to women's refusal to adhere (or, to use Ahmed's term, 'stick') to what is expected of them:

One afternoon in a focus group session, the writer-in-residence, Mary Fox, was asking women whether they would be willing to cooperate and co-host a session with an incoming motivational speaker who was invited to speak to two large groups of women. The speaker would be a former resident at Drake Hall, who had subsequently made a success of her pathway out of prison as an entrepreneurial businesswoman. The women were immediately resistant. Mary tried to argue that the speaker was a woman coming from the same place as them – prison – but their responses indicated that they refused that association without knowing more about her 'backstory'. For them, being on a discussion panel would mean the audience of their peers might interrogate them as much as the invited speaker. Some of their questions were 'How can I get involved

114   *Applied Theatre: Women and the Criminal Justice System*

when I would have issues about disclosure?' and 'How does her story relate to my own story of offending?' They were trying to assert their difference from the majority of the women in the prison. Ultimately, they reminded Mary that 'we have to live here, and have to deal with the fallout from the other women'.

Research Journal, August 2012

While we could read their refusal as just one example of stubborn lack of cooperation, on another level it indicated a profound awareness of the ongoing narratives of survival within the prison. The women were professing their right to maintain secrecy and hold back their personal information, in the belief that other women (and officers) could use the information as a means of interfering with their sentence progression.[7] This highlights the assumptions that cooperation would be risk-free for these women, and it reminded me of the enormous gesture of faith that women make when participating in performance-making processes. This story, however, carved out a space within the prison, where these five women could assert their vulnerability while at the same time resisting being 'read' or stigmatized as such by the wider institution (other prisoners and staff). On another level, they were resisting being cast as merely 'women in prison' as if the general category were a levelling measure. Rather, they preferred to be seen as individual, specific and with particular criminogenic backgrounds, case histories and pathways out of prison. It was this group that highlighted a tension between the general system/specific story. My experiences as artist facilitator/researcher in Drake Hall was characterized by the multiple subjectivities of women in prison, their own tendencies to be self-critical and the pervasive illusions of hope despite 'failure' and the cycles of reoffending looming large.[8] They seemed to want to believe that prison had worked. In this next example, one of the women told of an experience that exemplified how the systemic approach to reducing rule-breaking does not allow space for affect:

During one of the coffee breaks, a woman recounted an experience she had as a cleaner in the visits' hall. The women have strict time frames for cleaning when visits are not underway. Dani was cleaning near the vending machines when she found a pound coin. Money, as she explained to me, is contraband, but when she found it she was so excited. However, she was concerned that someone would notice her picking it up, so she moved elsewhere to vacuum, returning to look at the renegade coin on the carpet several times before she felt safe enough to slip it into her pocket. She narrated her sense of breathlessness as she left her job that

The Affective and Gendered Performance of Prison   115

day, feeling the pound coin in her pocket, to check whether it was real or not. She said, 'I found a pound coin and you woulda thought I won the bloody lottery!' Dani's willingness to risk being discovered with contraband highlights the absurdity of institutionalization. She knew that she would not be able to use the money inside the prison, but, nevertheless, the lure of money was too great to avoid. Her risk would be to get 'statemented' – where a red statement is notated in the prisoner's file. Most likely, she would need to hide the pound coin, keeping it as a memento of her discovery.

Research Journal, August 2012

Dani's treasure served as a symbolic, rather than actual, capital, to gloss Pierre Bourdieu's most widely adopted concept (1984). His thinking here relates to the sense of value placed in a range of spheres, aside from simply economic, and that these correlate with how status can be fluid according to influence and importance. As this example shows, wealth in prison has no currency. Her pleasure derived from possessing the coin, despite it being worthless in prison because there is no use of currency within institutions, demonstrates the performative impact of believing that one possesses agency. She grappled with the fear of discovery, but, ultimately, took the coin. There is a sense of investment in her identity as an agent capable of making choices that run counter to the institutional regulations. The coin symbolically links her to her Self outside. What is more, her subsequent retelling of the finding and keeping of the coin was a re-enactment in which she explicitly contrasted the stakes she experienced with the small 'reward'. In her retelling, she modelled a reflexivity of her imagined Self outside and the disbelief of winning large amounts of money in the lottery with its correlative luck in prison. Her story highlights the dearth of opportunities that women in prison have for breaking through the limiting discourse of the institution to alternative performativities in which rewards and good fortune are possibilities.

The work of gender in the project

I return here to Ahmed's theorization of affective economies as being based upon the circulation, and creation, of surplus value. She demonstrates that the social and material circulation of affect is a process by which both the subject and the institution are constituted (2004: 121). Further, Ahmed's sense of how emotions make and remake the discourses about marginalized types of subjects helps expand and extend thinking about women in prison. My own reading of the applied theatre practices I conducted in HMP Drake

116   *Applied Theatre: Women and the Criminal Justice System*

Hall as also contributing to the circulation of affective economies by necessity draws attention to the means by which women in the workshops (and their representation in my research journal vignettes) are sticky with institutional affect. The following vignette offers a metaphor of a sticking plaster as an object the women used in dramatic improvisation. By deploying this example here, I am shifting away from the wider context to engage with accessing practice. I propose that play with metaphoric objects contributes towards the illusion that applied theatre projects can briefly shift attention away from the real, embodied affective economies of prison life, but do not adequately serve to challenge, or transform, the conditions of the institution.

Within the performance sessions, the women were asked to improvise with objects that formed materials for the final performance we shared with other prisoners and invited staff. In one session, each woman developed an improvisation with a bright blue plaster that she would 'sell' to the others as if it were anything but a plaster:[9]

> Many of the improvisation routines perpetuated a sense of salvation – an item that could 'magic' away pain, fear or trauma. But what was most surprising was the repetition of the 'ideal' woman. One woman used the plaster as a magic patch that would augment one's womanly assets to make her more desirable to men; another showed the plaster as a protective private space to which she could retreat from external harms.
>
> Research Journal, August 2012[10]

In performance, these 'selling' sequences punctuated longer scenes, and audience reactions to the humour and familiarity of selling illusions reminded me that these pervasive understandings of women as sexual objects proliferate in prison. Yet, beneath the comedy, there was a sense of inevitability – that performing ideals demands a normative audience. In other words, the 'performance' of hyperfemininity or butch presentation gains prominence in the homosocial space of prison (Millbank 2004; Sedgwick 1985).[11] This is often explained in relation to 'offending' women's rejection of normative female traits and tendency to aggression and dominance (which is, of course, a limiting view of women's 'proper' behaviour, and fetishizes female subjugation). While aggression is most often associated with 'butch' performativity (and assumptions of lesbianism), my experiences with women in prison include a wide range of exaggerated performances of sexual availability that could be unrelated to actual sexual preference. In these cases, the body becomes a currency – a means of manipulation, exploitation or, indeed, comfort. In other words, women's gender and sexual identities were not important in themselves, except insofar as they could be put to work –

The Affective and Gendered Performance of Prison   117

both between women themselves and in relation to the status of the outsider, prison worker or practitioner.

In terms of gender and its sticky residue, it was especially evident that women made use of multiple grooming routines when there were family visits, but often 'let themselves go' (in the words of a participant) between visits. While interfacing with 'the public' (or anyone outside the day-to-day prison regime), some women rose to ever more extreme performances of femininity that tended to be directed towards men, in line with my observation above. In years of working in the prison context, it has become clear that sexuality and the sexualized body become a form of currency or 'capital'. I propose that in the institutional field that impoverishes women of 'positive' or affirmative attentions (Haney 2010), these deployments of the sexualized body work differently to interventions that are led by external practitioners. The operations of sex and sexuality as a form of affective labour that women can leverage outside the legitimized realm of work or education suggests the need for further research. So, too, does the link between the performance of gender and sexuality and the body's performative presence in applied theatre. Thinking, then, about the potential to attend to affect and the relation to the body, the following vignette explores the aesthetic framing of women's survival tactics as a form of affective labour:

> The performance developed around the rituals characters found to 'put on a brave face'. The women constructed a series of short scenes in pairs where they embodied a range of rituals the women employ in order to, in the words of one participant, 'focus and go on with the sentence', and also tactics to 'keep from thinking of self-harm' (Interview participant Julie, August 2012). In our conversations, Julie mentioned several of the concerns that feminist criminology raises, namely that prison is a set of reports and sentences that can in no way capture the chaos and confusion of women's lives. There is enormous pressure on women to 'put their heads down' and 'get on with it'. Yet the statistics relating to mental health show that there are complex considerations related to the ways women manage both pre-existing mental health issues alongside the stresses of surviving the prison system itself.[12]
>
> Research Journal, September 2012

For Haney (2010), long-term research engagement with the criminal justice context required thinking about how governance of women's desires and plans for reintegration were gendered. This chapter's examples of intimate moments of insight into how gender is reinforced relate to assumptions about women and transgression that feminist criminology shows as affecting how women are criminalized, sentenced and stigmatized post-release.

Concluding remarks

In closing, taking a lead from radical theorist Stevphen Shukaitis' (2012) work on the performance of labour and value, I am keen to consider how affect and gender in prison circulate and produce an ideal subject. This ideal subject in the case of women's prisons maintains normative, often limiting, narratives of women's roles outside prison. Thinking about the 'what works' agenda in relation to long-term reduction of reoffending, men's redemption narratives after prison often include a return to the labour force. This assumption that men's value is as economic providers is itself sticky, although the majority of ex-prisoners of all genders face challenges and barriers to finding employment. By contrast women's value after release from prison is not often articulated as value of the individual subject but in value *as women* – for example, as mothers returning to care for children, if they have not been removed to care. As such, applied theatre's potential in criminal justice contexts is in its aesthetics, antagonisms to institutionalization and reliance on value that is explicitly not related to value or profit in capitalist terms, as well as extending gender repertoires.

This chapter deploys a particular example of applied theatre practice as a contributing narrative to the theorization of prison's performance as affective and gendered. Thus, instead of being introduced as exemplary of practice in the UK, the moments from the project and the research journal are positioned as a critical interrogation of the spaces and possibilities of creative arts within the institutional paradigm. I have attempted to avoid positioning the aesthetic labour of performance as somehow extant outside institutional dynamics, grammars of power and sociopolitical structures. Rather, the chapter reads what practitioner/scholar Balfour calls the 'drama of little changes' (2009) alongside and through the competing interventions that explicitly put women's labour in service of the institution. His view is that the tension inherent in gaining support for project resourcing means that the 'artistic dimension therefore is often relegated to the second division, a footnote to the value or purpose of the project' (2009: 356). This suggests that applied theatre practitioners must be cognisant of how their practices work within the institution, and alongside other interventions. Thompson's (2009) rejoinder to consider affects suggests the need to consider the intimacy of the work in relation to 'contexts and discourse in which the work is located' (2009: 34). Although there is lots of important work in the UK that relates to evaluating practices (primarily collected by the National Criminal Justice Arts Alliance), there is the need to access practice and research that engages with the kinds of critical issues raised by practice. To reflect on 'what works' is not intended to marginalize or disparage the profound impact of applied theatre projects for those involved, but instead serves as a reminder of the distinction between often short-term projects and their relationship to sentences. It is also a timely reminder to ensure that evaluations attend to aesthetics and affect in addition to representing applied theatre interventions as at work in the grammar of the institution.

Some of the vignettes suggest that 'what works' is when women can rehearse and enjoy an expanded repertoire of gender. What works in relation to aesthetics is when the restrictions of the prison regime can generate significant imaginative wonder, humour and counternarratives that also point towards the possibilities for future behaviours or opportunities for women. Yet I am aware of the need to avoid unrealistic demands of single interventions, given that reducing reoffending is such a complex matter (McNeill, Anderson, Colvin, Sparks and Tett 2011). Thus, rather than offer hopeful narratives of change, I consider how this example of applied theatre practice, drawing on Ahmed and Goffman, considers gendered labour as an affective economy. I propose that when the work of creative collaboration can generate critical conversations on the risks, benefits and implications of participation within the institutional frame, then applied theatre projects can edge towards the profound. In the prison context, this can occur when women work together and feel supported in expressing vulnerabilities as well as practising strength or resilience. These kinds of processes can be productive for reducing reoffending, but cannot work alone. Women developing a sense of motivation, responsibility and hope; or developing social ties that work to construct belonging and a sense of community that may serve as a support after release. But these also suggest the need for individual women to have developed confidence and agency to be able to manage the challenges of institutional life and resettlement. Therefore, a radical, but nevertheless necessary, drive in my applied theatre practice in prison is to work towards the decoupling of notions of 'what works' that attend to the individuals from the institutional values (particularly when these are related to profit – as in the prison industrial complex). Practices and research must offer considerations of prisons' affects and effects: 'what works' is when projects can delegitimize the prevailing 'sticky' residue of stigma within and beyond the prison walls.

Notes

1 See, for example, New Philanthropy Capital's attempt to capture the value of the arts in criminal justice in economic terms (*Unlocking Value: The Economic Benefit of the Arts in Criminal Justice*, 2011).

120   *Applied Theatre: Women and the Criminal Justice System*

2 See Antonio Negri's (1999) formulation of value and affect 'from below' as a means of theorizing beyond value and labour.

3 It is worth reflecting on the difference between the regime style that is punitive and that of other countries (such as Norway and other Scandinavian countries), in which well-being and rehabilitation are prioritized, resulting in very different opportunities for work, learning and living conditions that is often said to be 'humane' (see James 2013).

4 See 'What Works? Evidence Centres for Social Policy' (Gov.uk 2013) for the coalition government's approach to commissioning due to evidence-based practices. McNeill et al. (2010) demonstrate how these are often tied to specific forms of evidence that are anathema to arts practice; in particular, evidence related to economic savings or cost–benefit analyses.

5 All prison work contracts are a means of supplying cheap labour and, as such, often include menial tasks and manual labour that has become less common in the largely deindustrialized UK. The work to keep the institution functioning (orderlies in kitchens, the library and gym and cleaners) often corresponds with vocational training (and certification). For men, these are often in skills such as industrial cleaning, brickwork and painting and decorating. By contrast to the gendered work and training I mention for women, men's work in prison can include fixing broken parts on wheelchairs, packing dog biscuits or fixing pins on badges.

6 For example, Geese Theatre's methodology retains a focus on cognitive-behavioural models of change. Clean Break theatre company's education programme is conducted in the community post-release, and is a more sustainable model for developing life skills outside of prison.

7 This is the prison service jargon for the processual, emergent performance enacted by prisoners according to the 'sentence plan' – determined by a range of prison service professionals. The 'script' or sentence plan is intended to be specific, tailored to maximizing individuals' potential to 'succeed'. A sentence might, for example, indicate that an individual needs to complete drug and alcohol awareness courses as well as engage in group work conducted by the psychology team in order to address offending behaviour. Such courses are generally connected to certification and accreditation, so that prisoners are able to measure achievement in terms of learning in addition to considering the legal requirements dictated by the script.

8 I am alluding to the findings from detailed quality of life questionnaires (see also Drake 2012) that I conducted from the core performance group. The findings indicate a veneer of hope and positivity that is not realistic in the current milieu (of cuts and economic austerity) and that, as Haney's US case study (2010) shows, may be predicated on the discursive framing of women's prisons as empowering rather than punitive. In this chapter, I have not made specific reference to the questionnaires aside from this, since I preferred to focus on the actual 'performances' of women in prison rather than their self-reported attitudes towards their offending background and belief in the future.

The Affective and Gendered Performance of Prison   121

9   This exercise is adapted from a common theatre improvisation exercise, 'this is not a bottle'. It is primarily about extending the visual imagination so that players and audience become aware of an augmentation of the realm of possibilities in the fictional context. The choice of objects related specifically to what I was allowed to bring into prison that provided openness for imaginative possibilities but also did not prove to be a security risk.

10 The following two extracts from research journals originally formed part of my PhD thesis (Walsh 2014a).

11 I am glossing Sedgwick's (1985) term here, which refers to the interplay between desire and power in relation to the ways patriarchal cultures are upheld by presumptions of a social glue of homosociality. In similar ways, prison cultures are formed around perpetuations of women's labour, women's habitus and women's 'place'. This is in addition to the manifestation of (female) homosexual desire.

12 The charity Women in Prison highlights the following critical statistics in relation to mental health: 'Women account for 47% of all incidents of self-harm. 30% of women (as compared to 10% of men) have had a previous psychiatric admission before they come into prison' (cited in Women in Prison 2016).

References

Ahmed, S. (2004), 'Affective Economies', *Social Text*, 22(2): 117–39.

Ahmed, S. (2014), *The Cultural Politics of Emotion* (2nd edn), Edinburgh: Edinburgh University Press.

Balfour, M. (2009), 'The Politics of Intention: Looking for a Theatre of Little Changes', *Research in Drama Education: The Journal of Applied Theatre and Performance* 14(3): 347–59.

Biggs, L. (2016), 'Serious Fun at Sun City: Theatre for Incarcerated Women in the "New" South Africa', *Theatre Survey* 57(1): 4–36.

Bilby, C., Caulfield, L. and L. Ridley (2013), *Re-imagining Futures: Exploring Arts Interventions and the Process of Desistance*, London: Arts Alliance.

Bourdieu, P. (1984), *Distinction: A Social Critique of the Judgment of Taste* (translated by R. Nice), Cambridge MA: Harvard University Press.

Britton, D. M. (2003), *At Work in the Iron Cage: The Prison as Gendered Organization*, New York: New York University Press.

Cheliotis, L. K. (ed.) (2012a), *The Arts of Imprisonment: Control, Resistance and Empowerment*, Ashgate: Farnham.

Cheliotis, L. K. (2012b), 'Theatre States: Probing the Politics of Arts-in-Prisons Programmes', *Criminal Justice Matters* 89(1): 32–4.

Cheliotis, L. K. (2014), 'Decorative Justice: Deconstructing the Relationship Between Arts and Imprisonment', *International Journal for Crime, Justice and Social Democracy* 3(1): 16–34.

122   *Applied Theatre: Women and the Criminal Justice System*

Chesney-Lind, M. and L. Pasko (eds) (2004), *Girls, Women and Crime: Selected Readings*, Thousand Oaks: Sage.

Davis, A. (2003), *Are Prisons Obsolete?* New York: Seven Stories Press.

Davis, A. (2004), 'On Teaching Women's Prison Writing: A Feminist Approach to Women, Crime, and Incarceration', *Women's Studies Quarterly* 3/4: 261–79.

Drake, D. (2012), *Prisons, Punishment and the Pursuit of Security*. Basingstoke: Palgrave Macmillan.

Ferraro, K. J. and A. M. Moe (2003), 'Women's Stories of Survival and Resistance', in B. H. Zaitzow and J. Thomas (eds), *Women in Prison: Gender and Social Control*, 65–94, Boulder: Lynne Reiner.

Goffman, E. (1963), *Stigma: Notes on the Management of a Spoiled Identity*, New York: Simon & Schuster.

Goffman, E. (2007), *Asylums: Essays on the Social Situation of Mental Patients and Other Inmates*, New Brunswick: Aldine Transaction.

Gov.uk (2013), 'What Works: Evidence Centres for Social Policy'. Available online: https://www.gov.uk/government/publications/what-works-evidence-centres-for-social-policy (accessed 11 May 2016).

Haney, L. A. (2010), *Offending Women: Power, Punishment, and the Regulation of Desire*, Berkeley: University of California Press.

Herrmann, A. (2009), '"The Mothership": Sustainability and Transformation in the Work of Clean Break', in T. Prentki and S. Preston (eds), *The Applied Theatre Reader*, 328–35, Abingdon and New York: Routledge.

James, E. (2013), 'Bastoy: The Norwegian Prison that Works', *Guardian*, 4 September. Available online: https://www.theguardian.com/society/2013/sep/04/bastoy-norwegian-prison-works (accessed 24 March 2016).

McNeill, F., Anderson, K., Colvin, S., Overy, K., Sparks, R. and L. Tett (2010), 'Inspiring Desistance? Arts Projects and "What Works"', *Justitiele verkenningen* 37(5): 80–101.

Millbank, J. (2004), 'It's About *This*: Lesbians, Prison, Desire', *Social & Legal Studies* 13(2): 155–90.

Negri, A. (1999), 'Value and Affect' (translated by M. Hardt), *Boundary 2* 26(2): 77–88.

New Philanthropy Capital (2011), *Unlocking Value: The Economic Benefit of the Arts in Criminal Justice*, London: National Alliance for Arts in Criminal Justice.

Prison Reform Trust (2015), 'Working It Out: Employment for Women Offenders', Briefing Document. Available online: http://www.prisonreformtrust.org.uk/Portals/0/Documents/Women/Employmentbriefing.pdf (accessed 10 January 2016).

Sedgwick, E. K. (1985), *Between Men: English Literature and Male Homosocial Desire*, New York: Columbia University Press.

Shukaitis, S. (2012), 'Symphony of the Surplus/Value: Notes on Labour, Valorization and Sabotage in the Metropolitan Factory', *Performance Research* 17(6): 48–55.

Simon, F. H. (1999), *Prisoners' Work and Vocational Training*, London: Routledge.

Thompson, J. (2004), 'From the Stocks to the Stage: Prison Theatre and the Theatre of Prison', in M. Balfour (ed.), *Theatre in Prison: Theory and Practice*, 57–76, Bristol: Intellect.

Thompson, J. (2009), *Performance Affects: Applied Theatre and the End of Effect*, Basingstoke: Palgrave Macmillan.

Tyler, I. (2013), *Revolting Subjects: Social Abjection and Resistance in Neoliberal Britain*, London: Zed Books.

UNODC (United Nations Office on Drugs and Crime) (2014), 'Handbook on Women and Imprisonment (2nd edn)', United Nations. Available online: https://www.unodc.org/documents/justice-and-prison-reform/women_and_imprisonment_-_2nd_edition.pdf (accessed 5 April 2016).

Women in Prison (2016), 'Key Facts'. Available online: http://www.womeninprison.org.uk/research/key-facts.php (accessed 20 March 2016).

Extract I from *Inside Bitch* (2019)

Conceived by Stacey Gregg and Deborah Pearson, devised with Lucy Edkins, Jennifer Joseph, TerriAnn Oudjar and Jade Small

Jade Okay so I know what you are thinking. You're thinking, 'Not another television show about women in prison.' Right?

You've seen *Orange Is the New Black*. You've seen *Locked Up*. You've seen *Bad Girls* – the TV show and the musical. So what have we got that's different? Well, for one, we've all been to prison. We know what it's like. We know what was funny, we know what was boring, we know what was sad. And we know what mum and dad sitting at home in front of a telly on a Saturday night want to see.

We've got the real shit, and trust me, it's dark as fuck, and it will knock your socks off.

Also, this would be set in the UK, yeah?

And it *won't* star a blonde woman.

From 1990, Clean Break primarily commissioned professional writers to develop plays which addressed issues of women, crime and punishment. As the company approached its fortieth anniversary, it made a commitment to return to its roots, repositioning women with lived experience of the criminal justice system at the heart of its artistic output – not only as subjects but as artists, storytellers and activists. *Inside Bitch* evolved from a collaborative research and devising process with the company over two years. It confronted public perceptions of women and prison through a playful, but profoundly serious and rigorous critique of stereotypical cultural representations in television and film, intercut with biographical material. *Inside Bitch* was a co-production with the Royal Court, London, staged in January 2019, the opening event of a year-long programme celebrating the lives and work of all the women who have, over four decades, created and sustained Clean Break.

5

Possible Fictions: Split Britches, Biography and Fantasy with Women in Prison

Caoimhe McAvinchey

Between 2001 and 2003, Lois Weaver and Peggy Shaw led a strand of People's Palace Projects' *Staging Human Rights* in England and Brazil. Four women's prisons hosted residencies: HMP Highpoint and HMP and YOI Bullwood Hall in England and Presídio Nelson Hungria and Penetenciaria Talavera Bruce in the state of Rio de Janeiro, Brazil. Shaw was very clear about the imperative for the work: 'We work with women. Prison is a place where women live' (2003). In each residency, Weaver and Shaw drew upon the approaches that shape all their work – a radical playfulness engaging with biography and fantasy, carefully attending to power, identity and representation – optimistic for the possibilities of performance as a social practice.

Weaver and Shaw worked with each group to create fantasy characters who revealed details of the lives of the women who created them. Each residency culminated in a performance within the prison but the format for this was not preset, rather it was determined by each group of women. These included a cabaret hosted by Lois's fantasy character, Tammy Whynot, in Presídio Nelson Hungria; a series of music videos with teenage girls in HMP and YOI Bullwood Hall; a public performance during a family visiting day in Talavera Bruce; and, in HMP Highpoint, *The Highpoint Big Breakfast* television show. The women gave testimony to their own lives through performance and offered this testimony to the world beyond the prison walls by sending messages through recorded statements and art works, curated and presented in *In The House,* an installation, performance and public discussion in Casa de Lapa, Rio de Janeiro (23 June 2003). I worked with Lois and Peggy as a researcher throughout this project. The following documentation of aspects of the first residency gives access to Weaver and Shaw's performance-making methodology and the ways in which a blurring of the real and the fantasy disrupted institutional life and disconfirmed a limited sense of self that is inscribed by it.[1]

126   *Applied Theatre: Women and the Criminal Justice System*

HMP Highpoint. 2 April 2002. Day 1. Morning.

We turn up for the first day of the workshop at 8.30 a.m. It is a cold, misty morning. The day after a bank holiday weekend. A residue of reluctance to go back to work hangs in the air which is in stark contrast to our own feelings of anticipation. We go to the gate, state our names and who we are here to see. There is a shift-change. Staff who have been awake through the night stumble into the sharp air. We wait, watching each officer leave, shouting messages of condolence to those beginning the next shift.

We pass through the outer gate into the compound. Our names are checked off against a list at the security hut. We are asked to leave our mobile phones there. We are then allowed, finally, to enter the building. We line up in front of a bulletproof glass window, drop our passports into a metal box under it and wait to have our names checked off another list. None of our bags have been checked, no one is searched.

We are met by a group of sixteen women in a room misty with cigarette smoke. Most of the women are in their mid-to-late twenties, and there are two women in their late fifties and early sixties. Although never explicitly asked, many of the women reveal the reason for their imprisonment. Drug-related crimes feature time and again. We join them, having a cup of tea, introducing ourselves and what we hope to do together. The session begins. We form a circle. Lois leads:

> Close your eyes, visualize yourself. What do you see? When I touch your shoulder, say a word or feeling that describes that image of yourself.
> If that feeling or word were an object, what would it be?
> Now, introduce yourself with your name and the object that describes your image of yourself.

The women, with little resistance, eyes closed, murmur:

> I am Jean the rose bush.
> I am Rachel the beach.
> I am Sam the sun.
> I am Natasha the sea.

Within moments the women have identified themselves as being something other than a mother, a prisoner, angry or bored. Lois continues:

> Find a partner and make up two things about them. Forget the things you already know for sure. What could they be? Then, introduce your friend to the group describing what they do when they are not here.

Possible Fictions   127

This is my friend Beccy, she is an ambassador for world peace; this is Michelle, she is in fact the Queen who likes giving away money; this is Tracey who is an undercover spy; this is Darcy, an Australian actress from Cell Block H; this is Sarah, a singing ice skater; this is Sam, a ballet dancer who used to have a moustache.

As each woman introduces the one next to her, the group laughs, imagining the women who they have lived with, had endless cups of tea and cigarettes with, as having another life. Imagine that, instead of going to the painting and decorating workshop, Sam rehearsed for her ballet solo. Imagine that, instead of inputting names into the census reports for five hours a day, Pauline actually was an undercover agent who filed reports on questionable international deals. Imagine that Beccy, instead of going to meds for more antidepressants, was having negotiations with key UN officials about diplomatic relations in the Middle East. Imagine. The possible fictions lingered:

Now, close your eyes and think about yourself. Think of two things about yourself which are true and one that is a lie. Then add these to the things that your partner invented for you. Introduce yourself to the group giving us these details, some true, some made up, in any order.

Hi, my name is Sam, I'm 23 and a ballet dancer. I'm from Birmingham but currently live in Russia. I have six kids.

Hi, my name is Jean, I am Mother Earth. I have a dog that I love and wish peace to all mankind. I have two children and live on the Moon.

My name is Pauline. I'm an undercover cop, I'm a mum to seven kids and grandmother to nine and have two toes missing.

Well I'm the Queen. I like giving money away. I went to Jamaica and I got shot in Jamaica and I robbed an aeroplane to come home.

As the new construction of the self is articulated, there is a hesitancy as people try to remember what they are prepared to divulge about themselves, what has been said about them and what untruth they will throw into the mix. The session moves on:

Let's pretend that all these people are in a play. Give them all a name.

Lois goes around the circle and asks the group to name each of the characters:

128 *Applied Theatre: Women and the Criminal Justice System*

Speedy
Earth Mother
Bright Eyes
Road Runner
CID Sid
Twinkle Toes
Bobby
Energy
Runaway Bride
Peace Keeper
Lily

The bell rings. The women leave for lunch. Fish mornay and chips. Again. There is a two-hour break. This first session, with a group of women who have no prior experience of performance making, reveals much about Lois's and Peggy's methodology: all the material you will ever need to make a piece of performance is already within and around you; a little bit of truth and a lot of imagination can bring you anywhere; just begin. Each of the exercises asked the women to think about, or refer to, something that was already within their frame of reference. They weren't being tested on something that they may or may not have known. Stepping into the realm of the imagination within minutes of beginning to work together, and inviting the women to share these imaginings with the rest of the group, established the parameters that the women would be working within – a created space where their participation was welcomed and valued, where they could be themselves while being something other than their everyday selves.

HMP Highpoint. 2 April 2002. Day 1. Afternoon. The creation of fantasy characters.

The mood among the group in the afternoon is different to the focus and nervous curiosity of the morning. There are some new additions to the group. The room feels both giddy and lethargic – the effect of a carbohydrate-heavy lunch, sleeping and medication. Eventually, with gentle persistence, Lois brings the group's concentration together. They begin to develop the characters that they created that morning with a guided writing exercise:

I live in . . .
I work in . . .
In my free time I like to . . .

Just before I get home I . . .
If you could have seen me the other night . . .
The thing I like most in the world is . . .
I would give anything for . . .

My name is Bright Eyes, I live in the Taj Mahal. I work in an ice-cream parlour and sell all kinds of flavours. In my free time I sing the blues. I always love having the children around for ice cream, cakes and stories. If you could have seen me the other night, I would have been so proud. I was fantastic. The thing I enjoy most of all is living and I would give anything for my liberty.

My name is Twinkle Toes. I live at 1, Ballet Close and I work as a ballet dancer. In my free time I relax and love watching *Swan Lake*. Just before I go home I usually go swimming. I always love having time to myself. Of course, that's only when I'm not working or having friends around. If you could have seen me the other night you would have loved my performance. I was so proud of my performance, I done it so well. The thing I love most of all in the whole world is performing. I would give anything for my ballet to be noticed.

My name is Flexi. I live in Amsterdam. I work in the circus. In my free time I make clothes. Just before I go home I usually stretch myself. I always love having chocolate. If you could have seen me the other night you would have thought, how did I do that? I was so proud of my position. The thing I like most in the world is stretching and I'd give anything for a day off.

My name is Bubby aka Marley. I live at 10300 Dinish Road, Waterhouse, Jamaica. I work at a banana plantation. In my free time I like to go swimming. Just before I get home I usually score a bit of weed. I always love having a spliff. Of course that's only when I have no work to do. If you could have seen me the other night I wrote a song. I was so proud of it. The thing I like most in the world is letting my mind wander and dream. The thing I'd give anything for is for those dreams to come true.

The women are sitting in a circle with their clip-boards. They share the same dilemma: wanting to share their stories yet anxious about how they will be received. As each person offers to read their story, the mood changes. There is a rising sense of pleasure and curiosity as the stories unfold. Belly laughs and small shrieks of disbelief interrupt the tales, reflecting the disparity between

130   *Applied Theatre: Women and the Criminal Justice System*

the teller and what is being told. The clear line that marks 'the real' and 'the imaginary' is blurred through the creation of these fictions with a root, in a person's biography that flies beyond our assumptions of who they were or could be. Etchells' comment, 'We talk as if the real and the playful were separate. But we know that isn't true', is repeatedly evidenced through this work (1999: 61).

The women are increasingly comfortable with their ability to create something and to present it to the group. Lois begins to shift the pace and direction of the work by inviting the women to make picture portraits of these characters. She chooses one of the stories we have just heard and reads it out to the group. She then invites the group to mould her body, to create a statue, a portrait of the character in the story. She offers her body as a piece of malleable but delicate clay and invites the group to consider what they have heard and to gently shape and manipulate her body. They can make facial expressions for her to mirror; they can give her props to illustrate her character. The group tentatively approach Lois. Lois is a woman who is visiting them, who has made them laugh, who has helped them make these stories. But Lois is also a figure of authority. The teacher. Can they really touch and manipulate her body? Gradually and with increasing confidence, as it becomes clear that their actions won't warrant punishment, the women touch and gently shape Lois's body. When they are satisfied, they step back. Lois holds the pose, a physical portrait of one of the characters created by the group. The group are happy with the likeness they have made and the manner in which they have made it. By offering herself as a model for the group, by literally putting herself in the group's hands, Lois articulates both her trust in the group and the expectation she has of the group to take responsibility for her. Lois then invites them to get into small groups to set about modelling each other. The women take the same level of care and attention when modelling each other as they did when working with Lois.

This seemingly simple exercise marks a considerable shift in the manner in which the group works together. Previously, there was a clear sense that the thing that enabled this group of women to identify with each other was the fact that they were in prison, in the same place at the same time. The room was always loud with banter. Now, there was a shift in the quality of the focus in the room as the women found they had something else in common – this project, this different way of spending time together with the strange group of visitors who invited them to make things up, to play games, to touch and shape each other's bodies.

We take photographs of the character's posed portraits. It is approaching the end of the day. There is a sense of pleasure and achievement in the room. When Lois asks the women to think about their characters for tomorrow,

Possible Fictions   131

Tracey says that she won't be there as she will be in court and Fiona says she is being released and going home. The starkness of these announcements, and the level of surprise and disappointment they generate within the group, reveal the complexity and scale of the imaginary world that had been created throughout the day.

HMP Highpoint. 3 April 2002. Day 2.

We stand in a circle and begin the day with Body Hoo-Ha, Lois's signature warm-up game. Each person allows their body to make a sound and gesture without consideration. Well, that's the theory anyway. Reluctant morning bodies shuffle into action. The energy levels are low. Rather than accepting this drab effort, Lois continues to encourage and cajole the women into action. They realize that they are not going to be able to stand there and do nothing or skulk away. Lois expects them to play this game with her. The women join in with increasing physical enthusiasm despite the ongoing groans and complaints. The energy in the room lifts. Soon gestures and sounds move the air around us, and the circle of women stand, slightly flushed, ready to play. Lois introduces the first exercise, another beginning which invites a response:

I have a story to tell and it's about . . .

One by one, the women complete the end of the sentence.

I have a story to tell and it's about . . . nests, prison food, a water fight, a dolphin, my marriage, my sister, my rabbit.

Then Lois asks them to say the sentence again but this time to let the end of it run on and on and on until they can't think of anything else to say. Most of the responses from the women are firmly rooted in the real, in the autobiographical:

I have a story to tell and it's about my marriage. I met my husband when I was 16 years old and he was 22. I was 18, nearly 19 when I got married and he was 25.

I have a story to tell about a water fight. I had a good laugh and I drowned Darcy and Sam with water and it stunk and we had a proper laugh and it was freezing cold water and after we had to clear the mess up. So that wasn't all that good.

132   *Applied Theatre: Women and the Criminal Justice System*

> I have a story to tell about the pain in my leg. I've had it for two days and all they give me is three ibuprofen.

> I have a story to tell about life. Life is hard here at prison. Being away from my children and my family.

> I've a story to tell about my sister. She is the best, I want to be like her.

> I have a story to tell about prison food. It's not very nice. The meat isn't seasoned and the custard has got lots of lumps in it. The sponges are always the same. The milk is always off so I've always got a bad stomach so I've stopped drinking milk which means I can't have cornflakes.

These stories were small insights into the lives of the women, the practicalities of prison life and the memory and desire for what lay beyond. One of the women rose to the challenge of dancing on the tightrope between the real and the imaginary:

> I have a story to tell about my pet rabbit. I'm not supposed to have it in prison. The authorities get a bit iffy about it and I'm getting a bit worried because I think it's pregnant. What am I supposed to do with twenty-six bunny rabbits? I've thought about trading them for a half ounce of tobacco each but I'm not sure. I was thinking about writing to *The Sun*'s agony page but the letter may not get through security.

The women's response to this was laughter and delight in the saga and in the performance of the telling of the story. We sit together and look through the material that was written yesterday. Lois suggests that we meet the characters again, and then we try to develop them. She asks each person to introduce their character and to tell us a little more about them. If someone is stuck we can help each other by asking questions of the character, by interviewing them. The women describe their characters in the third person. Jude begins:

> Lily lives in a big house. It's peaceful and quiet. It looks like the sky. It's in the middle of nowhere with fields all around it, with flowers and trees and a stream and swans and geese.

One of the girls, swept up in the serenity of the image, interrupts: 'Got any spare rooms? Can we all come?' Everyone laughs and joins in, gathering a momentum and catalogue of favourite things:

Possible Fictions 133

Rachel Do you have puppies?

Jude Oh yes, and kittens.

Rachel In the fantasy they can always stay puppies, can't they?

Jude Yes.

Vicki She has a bike.

Sarah If her character was a part of the body it would be a heart – a puffy, duvet cover-like heart.

Jude It feels great. It's midday. It's a very bright house.

Jean How do you make your living?

Jude She is a retired librarian who is an artist.

Sam She eats when she's hungry and grows her own vegetables.

Beccy She eats soft cheese – doorsteps of cheese and hunks of bread and a fresh cup of unpasteurized goat's milk.

There is a pause in the crescendo of ideas. Sam laughs and says, 'We got carried away there, didn't we?'

Jude's character, and the group's engagement with her, allowed each of us to step beyond the reality of the hum and glare of the fluorescent lights, into another world, Lily's world. Jude had created a liminal space that, however briefly, allowed us to travel beyond the here and now before returning to it. The group is eager to feel this sensation again and encourage another woman, Jean, to speak. Her character is called Peace Keeper. She invites questions from the group and they begin:

Vicki What's she like?

Jean Quiet, tranquil, busy, strong.

Jude Where do you see yourself living?

Jean A castle – not a mansion; that's too pretentious.

Sam How do you get there?

Jean A flying horse, a centaur.

Rachel What time is it?

Jean It's dusk on a summer's night.

134   *Applied Theatre: Women and the Criminal Justice System*

Jude   What do you hold most dear to you?

Jean   Family.

Beccy   What do you mean?

Jean   Those nearest and dearest.

Beccy   Not necessarily blood.

Jean   No.

Beccy   Rather people you care about.

Sam   Like us?

Jean   Yes, people I can look after.

Jude   If you were an object, what would you be?

Jean   Something I can look after – a bird's egg, something that is delicate and needs taking care of. I'd be dressed in lilac.

Throughout the morning, people have been going to legal and family visits and to meds. There are now only seven women in the room, which is very quiet and focused. Sam begins to describe her character. She is not interrupted by the group:

> My character is called Twinkle Toes. She doesn't dance to ballet music – it's too slow. She needs something quicker, a polka. Quiet music can't contain her, she needs bigger music to wrap itself around her and let her spin out. She is on the stage in the spotlight. The theatre is empty. The spotlight is moving, anticipating her moves, even though there is no one manually moving it. Outside the theatre there is a bustling little town oblivious to her joy and dancing. She is wearing her own clothes, not a costume, and ballet shoes. It could be any time of the day.

There is a long silence when Sam finishes speaking. We are in the theatre with Twinkle Toes, crouching behind the seats in the darkness, watching this woman dance, hoping we don't interrupt her. We realize that she has left the stage to walk home through the bustling little town. We clap the empty stage still resonating with the joy of the dancer. We clap Sam who is sitting before us beaming.

Again, there has been another change in the group. They are really allowing themselves to imagine their characters. They are allowing themselves, and each other, to think in the abstract, to cross the line between the real and the imaginary. Pauline has just come in after having a visit. It's 4.10 p.m. There are only ten minutes left in the session so she could have gone back to the wing but chose not to. She wants to know what's been happening.

HMP Highpoint. 4 April 2002. Day 3. Tammy Whynot.

Today, Lois introduces us to her fantasy character, Tammy Whynot. Tammy Whynot is a country-and-western singer from Virginia who has reached middle age and realizes that there is much in the world that she doesn't know. As well as having a passion for all things pink, orange and sparkly, Tammy has a burning curiosity to find out as much as she can about things that have, until now, been beyond the realm of her experience. Tammy is a gregarious and generous-spirited character who flicks her peroxide curls out of the way as she takes a closer look at life.

Tammy first appeared in Split Britches' *Upwardly Mobile Home* in the spring of 1984 and took on a life of her own beyond the play to become a regular MC at the WOW Café throughout the 1980s. She is, as Carlson identifies, 'a character that lives in no play but roams in the real' (1996: 152). However, Tammy Whynot is more than this. She is a character who was born into a play but has rebelled against its confinements and frolics in the real. Within these prison walls, she is a delightful anathema.

It is another grey morning. Lois says that she would like to introduce someone to the group. As she sits, as Lois, on a chair in the circle with the women, she begins to describe Tammy. She takes off her boots and slips on a pair of sparkly mules. As she takes off her jumper and puts on a sheer leopard-skin blouse, her voice begins to change, morphing from educated East Coast to a more cascading, playful Southern drawl. She moves from talking about Tammy in the third person to talking *as* Tammy in the first person. She leans forwards and, when she snaps her head back, Lois's short blond bob has been replaced by a river of white-blond locks.

Tammy tells us all about the trailer where she lives and the songs she likes to sing as she glues on her eyelashes and swipes a dash of lipstick across her mouth. She smiles. Her orange bangles clack as she waves hello to the women in the room who are transfixed by this metamorphosis from the drama teacher who gets them to do annoying warm-ups to this effervescent creature with a mischievous look in her eye. Who is she? Where did she come from? Where is Lois? How is that possible? There is a hiatus of disbelief and pleasure as we all realize that Lois's fantasy character has become a reality. Go on, say something, Tammy. Tammy explains that she is in the process of educating herself and has never been to a women's prison before. She asks the women

136 *Applied Theatre: Women and the Criminal Justice System*

to host a session called *What Tammy Needs To Know About Prison*. The shift of dynamic in the room is dramatic. Women who had to be gently encouraged to speak were now talking over each other in an attempt to tell this woman all she needed to know about prison – how it works and how to survive it.

The room has been transformed. It is no longer the glaringly lit old aircraft hangar with monochrome aspirational prints on the wall, humming with sounds spilling over from the painting and decorating workshop. It is now a salon of curious and opinionated women, hosted by the most delightful, irreverent and engaging hostess. There is laughter and coy disbelief as Tammy sings her manifesto for loving life, a call to put 'the cunt back in country', encouraging them to join in the chorus. The women raucously respond, yet occasionally shoot nervous glances towards the door, listening for the jangle of keys or the squelch of rubber-soled patrolling shoes. The staff from the pre-release education course emerge from their offices grinning at this sight. Tammy gathers her things and says:

> Well, I just love you all to pieces and I'm telling you what, I would love for you all to come on tour with me. In fact, one of the things I'm going to do is buy a bus that is so big and so strong that I'm just going to drive that bus straight through the front gate and load you all up and take you just everywhere!

At the end of the session Tammy thanks the women for her education and grins before sliding off her wig. Lois then asks the women to think about the props and costumes they want for their fantasy characters. We set off at lunchtime with a shopping list for gold bustiers, trench coats and tutus.

When we arrive after lunch, the women are waiting for us. They are relating to Lois in a different way. They keep looking at her, waiting for any hint of Tammy's return. They position themselves closer to her. They don't want to be too far away in case something else happens. Lois wheels a bulging suitcase into the middle of the floor, unzips it and invites everyone to find their character's costume. Brightly coloured clothes and lengths of material spill out. There are whoops of surprise and excitement as everyone rummages around to find something specific to their character. We spend the afternoon dressing up and playing. A pair of orange plastic bracelets is gaffer-taped together to create handcuffs. A length of floral material becomes Mother Earth's robe. A gold bustier, peroxide wig and pink feather boa transform one pale, tired-looking woman into Bright Eyes. We couldn't find a tutu so we set about making one out of pieces of white paper sellotaped together, folded into pleats and threaded with string to tie at the back. Initially dubious about the invention, Sam puts it on over her tracksuit and trainers, and grins as she

Possible Fictions

sees that she is, now, a ballerina. A fake rose and application of red lipstick completes the look.

Lois asks them to take the text that they have written about their character and to read it as if they are the character. Instead of introducing their character by saying 'she is', she asks the women to introduce them by saying 'I am'. Dressed in their costumes, the women begin to introduce themselves *as* their fantasy characters:

My name is Bright Eyes and I'm going to the sea and I walk around and take things in and don't eat candyfloss, just smell it. I sleep under the pier, it's cold in winter, but it's lovely. Other people sleep there, too. There are lots of rocks on the beach.

My name is Energy and I'm full of life. I love clubbing, I love E. I have lots of friends. I mix records in my free time. I get paid for mixing records. I live alone. Clubbing is the most important thing to me in the whole world.

My name is Verge. I'm on the Edge of Life. I fall off all the time. I'm 10. I'm not a gymnast. I don't live with my mum and dad. I live in a nursery with all my friends – they're not on the edge. I eat sweets. I want to learn to balance when I grow up.

My name is CID Sid. I fry fish and I like fish and I love eel. I fry lots of things – chicken, sausages, but not a Mars bars in batter. My chip shop is called Star Bar and there are a few other people there – Darcy, Twinkle Toes and Bright Eyes. I pay them ... not a lot. When I'm not frying I'm an undercover for the police. I chase criminals. I can't tell you if I work for the FBI.

The performance residency culminated in a performance, *The Highpoint Big Breakfast* television show. The following extract considers how the group identified a medium through which to present their fantasy characters while engaging in the very real issues at play within the group.

HMP Highpoint. 12 April 2002. Final day.
Betty No-Boobs changes her mind.

The group decided that two of the women would host a programme in which they would interview the fantasy characters which had been created during

138   *Applied Theatre: Women and the Criminal Justice System*

the previous weeks. Garden experts, agony aunts and entertainers were welcomed onto the show which was filmed by one of the characters who also happened to be the show's resident fitness guru. There is one character, in particular, that I would like to introduce you to:

> My name is Betty No-Boobs and I like being the centre of attention. I want a boob job, 36DD. I live alone. I have hundreds of bikinis and a pet snake called Timmy that I've had for ten years and I wrap him around my boobs and I'm a lap dancer. I've a partner. A man and a woman partner.

Betty No-Boobs was, in fact, a quiet 22-year-old woman who had a very low self-image and, throughout the course of the residency, became a focal point for the gentle, humorous and persistent support of the group. This was never explicitly discussed or made a big deal of in any way. However, on the final day of the workshops, during *The Highpoint Big Breakfast*, it became extraordinarily clear how concerned the women were about this girl, and how they used the performance to address this. The following transcriptions from the performance illustrate this. The stage is set with the resident agony aunt, Rachel. She reads a letter that has been written on behalf of Betty No-Boobs:

> Dear Rachel, I want you to tell me why you think I need to have lots of operations to feel good. I hate it that I can't be happy being just me. I get depressed when I see a beautiful woman with big natural boobs and glowing skin and a size 8 body with no cellulite. It makes me self-conscious and I dread going to the beach. What do you think I should do as I'm not happy eating just salads and exercising for hours every day. I know that even when I have my 36DD boobs and all the rest of it I won't be satisfied. So please, can you tell me what I should do to feel better about myself and why I feel so awful about myself?
> Love, Betty No-Boobs.

Then Rachel responds as the agony aunt:

> Well I would reply to that that you should look within yourself before you have the boob job done because until you love yourself no one will love you. You can have a boob job done and do what you want but at the end of the day you are still going to be the same person inside so you need to look inside yourself before you start looking on the outside.

No sooner has the agony aunt left the stage than Jean, one of the hostesses, begins to speak:

Possible Fictions

I've decided today to express some views that may be useful to one of our earlier guests. Now, Betty No-Boobs seems intent on having a boob job, 36DD or maybe even bigger. I want to tell you what it's like to have big boobs. Believe me, Betty No-Boobs, this is not as nice and comfortable as you may think. Let me just give you a few examples. When you go to bed at night and turn on your side, the right boob knocks you in the eye. Not comfortable at all. If you have to run for a bus, right and left boob, over shoulders. Once again, not very nice. When we come to the summer and you think OK, no bra, let's go braless. How can you go braless with boobs waltzing over one arm and under the other arm? I beg of you. You may ask me why haven't I got a boob reduction, but I believe in living with what God gave me and I think you should do the same or you'll be struggling to get a bra big enough to fit you. If you perspire a lot, you are permanently wet under your boobs. This is not nice, this is not pleasant. Please, Betty No-Boobs, take it from one who knows: little is best.

These excerpts reveal much about the distance travelled by this group of women throughout the performance workshops. During a feedback session with the group, Betty No-Boobs thanked everyone for helping her realize that she didn't need a boob job. This change in perspective is not something we could have imagined or prescribed when we turned up at the prison gates on the first day, nor is it one that the prison administration would necessarily value as a useful indicator of change. We have no idea if the young woman still feels the same way. All we do know is that, in the midst of creating fantasy characters, these women were firmly rooted in the real, listening to each other, being playful when they could, being serious when they needed to be. Behind the bravura of Betty No-Boobs, they heard a young person asking for help and for acceptance. They used their fantasy characters to stage a conversation that would otherwise have been too difficult to have in their everyday lives.

Note

1 This documentation is drawn from McAvinchey (2007: 173–201).

References

Carlson, M. (1996), *Performance: A Critical Introduction*, London and New York: Routledge.

Etchells, T. (1999), *Certain Fragments: Contemporary Performance and Forced Entertainment*, London: Routledge.

McAvinchey, C. (2007), 'Possible Fictions: The Testimony of Applied Performance with Women in Prisons in England and Brazil'. Unpublished PhD Thesis, QMUL.

Shaw, P. (2003), Interview with the author, 22 March. HMP Highpoint, Suffolk.

Extract I from *Killers* (1980)

Jacqueline Holborough

The Prisoner   How absurd it seems that we should be kept here like this. In separate little compartments, filed away – for three years ... or thirty. A matter of numbers. What you or anyone else is supposed to have done recedes into a dusty pile of papers that ceases to have meaning. Left only with isolated individuals coming together for group identification at times specified by system routine. You may mix together. You may not mix together, two or three of you may mix in that corner, four or five of you in this space here. And the times and patterns at which this association may occur are worked out as carefully as an abstract painting – seeming haphazard but having, one suspects, all the skill of purposeful planning.

Every day of the week has some small variation worked into it. An incentive to keep on moving. Kit change day, library day, canteen day – and so on. So the days of the week are marked, and with them go the months and, I suppose, the years, as the industry ticks on. Everybody behaving as though trees and grass no longer exist. Animals and children almost extinct. Private conversation, personal actions and life away from the antiseptic glare – all a long time ago.

Even after a few days it seems somehow acceptable. Nobody complains. When the men were here there were protests. Demonstrations every day. Hunger strikes, mutinies, escape attempts. Questions in the House. The media waited eagerly for news of fresh disturbance from Durham's E Wing. Committees of experts came and went filing reports about psychological damage and conditions intolerable to civilized society. So they moved the men out. And after a decent lapse of time and a change of title, they moved the women in. Since which time the wing has hardly been known to exist. There are only women here now. Tension is all premenstrual. Give 'em enough Valium and they'll fade from view.

142   *Applied Theatre: Women and the Criminal Justice System*

Killers was written and performed by Jacqueline Holborough, one of Clean Break's founder members. While in prison, the theatre collective was not allowed to create work that directly engaged with the ideology or experience of incarceration. *Killers* was the first Clean Break production to directly address the material conditions and political implications of women's incarceration. Staged at the Pleasance Theatre, Edinburgh (1980), it was subsequently adapted for radio (*Wednesday Is Yoga Day,* 1982, BBC Radio 4, dir. Kay Patrick) and for television (1984, Channel 4, dir. Bob Long). Like *Decade* (Holborough, 1984), *Killers* is set in HMP Durham's maximum security unit for women, H Wing in the 1970s. Despite the fact that very few women were convicted for serious and violent offences, all thirty-six places in the wing were filled with women, most of whom had short-term sentences for less serious crimes.

Killers is an unpublished play text held in the Clean Break archive, Bishopsgate Institute, London.

6

Theatre as Collective Casework: Clean Break Theatre Company's *Charged* (2010)

Molly McPhee

Seventeenth-century poet and fabulist La Fontaine begins his fable 'The Wolf and the Lamb' with a pithy construction of casework:

> The strong are always best at proving they're right.
> Witness the case we're now going to cite.

In 'The Wolf and the Lamb', a hungry wolf accuses a young lamb of speaking badly of him in the previous year. When the lamb protests that it is not yet a year old and, therefore, can't be the source of any bad talk, the wolf declares it must be one of the lamb's associates, and eats the lamb anyway: 'So trial and judgment stood.' The 'case' of the wolf and the lamb, La Fontaine tells the reader, will illustrate the point he gives in his first line: that the strong are best at proving they're right. Meanwhile, the reader is instructed to witness the infallible narration of the case, in lamb-like fashion, as each line flows from the first to produce the general through the example.

Cases are ubiquitous across modes of discourse: the cases of fabulists stand in direct relation to the medical case, the criminal case, the academic case, the social work case, the case study as a methodology. Formally, cases work to both clarify and diagnose an overarching problem or question at hand. They propose, as Lauren Berlant puts it, 'a problem-event that has animated some kind of judgment. Any enigma could do – a symptom, a crime, a causal variable, a situation, a stranger, or any irritating obstacle to clarity. What matters is the idiom of the judgment' (2007: 663). As such, cases are complex adjudicators: parts illustrating the whole, parts questioning the whole, parts disciplining the whole, parts becoming the whole. The practice of British case law, for example, expresses the role of the fractional legal case as an arbiter of common law: hundreds-of-years-old cases continue to set judicial precedent, define acts of parliament and explain the common law.

144   *Applied Theatre: Women and the Criminal Justice System*

In this way, case law provides a clear illustration of not only how 'law mirrors social and political attitudes', but how the case itself, in form and content, shapes social and political attitudes (Clapham 2018). Cases are systems of meaning-making.

They are also popular systems of media-making, as demonstrated by a global entertainment industry awash in case-led investigative procedural formats, from detective dramas to true-crime podcasts. Both as a narrative format and as an idiom of judgement invested in shaping society, the case in criminal justice contexts plays a fundamental role in maintaining a collective 'carceral imaginary' (Fludernik 2005), in which cultural assumptions about criminality accrete and reify the institution of prison and practice of imprisonment. Yet the majority of case-led narratives that shape a collectively held carceral imaginary come at audiences through heavily mediated channels, offering minimal capacity for live response.

Theatre, as a cultural product predicated on physical proximity and collectivity, proposes a form with unique capacity to agitate audience awareness of how the constructs of casework motivate carceral society through a shared carceral imaginary. In this chapter, I investigate Clean Break theatre company's *Charged* at Soho Theatre (2010) as operating within, and critiquing, the syntax of a criminal case by engaging audiences in collective casework at the theatre.[1] When it suddenly becomes a live encounter, in what ways might casework at the theatre reveal carceral sites – and site-making processes – as immediate, material and specific to the context of the audience?

London-based Clean Break, who work with women in prison and women at risk in the community, summon the audiences of *Charged* to collective casework through an image of a woman styled as a booking photo in the foyer at Soho Theatre. As the theatrical event proceeds, however, the nature of the criminal 'charge' is never specified in any detail. A charge in this theatre does not attempt to result in audience determination of conviction or release of any singular character. Instead, the charge of *Charged* works to generate a broader question of what an ambient 'charge' might mean within carceral society: can an ever-manifesting identity site of 'becoming-criminal' be completely disestablished, even if the charge never lands? Through a production comprised of multiple narratives, casts, performance spaces and audience movement through Soho Theatre's building, *Charged* provokes audiences to explore personal and collective responsibility in a society that routinely criminalizes women through social bias. Here, I examine the collective casework within *Charged* as facilitating what Elaine Aston calls 'networks of resistance', in which 'political subjectivities [occur] across multiple sites of potential emancipatory possibility' (2016: 8). Tracing the

Theatre as Collective Casework

casework of *Charged* advances a broader development in this chapter around theatre's capacity to destabilize linear causality in criminal justice narratives, and to critique the carceral function of audiences.

Witness the case we're now going to cite.

Setting the conditions for casework: The *Charged* poster and structure of the production

Clean Break's 2010 production *Charged* convened its audiences in the foyer of Soho Theatre, next to large posters of a woman apparently under investigation, the production title stamped under her chin. Framed up large at the theatre, her face seems plucked from a rogue's gallery: a white face looks out, defiantly pursing her lips around a cigarette. The freckles on her face condense into a patina of green, loading her with the hue of oxidized copper. A bad penny. This mugshot declares: CHARGED. But with what? The nature of the charge is not given, yet audiences are nevertheless called to the theatre to adjudicate. 'Punish me or pray for me,' ran the marketing copy. 'Lock me up or look away. I'm not going anywhere' (Clean Break 2010). A poster styled up as a booking photo, accompanied by an invocation to judgement ('Lock me up or look away'): proffering a *Charged* woman to the audience, the production formed from the outset a dynamic that challenged audiences to investigate a fictive charged identity – to punish, pray for, lock up or look away.

The *Charged* poster is the first point of activation for a production concerned with provoking and challenging a collective carceral imaginary around women under criminal investigation. Through the semiotics of a long tradition of Wanted posters, from Wild West villains to police booking photos, *Charged* set up audiences as apprehenders at the precipice of judgement. 'Charged', as a word, and as a word conferred upon an image of a woman, works as a punitive performative, in Judith Butler's sense (2011; also McKenzie 2001: 166–70). The word endows a loaded (literally charged) subjectivity, conferred with a 'binding power': 'Here it is not only a question of how discourse injures bodies, but how certain injuries establish certain bodies at the limits of available ontologies, available schemes of intelligibility' (Butler 2011: 170). The binding power of a criminal charge – 'I charge you' – may yet be one that can *potentially* be slipped out of: a transitional identity state, in other words, changing upon release or conviction. Superimposing a 'charge' on a poster styled as a booking photo, the *Charged* poster gathers carceral traditions around spectatorship and criminality as an explicit theatre of judgement.[2] The poster promises an investigation and, in this, a clinical

146 *Applied Theatre: Women and the Criminal Justice System*

casework in which audiences will assess the charge. Yet a singular case, though promised, never seems to arrive. And so: what is being articulated when the company presents the case of a charged woman, yet the charge is never given or resolved?

The overall challenge of the production to witness and ultimately adjudicate on a charged identity quickly falls into disarray, as audiences encounter six short plays, narratively unconnected to each other: *Doris Day* by E. V. Crowe, *Dancing Bears* by Sam Holcroft, *That Almost Unnameable Lust* by Rebecca Lenkiewicz, *Fatal Light* by Chloë Moss, *Taken* by Winsome Pinnock and *Dream Pill* by Rebecca Prichard. *Charged* was performed in two-night cycles, over three weeks – three plays on night one ('Charged 1') and three plays on the following, night two ('Charged 2').[3] The plays were performed across three spaces, each on a different floor within Soho Theatre: the basement, the middle-level mainstage theatre and the studio at the top of the building. Once assembled under the poster in the foyer of Soho Theatre, audiences were randomly split, such that half would start with a play in the basement and half in the top-floor studio; the two groups then travelled up- or downstairs to the middle level to watch the second play together as one audience; finally, for the third play, audiences split back into their groups again and continued either down to the basement or up to the studio. On any given night, the studio and basement plays were performed twice, once for each half of the split audience; the middle-level play was performed only once for the whole audience together.

Plays performed in the basement and studio spaces dramatized 'at risk' or criminal justice-adjacent thematics – addiction (*Taken*), sex trafficking (*Dream Pill*), girl gangs (*Dancing Bears*) and gender discrimination (*Doris Day*). Prison is not the setting of these plays and, in most of them, prison is not mentioned. Only on the middle-level, proscenium mainstage did audiences encounter settings and narratives that worked explicitly with prison or police custody: deaths in custody (*Fatal Light*) and ageing in prison (*That Almost Unnameable Lust*). Physically moving from risk narrative (studio or basement) to custody narrative (mainstage) and back into risk narrative (basement or studio), audiences investigate some of the categories of social risk routinely linked to the criminal justice system. The production agitates the dramaturgical link between, for example, gangs and prison, addiction and prison, sex trafficking and prison, as sites where an inevitable criminal charge has yet to land. Prison both follows and predicts these risk spaces, figuring the criminal justice system as on an Ourobotic continuum of disciplines, aftermaths, re-entries.

Fostering these dramaturgical connections is at the core of Clean Break's artistic vision:

Theatre as Collective Casework 147

The treatment of women by the criminal justice system is one of the clearest demonstrations that our society is still unequal and that women are judged by different standards to men. ... we believe that theatre enables women to challenge their oppression by society in general and by the criminal justice system in particular.

Clean Break 2019

As a significant body of critical work by sociologists, feminist criminologists, activists and legal scholars attests, women in the criminal justice system represent a demographic where the assignation of the criminal identity, the 'at risk' and the becoming-criminal stems from a terrain where legal identity is vastly overdetermined by cultural norms arising from prejudice and stigma (see, for example, Kennedy 2005; Pemberton 2013; Gelsthorpe 2004, 2010; Davis 2003; Wacquant 2009; Tyler 2013). In the United Kingdom, stigma-driven gendered sentencing (and its analogon, gender enforcement) lead most women to be arrested, cautioned or sentenced for non-violent offences linked to poverty, mental health, addiction, racism and lack of education. Physical health (including HIV and Hepatitis-C diagnosis), disability and parenting status are also factors (Corston 2007), as is a background of domestic violence and sexual abuse.

Despite prodigious research demonstrating the damaging impacts of imprisonment on British society, the number of women incarcerated in the UK continues to grow. The casework of *Charged* relies on setting up the social norms that drive conditions of hyperincarceration: it is not the deviation from the norm, but the norm itself that will become investigated. Correspondingly, *Charged* is structured to produce scenarios of criminalization in direct relationship to categories of social normativity. The *Charged* poster, styled as a booking photo, works from the outset as a lure to establish the audience as arbiters of social norms, 'infallible narrators' of criminality. This is a technique with long traditions in Europe, as Michael Herzog writes, beginning with the eighteenth-century practice of widely disseminating criminal dossiers:

the criminal is presented as a curiosity, an aberration from the norm that makes him [*sic*] an interesting case. The powers that judge the criminal are thrust into the background as the individual criminal takes center stage to be documented, classified, and distinguished – by an invisible, purportedly infallible, and generally anonymous narrator.

Herzog 2009: 37

This staging of the criminal by an infallible narrator sets up a concept of the case as mode by which to document one (or many) deviance(s) from the norm,

148   *Applied Theatre: Women and the Criminal Justice System*

as Foucault theorizes in *The Birth of the Prison* (1995: 184ff). For other theorists, however, the shifting nature of the case provides not only documentation and assessment of deviance, but consistently re-establishes and reframes the conventions of the norm itself (Jolles in Chandler 1998; Herzog 2009; Berlant 2007). It is in this sense that Diana Taylor affiliates case-study methodologies to the normalization of torture: 'Particular case studies seem to transparently illustrate patterns and produce generalizable theories. They generate evidence that is objective and replicable – any investigator should be able to reproduce the findings' (2007: 715). In *Charged*, basement and studio dramatizations of risk become scenarios of criminalization. With no connecting narrative ligature between the scenarios, a core underlying operation of the casework within *Charged* is to reactivate the 'known' through bias and prejudice. Any investigator should be able to reproduce the findings – under the sheen of new risk variables, the case of *Charged* always progresses through the middle-level imprisonment narrative, reaffirming social attitudes and fears.

In creating a piece of theatre that revolves around an *ambient* criminal charge – a charge never clarified, but physically carried by each audience member from each performance space to the next – Clean Break generates a multicausal dramaturgical model, in which criminalization becomes motivated by stigmatic idioms of judgement. *Charged* configures and draws on multiple identity positions, descending and ascending through topoi of the carceral imaginary, emotional events, contexts of risk and, not least, the many ages and ethnicities of performers and audience members alike. The production is thus *charged*, as in loaded or supercharged, with bodies, stories and knowledges. It is also charged with stigmas of various kinds, creating an excess of pre-, post- and paracriminal identities through dramaturgical surplus that engages the audience in carceral overflow.

In part, this multiply-valenced load on the production occurs through sheer numbers of creative team, consultants and crew. Six playwrights engaged with the company via residencies onsite at Clean Break's studios and in prisons, and via consultations with staff at drug and alcohol rehabilitation centres, probation and with police.[4] As a performance event, *Charged* extended into ambitious terrains, on a scale never before attempted by the company: in her foreword to the play text, Executive Director Lucy Perman MBE writes of the production as 'an epic moment for Clean Break' (2010: iv). Three directors – Tessa Walker, Caroline Steinbeis and Lucy Morrison – helmed a creative and production team of thirty women theatre practitioners, including three companies of actors whose ages spanned eight decades on stage. They, in turn, were supported by producers, staff, consultants and board based year round at the company's London studios. *Charged* was a multiply-stranded event on three levels, therefore: multiple physical passages through the plays; multiple dramaturgical passages through an overarching narrative of the *Charged* woman; and a heterogeneity in artistic vision and execution, with several companies of playwrights, directors, designers and performers working across six plays.

By offering such a large number of variables to the audience, the case of *Charged* isolates social preconceptions about women and criminality – the carceral imaginary – as one of the only constants of the production. Where in *Charged* each physical and narrative space operates along a referential axis to the word 'charged' (sex-trafficked girls – charged; families dealing with addiction – charged; girl gangs – charged), the plays also use their multicausal charge (as excess) to activate each other along resistive networks *against* the charge (as legal event).

Charged occasioned surprise among critics who had clear expectations of what a play about women in the criminal justice system might be like. In a preview press interview, *Guardian* critic Lyn Gardner faithfully reports her own suggestion that the plays 'don't sound like the most cheerful of nights out', to which *Charged* playwright Rebecca Prichard responds, 'I'm confident we will surprise you' (Gardner 2010). The surprise was, in fact, experienced by several reviewers, who highlighted the disparity between anticipations of 'an orgy of narrowly issue-driven drama and tub-thumping political correctness' and the 'unexpected directions' in which *Charged* took audiences (Taylor 2010). In their reviews of *Charged*, Hazel Tsoi and Carole Woddis both note a lack of resolution-oriented dramaturgy. For Woddis, 'Offering no solution [...] *Charged* confronts us with complex realities of crime, the criminal justice system and those who become entangled in its web either as victims, perpetrators or custodians' (2010). Tsoi echoes: 'the incredible power of *Charged* is the absence of solutions to the situations investigated [...] you are free to feel scared, angry, dismayed, uplifted, uncomfortable or happy as you wish' (2010). If this small selection of notices is any indication, then it makes clear than an aspect of the carceral imaginary (at an intersection with theatre) is punitive to audiences: when provoked to imagine an exposure to carceral spaces at the theatre, audience members expect that they, too, will be implicated in a disciplinary way.

These are normative case-led expectations, in the sense that these reviewers appear to bring their experience with, and imagination of, theatre for social justice ('tub-thumping') to bear on their experience with mass-mediatized narratives of carcerality, a kind of doubly punitive scenario. They were surprised because, to use Tsoi's terms, 'the situations investigated' did not force them to feel or think any particular way. For these reviewers, and for me, *Charged* proposed instead what Berlant calls 'an altered way of feeling things out' (2007: 666): a potential within casework to undo or mitigate the

150   *Applied Theatre: Women and the Criminal Justice System*

teleological bent to reaffirm the known, which normally accompanies the space of the case.

Beginning and ending in risk environments: The basement and studio plays

In keeping with their fundamental role in assessing risk (to the social norm, as well as more broadly), cases can become risky events. 'Cases' in the criminal justice system – in an expanded sense of legal cases, police cases and the casework of probation and social services – significantly magnify the actuarial aspect of the case, as risk-led idioms further assess people already defined as 'at risk' in society. In the theatre of *Charged*, these propensities of the case become heightened; they also become in some ways overturned, offering ways to productively 'fall out of line'[5] with the normativity of case-led narrative:

> [The case] raises questions of precedent and futurity, of canons of contextualization, of narrative elucidation. This is what's disciplinary about the normativity of caseness. ... Case almost closed: the marked subject is a walking exemplar, a person trailing an already-known story. Not always, though – [...] the case can incite an opening, an altered way of feeling things out, of falling out of line.
>
> Berlant 2007: 666

Charged immediately set up the audience for casework predicated on an 'altered way of feeling things out' through the settings of the first short plays of the production. The basement and studio plays amplified 'at risk' thematics, creating cramped and precarious environments in which distinctions between criminal and investigator, as much as performer and audience, begin to lose carceral power.

In the basement, *Dream Pill* (Prichard, 'Charged 1') audiences encounter Bola and Tunde, two young Nigerian girls sex-trafficked to the UK; in 'Charged 2', *Dancing Bears* (Holcroft), four teenagers navigate life on the streets as part of a gang. Both basement plays employed a semi-immersive performance space; while both settings were end-on, actors moved into and among audiences. The aesthetics of *Dancing Bears* and *Dream Pill* manifested both a vulnerability, and a volatility, resonant to chaotic environments in which children at risk live. Throughout *Dancing Bears*, four teenagers keep themselves moving, hopping from foot to foot across a stage envisaged by Holcroft as a bed of hot coals. This movement is met by constant character

Theatre as Collective Casework 151

transfigurations between male and female, pregnant and not-pregnant, and human-animalness within the proxy family of the gang. Where in *Dancing Bears* characters explore continuums of love, fear, desire and violence through multiple subject positions, in *Dream Pill* it is the audience that becomes implicated in such shifts. Bola and Tunde, as girls not yet 10 years of age, speak to the audience, tell them stories, give them objects; the audience vacillate between figurations, addressed sometimes as punters, sometimes as other girls trafficked to the basement for sex work, at other times as rescuers. These characterizations propose a hybrid narrative of theatre and criminality via shifting, scrambling subject positions, in which kinetic engagements with young characters in risk environments underscore the nature of risk itself as a becoming, with uncertain temporalities (Van Loon 2000: 176). As such, *Dream Pill* and *Dancing Bears* set a scenario in which the fallibility of criminal justice casework from a superposition of an investigative eye becomes evident.

The basement plays also manifested risk as *material* sites bound by precarity. This latter aesthetic was made possible through a heterotopic dynamic in the basement, which functioned during the production as both performance space and as a working kitchen for the theatre's bar directly above.[6] The sounds of the theatre's bar, along with the chip fryer going off intermittently as the kitchen filled orders, suffused the plays with heterotopic tension. A partially converted space gave these plays a palpably differential, and vulnerable, status – they were not in a sense 'protected' by theatre anymore; instead they circulated through an undetermined, semi-converted social space. As the audience experienced the audible encroachment of a public in the bar above and chefs in the kitchen at the back, the vulnerable porosity of the performance space echoed the social themes of the plays; it also evoked the porosity of carceral society itself, in which the narratives, techniques and technologies of the criminal justice system bleed throughout the socius, including from the basement up into the Soho Theatre bar.

The small top-floor studio space, by contrast, presented as exceptionally sealed. A cramped aesthetic here amplified the topics of the studio plays: addiction in the family, in *Taken* (Pinnock) for 'Charged 1'; and gender discrimination in the police force in *Doris Day* (Crowe) for 'Charged 2'. *Taken* pivoted off themes of generational trauma, and transmissions of post-traumatic stress between family members. The play's recursive patterns of addiction drew the performers and audience into an ever-increasing claustrophobia of trauma, intensified by traverse staging, as each half of the audience stared down their own counterparts on the other side of the stage.

In an exploration of institutional violence and gender discrimination within the police force, *Doris Day* also benefited from the tight, sealed space.

152   *Applied Theatre: Women and the Criminal Justice System*

Doris Day expanded *Charged*'s overall investigation into 'women in the criminal justice system' beyond the traditional sense of women under criminal charge, to also include those women who police them. This inclusion compacted the relative airlessness of the studio, in its scrutiny of a discriminatory system that punishes the (supposed) punisher. In the studio, various stucknesses coalesced within *Charged*'s macro-trap of imprisonment themes: stuckness of addiction joined the stuckness of rank-and-file policing experienced by women officers continually passed over for promotion joined the stuckness of family and friendship (in *Taken* and *Doris Day*, these stucknesses each have positive and negative cadences).

Cops, friends, kids, parents, resilient, funny, heartbreaking: both *Taken* and *Doris Day*, as well as *Dream Pill* and *Dancing Bears*, work hard to shift the narrative onus off victims of the criminal justice system as 'tragic protagonists'. In this, the basement and studio plays heed Rustom Bharucha's warning that '[n]ot only can this singular focus on the tragic protagonist blind one to the suffering and social exclusion of others, it can also pre-empt the actual possibilities of radical transformation in society at large' (2014: 46). To dismantle the casework of the carceral imaginary, it becomes critical to provoke instead a contingency of figurations, both within and beyond the 'already known' of criminal identities, which can sweep the audience into a relationality that prohibits exoticizing the criminal woman. Crucial to the transformative impact of *Charged* is this multiplicity which, while shifting focus off any one protagonist – let alone any one tragedy – does not altogether eliminate protagonists and tragedies.

Unlike the characters in the plays, who operate within conditions of social and environmental stuckness, and the performers, who do not move between performance spaces, the audience *can* move – and this very exercise of movement becomes part of the production's meaning through exclusionary space and narrative. Yet, at the same time, audiences did not choose an order of plays or drift in and out of performance spaces at will. A curated movement through the space thus serves to intensify the effect of carceral stuckness: there is movement, but even this movement is processional, almost – to borrow a term from prison contexts – a *decanting* of audiences between performance spaces. Cases, like risk definition, are predicated on maintenance of a clear power differential (Beck 2006: 333); accordingly the audience is pressured, in some ways, to allocate certain risk states to criminal states (and vice versa). Stilted, curated movement for the audience implicates them in the overall carceral atmosphere at work in the production, as predictable risk spaces convene together through a collective passage. In these ways, audience movement within *Charged* illustrates the carceral function of audiences as they perform what Lefebvre terms social *dressage*: 'To enter into a society,

Theatre as Collective Casework

group or nationality is to accept values (that are taught), to learn a trade by following the right channels, but also to bend oneself (to be bent) to its ways' (2004 [1992]: 39). The means by which individuals and communities break themselves in, or come to be broken into representations of self, versus and among other selves and other objects, are often non-discursive performances, as *Charged* expresses through its phenomenological linkage of narrative domains. Processes of movement and affect, trailing through the social domain and in the social encounter, reflect the self's adaptation to a collective will, in which visibility and viability of persons is ordered in strata of standardization. Dressage, up and down the levels of Soho Theatre, choreographs this movement into and around identities legible to the state and, correspondingly, to the carceral imaginary.

Yet *Charged* undercuts this power differential, both through a split audience and through studio and basement narratives that demonstrate the reflexivity of risk. Squeezing by each other along narrow passageways between performance spaces, audiences linked 'at risk' narratives phenomenologically through their own movement, creating a site-responsive dramaturgy of multiply-noded causalities and fractured subject positions. Through these interruptions of linear causality, the spaces of performance accreted dynamic connections and outcomes, related purely through audience movement within a dramaturgical space in which both simultaneous and sequential narratives were performed within the same building.

Proscenium prisons: Staging custodial settings on the middle level

Berlant draws a distinction between casework that rehearses normativity and casework that can resist or change it: 'When it doesn't work to change the conditions of exemplarity or explanation, something is deemed merely a case study, remanded to banal particularity', she writes. 'When it does, a personal or collective sensorium shifts' (2007: 667). Brushing by each other, audiences became cross-contaminating hosts not only of the detecting position of social control, but of a carceral imaginary that could only come into being through the audience's own movement through 'at risk' narratives under the banner of a 'charged' woman. As the audiences continue their trajectories, some ascending, others descending, they cross-pollinate subject formations. Fredric Jameson writes of stereotypes as the friction between the epidermis of groups, 'precisely the outer edge of the group that – all the while remaining unrepresentable – brushes against that of the other' (in Chow 2010: 49). Filing past each other in the ascent and descent, the audience chafes; sloughs

154   *Applied Theatre: Women and the Criminal Justice System*

off some of the skins of cultural prejudice; litters them in the midden of the theatre.

The settings of the studio and basement plays connected notions of social cohesion and exclusion with hierarchies of space, and embedded them in the performance dynamic and audience's reception mode. These conditionings of the audience become most starkly evocative when considering the 'at risk' studio and basement plays in relation to the middle-level performance space and its plays. The middle-level plays, presented on Soho Theatre's most traditional, proscenium stage with raked auditorium seating, offered the only perspectives on imprisonment in the production, overtly matching the institutional theme of the plays to the institutionalized setting of the proscenium. Subject formations of the risk space, pre-, post- or paracriminal – addicted but not criminal, sex-trafficked but not criminal, not yet – meet in the middle as the audience becomes exposed to characters pulled into custody. In *That Almost Unnameable Lust* by Rebecca Lenkiewicz, a writer delivers workshops with older women serving long sentences ('Charged 2'). *Fatal Light* by Chloë Moss ('Charged 1'), on mental health and deaths in custody, is told in reverse order, gradually unpeeling connections between social isolation and single motherhood. A kind of 'proscenium imprisonment' thus operates here as a fulcrum for space (the middle level of the theatre) and for audience (the only space in which the audience comes together to watch a play as one group); it also provides a thematic fulcrum, in that it manifests conditions of imprisonment as inherent to the semantics of the criminal charge under investigation. However, these 'middle plays' of imprisonment do not provide thematic resolution, or even a single point of connection, between the 'at risk' thematics of top- and lower-floor plays. What narrative through lines there may be are created only via the connecting ligature of the audience's movement from risk space to imprisonment to risk space. Without conscious intention, as cross-contaminating bodies themselves, audience members encounter characters in risk spaces, and then enter a totalizing mainstage framework of custody narrative. Coming back out of the custody space, the final risk narrative carries an immediate history of criminality that overshadows and pressures the dramaturgical arc.

Although collective casework in *Charged* pulls audience members into a kind of contaminating carceral dressage, this does not foreclose an ability to break gait from the narrative expectations fostered by the carceral imaginary. As Elaine Aston proposes, 'networks of resistance' in theatre and performance practice become formed via an 'amalgam of dissensual and reparative practices [...] agitating for change' (2016: 9):

> Agitating for change requires not only oppositional strategies, but also reparative tactics to help envision the remaking of an alternative, socially

Theatre as Collective Casework

progressive hegemony … both imagining and working towards a systemic change that is not yet, while at the same time surviving the here-and-now conditions of a sociopolitical given.

Aston 2016: 8–9

Where some aspects of the production's dramaturgy were overtly dissensual – idiosyncratic environments pulled together in deliberate disconnect – *Charged* employed 'reparative tactics' in its staging of the middle-level imprisonment plays. As within Aston's networks of resistance, this amalgam of dissent and reparation supports a shift in the audience sensorium. The proscenium-imprisonment of the middle level inaugurates anew the role of case-building investigator, looking to normalize the custodial narrative. *Fatal Light* takes a clear investigatory line – working backwards in the narrative to reveal how a death in custody could have occurred/been allowed to occur. *That Almost Unnameable Lust* organizes around the difficulties and misconceptions of a writer running workshops in prison: her experiences as an outsider trying to understand the world of the women inside define the course of a narrative fuelled by the mystery of why the characters are serving long sentences. In the former, why did a woman die? In the latter, how did these older women in prison become lifers? Suddenly confronted with explicitly case-driven scenarios on the hegemonic mainstage, the atmosphere becomes explicitly redolent of the Wanted poster of the *Charged* woman.

The impulses to case normativity on the mainstage coalesce through characters and content endowed with investigator/coroner consciousness. These pieces agitate a very 'writerly' zone – through Moss's play, a formal conceit, walking back in time; and in Lenkiewicz's play, a framing narrative of an inexperienced writer accompanies stylized passages, which convey the inner thoughts of an imprisoned woman who no longer speaks. In these narratives, the writer becomes drawn into allegiance with the investigating aptitudes of the audience. On the mainstage in *Charged*, narrative through lines move in from risk spaces of the anticipated-yet-not-arrived, into the proscenium prison. Both the mainstage theatre and its narrative, situated physically on the middle level of the theatre, exist in a suspension between studio and basement sites. The audience in its split has become both reparative and dissensual to itself; in this strange suspension, the fragments of the narrative come into a restructuring of relationships, driven by a frustrated desire to close the case.

Because it is suspended between the performances of risk narrative in the basement and studio, the middle-level palimpsest of deeply culturally inscribed sites – prison and proscenium theatre, layered on one another –

becomes in some ways the most transparently constructed site, allowing for transformative work. The reparative middleness of the mainstage – a return to seemingly normative scenarios of imprisonment – becomes scrambled or 'broken', an effect aligned to what literary scholar Isobel Armstrong has called the 'broken middle' aesthetic: 'not a representation of the subject, but the subject of a representation, which is not a self, not an object, or a thematics, but the structuring movement of thought and feeling' (in Shaughnessy 2015: 99). The deepest struggle of *Charged* to divest prison from its representation within the carceral imaginary becomes articulated here as imprisonment narratives on the mainstage are not the representations of prison, but show the concept of prison as a totalizing representation itself.[7] By that very turning point, 'prison' becomes fallible: the subject of representation of something else – 'a movement of thought and feeling'.

The 'broken middle' enacts a breaking down in order to reveal what has long been broken about the criminal justice system. Performance theorist and practitioner Nicola Shaughnessy applies Armstrong's 'broken middle' in performance aesthetics to that moment when:

> the movement between opposites creates breakdown, contradiction and a restructuring of relationships [... This is the] notion of the in between space of the broken middle, and the bridging of affect and thought, emotion and cognition.
>
> Shaughnessy 2015: 99

The broken middle of the mainstage forces the audience to rationalize the preceding and coming risk spaces into imprisonment narrative and, I suggest, to reject such a rationalization. Personally, I found the mainstage plays involved me in just such a restructuring of relationships, which I experienced as a disassociation from, or a frozenness between, 'affect and thought', as Shaughnessy puts it. I remember crying during *Fatal Light* and, at the same time, wondering why.[8] It was not because the play and performances weren't 'affecting', but because I had cathected the proscenium prison into the ultimate articulation of how common the connection between risk and imprisonment is within carceral society. It was as simply illustrated as taking a lift, or walking up and down some stairs between performance spaces.

By offering no singular causality in the creation of the *Charged* woman beyond the movement of one's own body through predictable topics of carceral topoi, collective encounters within criminal justice narrative spaces cause a surfeit of assigned subjectivities to haze in shifting relation both to each other and to the macro-concept of the 'criminal'. The travelling audience reveals the co-creation of criminal justice narratives in domains both in and

Theatre as Collective Casework 157

out of the theatre, awakening the notion of positionality as, through the carceral imaginary, it/we/they co-create criminal subjectivities. In this sense, the production complicates not only the audience's perception of personal agency in carceral society, but also dramaturgical agency: what narrative does do, and what it can do, to disturb normative idioms of the carceral imaginary. *Charged*'s dramaturgy of criminality creates the conditions for audiences to reflect on how they are agents of stigmatization through their expectations of narrative closure in the criminal charge. Because *Charged* refuses to provide any narrative connections between the six plays, the audience performs a dramaturgy of criminality as an interpretive act. This dynamic speaks to the carceral function of audience within carceral imaginary. What *Charged* offers by way of the breakdowns of linear causality in the formation of the criminal subject, as such, also translates to an understanding of audience as sensorially, intellectually and socially present within carceral narrative production; audiences are not passive here as they are (intended to be) within carceral society. Passing through risk states connected together as carceral topoi, the audience are 'doing' carceral narrative: this is what makes *Charged* a spectacle of seepage between subject positions of individuality and collectivity within a criminal justice framework. The criminal charge in the theatre as live encounter intensifies the experience of the liveness of the criminal charge in social domains outside the theatre.

For *Charged* to provoke such seepages within a multicausal model defined by casework, then, proposes an understanding of how models of justice and support should be, or can become, themselves dynamic dramaturgical spaces, comprised discursively of multiple risks, multiple needs, multiple ideologies and multiple movements of audience and performers. This heterogeneity foments resistance, care and perhaps even emancipation, by disallowing a panoptic compulsion to render 'criminal' identity scrutable, and (in this scrutability) scriptable via anticipatory, simple models of risk identification and support. As such, *Charged* becomes a powerful example of Clean Break's ability to agitate deeply for social change.

Conclusion

In this chapter, I have positioned *Charged* as undermining the carceral imaginary through a dramaturgical event space modelled on investigative case structure. *Charged* brings a critical perspective on the supposed fleetingness, or ephemerality, of the charge: it challenges the audience to experience several sites of identity-injury through dramatized risk and imprisonment – to investigate how the charge never leaves and can become,

158   *Applied Theatre: Women and the Criminal Justice System*

in fact, a foregone conclusion or a delimiting technology to 'establish certain bodies at the limits of available ontologies' (Butler 2011: 170) of identity within carceral society. The process by which an ambient charge may land on stigmatized social situations and identities becomes reflexive through the site-responsive form of the production. As audience members travel up and down the theatre, they create a ligature of infinite variation between pathways to criminality. Brushing by each other, I contend here, audiences became cross-contaminating hosts not only of the detecting position of social control, but of a nascent criminal subjectivity that could only come into being through the audience's own movement through 'at risk' narratives under the banner of a 'charged' woman.

The fluidity of the state of becoming-criminal is the transmission generated by the casework of *Charged*: multiple perspectives, voices and bodies in the dramaturgy of the event preclude events of anagnorisis for character or audience member – there is no reintegration into a fluid procession from risk to criminality, nor is there rescue, or resettlement, in the wake of these narratives. Instead, by eliminating any possibility of dramaturgical closure, ruling, diagnosis or findings, the risk-states manifested by *Charged* allow it to precipitate a shift in audience sensorium (or to make such a shift available). Predicated on a *contingency* of identities, both within physical and narrative space, the production's evocation of multiple identities on the precipice inculcates a sustained focus on what social stigma needlessly, and ruthlessly, forecloses about marginalized identity – and stigma's participation in material conditions of oppression. *Charged* both engages and rejects expectations of narrative closure around a case-led dramaturgical structure, proposing instead a multicausal model of entry into criminal justice narratives.

Notes

1 I write as a specialist audience member. As a former staff member of Clean Break theatre company (2009–15), I both worked on *Charged* and I attended various iterations of the production countless times. I was not a member of the creative team for *Charged*, and as such the analysis in this chapter is based on my own interpretations of the production's aesthetics and politics, rather than reflecting on the express artistic brief of the production.

2 Spectacles of the criminal body have a long-limbed history as forms of theatre. Indeed, Erika Fischer-Lichte begins her 2014 *Introduction to Performance and Theatre* textbook with a verbatim reprint of a 1723 invitation to the public to attend 'the dissection of a female corpse of a child murderess' (18). In *Charged,* the crux of judgment at the theatre occurs not merely through an audience called to advance a disciplining of identity

Theatre as Collective Casework 159

through a legal charge; this production digs deeper into the exertion of an unquestioned right to look upon the *Charged* woman, and to judge the vicissitudes and viscera she holds within her.

3 Some audience members bought tickets to see both nights; others attended only one night of performances.

4 Among these were staff at INQUEST, a charity monitoring deaths in UK custody; HMP Peterborough; Metropolitan Police; Hope House, a drugs and alcohol treatment centre; and social policy think tank Race on the Agenda.

5 The English word 'case' derives from the Latin word, *casus* ('fall, chance, occurrence'), but also sounds like the Latin *cassus* ('void, hollow'), 'as though', Berlant notes, 'a falling out of the fabric of things produces an event that requires explanation' (2007: 666 n.11).

6 Though the basement is now a permanent performance space for Soho Theatre, when *Charged* was produced in 2010, a restaurant occupied the theatre's lower level; Clean Break took over the dining area for the production, making it a performance space.

7 As carceral geographers Sarah Armstrong and Andrew Jefferson write, 'When it comes to prison, our imagination seems to clog up. It is the political solution to its own failure, and the preferred metaphor for its own representation' (2017: 237–8).

8 Elsewhere I explore the necropolitics of tears and 'tearjerking' in one of the *Charged* plays – Rebecca Prichard's *Dream Pill* – and Alice Birch's *Little on the Inside* (McPhee 2019).

References

Aston, E. (2016), 'Agitating for Change: Theatre and a Feminist "Network of Resistance"', *Theatre Research International* 41(1): 5–20.

Beck, U. (2006), 'Living in the World Risk Society', *Economy and Society* 35(3): 329–45.

Berlant, L. (2007), 'On the Case', *Critical Inquiry* 33(4): 663–72.

Bharucha, R. (2014), *Terror and Performance*, London and New York: Routledge.

Bowie-Sell, D. (2010), '*Charged*, Clean Break, Soho Theatre, Review', *Daily Telegraph*. Available online: https://www.telegraph.co.uk/culture/theatre/theatre-reviews/8138516/Charged-Clean-Break-Soho-Theatre-review.html (accessed 15 March 2017).

Butler, J. (2011 [1993]), *Bodies That Matter: On the Discursive Limits of 'Sex'*, London and New York: Routledge.

Chow, R. (2010), 'Brushes with the-Other-as-Face: Stereotyping and Cross-Ethnic Representation', in P. Bowman (ed.), *The Rey Chow Reader*, 49–54, New York: Columbia University Press.

Clapham, N. (2018), 'Eight Cases from Across History Which Still Shape the Law Today', *The Conversation*, 26 September.

Corston, J. (2007), *The Corston Report*, London: Home Office.

Costa, M. (2010), 'Charged – Review', *Guardian*, 15 November. Available online: https://www.theguardian.com/stage/2010/nov/15/charged-review (accessed 15 March 2017).

Davis, A.Y. (2003), *Are Prisons Obsolete?*, New York: Seven Stories Press.

Fischer-Lichte, E. (2014), *The Routledge Introduction to Theatre and Performance Studies* (translated by M. Arjomand), London and New York: Routledge.

Fludernik, M. (2005), 'Metaphoric (Im)Prison(ment) and the Constitution of a Carceral Imaginary', *Anglia: Journal of English Philology* 123(1): 1–25.

Foucault, M. (1995 [1975]), *Discipline and Punish: The Birth of the Prison* (translated by A. Sheridan), New York: Vintage.

Gardner, L. (2010), 'Clean Break and the Invisible Women', *Guardian*. Available online: https://www.theguardian.com/stage/2010/nov/08/clean-break-women-prison-theatre (accessed 15 March 2017).

Gelsthorpe, L. (2004), 'Back to Basics in Crime Control: Weaving in Women', *Critical Review of International Social and Political Philosophy* 7(2): 76–103.

Gelsthorpe, L. 2010, 'Women, Crime and Control', *Criminology & Criminal Justice* 10(4): 375–86.

Herzog, M. (2009), *Crime Stories: Criminalistic Fantasy and the Culture of Crisis in Weimar Germany*, New York and Oxford: Berghahn Books.

Kennedy, H. (2005 [1992]), *Eve Was Framed: Women and British Justice*, London: Vintage.

La Fontaine, J. de (2005), 'The Wolf and the Lamb', in J. Derrida, *Rogues: Two Essays on Reason* (translated by P.-A. Brault and M. Nass), x–xi, Stanford: Stanford University Press.

Lefebvre, H. (2004 [1992]), *Rhythmanalysis: Space, Time and Everyday Life* (translated by S. Elden and G. Moore), London and New York: Continuum.

McKenzie, J. (2001), *Perform or Else: From Discipline to Performance*, London and New York: Routledge.

McPhee, M. (2019), '"I don't know why she's crying": Contagion and Criminality in *Dream Pill* and *Little on the Inside*', in F. Walsh (ed.), *Theatres of Contagion: Transmitting Early Modern to Contemporary Performance*, 121–35. London and New York: Bloomsbury.

Pemberton, S. (2013), 'Enforcing Gender: The Constitution of Sex and Gender in Prison Regimes', *Signs: Journal of Women in Culture and Society* 39(1): 151–75.

Perman, L. (2010), 'Foreword', in E. V. Crowe, S. Holcroft, R. Lenkiewicz, C. Moss, W. Pinnock and R. Prichard, *Charged*, iv, London: Nick Hern Books.

Shaughnessy, N. (2015), 'Dancing with Difference: Moving Towards a New Aesthetics', in G. White (ed.), *Applied Theatre Aesthetics*, 87–122, London and New York: Bloomsbury.

Taylor, D. (2007), 'Double-Blind: The Torture Case', *Critical Inquiry* 33(4): 710–33.

Taylor, P. (2010), '*Charged*, Soho Theatre, London', *The Independent*. Available online: https://www.independent.co.uk/arts-entertainment/theatre-dance/

reviews/charged-soho-theatre-london-2135919.html (accessed 18 March 2017).

Tsoi, H. (2010), 'Review: *Charged* @ Soho Theatre', *Londonist*. Available online: https://londonist.com/2010/11/review_charged_soho_theatre (accessed 18 March 2017).

Tyler, I. (2013), *Revolting Subjects: Social Abjection and Resistance in Neoliberal Britain*, London and New York: Zed Books.

Wacquant, L. (2009), *Punishing the Poor: The Neoliberal Government of Social Insecurity*, Durham NC and London: Duke University Press.

Woddis, C. (2010), '*Charged* 1 & 2, Soho Theatre', *The Arts Desk*. Available online: https://theartsdesk.com/theatre/charged-1-2-soho-theatre (accessed 15 March 2017).

'Prison Loves, Prison Hates', *Voices from Prison* (1987)

Bonni, HMP Styal

Prison loves, Prison hates,
Prison rules, Prison gates,
Prison walls, Prison cells,
Prison screws, Prison hell,
Prison food, Prison shit,
Fucking Prison, sick of it.

For information on *Voices from Prison,* please see p. 56.

7

Somebody's Daughter Theatre Company: The Arts – Unapologetically Transcendent

Maud Clark AM

I came into contact with Somebody's Daughter Theatre at a time in my life where I was looking for change. I didn't recognize that I was, I just had a feeling. The judge had said I was a pest. I was, and he had given me a chance, sentencing me to a substantial term of imprisonment for the sake of the community and, I believe, myself. I had been holding my breath for most of my adult life. I quickly joined the theatre group within the prison and was taught to just breathe. I did. I breathed, sang, danced, laughed, was nurtured and encouraged. I was released.

Cath Brigal

Somebody's Daughter Theatre is based in Melbourne, Australia: we work in theatre, art, film and music with women while in prison and after their release. We currently lead a unique, full-time arts, education and health partnership for young people who are 'school refusers' called Nobody's Fool Theatre in Geelong. This is modelled on the ground-breaking work we led with HighWater Theatre in Wodonga for fifteen years. The work with women and young people is intensive and ongoing. By this I mean years not months.

There are regular workshops every week in the two women's prisons in Victoria, and every year the workshops culminate in a major new performance work and visual art exhibition staged inside the prison. Outside audiences are invited to attend. The shows are devised and performed by the women and, most importantly, the women have the opportunity to perform to family, friends, workers and policy-makers, and afterwards to talk and mingle freely.

For young people, Nobody's Fool Theatre is their 'full-time' school; the creative work is the bridge to education. New Australian work is devised and performed by them and they tour to theatres and communities throughout Australia.

Nearly all those we work with – young and old – are born into a life of violence and poverty. Infancy to childhood to teens – a relentless assault of

164   *Applied Theatre: Women and the Criminal Justice System*

physical, verbal and often sexual abuse. There is no quick fix for a lifetime of abuse, and it is recognized by all partners we collaborate with in Health, Education and Justice that the arts work where, most often, all else has failed. This is very dependent on one factor: we are artists. Our training is in the arts. Our job is the arts. Somebody's Daughter Theatre is a company of artists.

We 'claim' our artistry as community artists and we are committed to using our art form to break through structural and ideological barriers of inequality. And, as community artists, we are committed to working *with* a community not *for* a community. Artists in Somebody's Daughter Theatre are not working to support their 'real artistic practice' – working with vulnerable communities *is* our 'artistic practice'. It is work we love, and all in Somebody's Daughter Theatre know that the arts can bring about not only personal, but also social and systemic, change. There is a great mutual trust and respect between Corrections and Somebody's Daughter Theatre, which is built upon thirty years of work.

Where did it all begin?

Somebody's Daughter Theatre had its beginnings at Fairlea Women's Prison in 1980 when I was a drama student at the Victorian College of the Arts and arranged for a play we were performing at the college to go into the prison. After the show, a woman asked us to come in and do drama. So we did. This is an important point. We were asked to do drama, to go into the prison to work with the women by the women themselves; we were not asked to go in by the management of the prison. From our very beginnings, there has never been any sense that we were going in to do drama because it is 'good' for people – we went in because we were truly, madly, deeply passionate about theatre, and there was a group of people who wanted to 'play' with us.

I'd like to be able to say that I was socially and politically aware – but I wasn't. What I know now is not what I knew then. When I first went into the prison I didn't know I had prejudice, that I saw women in prison as 'other'. It was only standing in a circle of women and realizing that I could be them – that my mother, my sister could be them – that I recognized my prejudice.

We did what we were passionate about. There was no lowering of the bar. We did what we were studying at drama school: commedia dell'arte, Shakespeare, text, improvisation, voice. We played. We played in a truly free environment with other women who wanted to play also. These women happened to be prisoners, and it was through the play that we met equally. And it was in prison that I began to understand the potency of the creative process as the great equalizer.

Somebody's Daughter Theatre Company 165

This is still what we do. We learnt on the way how little access women in prison and communities of disadvantage have to the arts, and we also learnt how powerful and subversive the arts can be in bringing down so many walls of inequality.

The arts can do this.

This cannot happen if you see individuals you are working with as 'other', so for Somebody's Daughter Theatre the potency of the arts is quite simple: if you are working creatively, you must work equally. In that clear space of equal meeting, which is the bedrock of the creative process, it is simply human beings coming together to create.

The reason we have survived for over thirty years is because of the power of the work produced. This is not only for those we work with but also for the wider audiences that come to these shows. Shows inside the prison and outside the prison have staggered audiences. Plays have been put on schools' lists – there have been performances all over the country in theatres, small halls, in drug rehabs, for members of parliament.

The work has not only had a huge impact on how performers view themselves but how audiences view prisons, prisoners and those who have left the prison: 'Having been involved in theatre for ten plus years, I have seen a lot. I have never been so moved, inspired and completely immersed in any production (theatre or film) before. I am so grateful to have witnessed the play tonight' (F., Theatre Producer); 'Deeply moving. Very real, explicit, wonderfully choreographed, directed and performed drama from the heart' (F., Film Critic); 'Amazingly impressive. Absolutely outstanding. Has put a human face on a side of life I have only heard about but had no contact with' (M., University Professor).

One of Somebody's Daughter Theatre's biggest challenges is the creep of the word 'therapy' into any creative work with the disadvantaged. Therapy is yet another word to add to the list that differentiates people from one another, that separates us from them – prisoner, ex-prisoner, offender, ex-offender, street kid, challenged. I wonder if there is any awareness of what we are doing in inferring that therapy is for the disadvantaged and art is for the rest of us.

Of course, the arts have huge impact on our emotional well-being – it's how we can all unravel the knots in heart and soul – and I would have no problems if this word were applied to us all: 'I'm off to the opera for some "opera therapy"' or 'we're going to see that great play for some theatre "therapy"'; if students in mainstream schools were doing not just art or drama but art therapy or drama therapy. That's not how it is: in the main the word 'therapy' is used for those already excluded from community, and this is simply another exclusion. Let me be clear, I am *not* addressing this to health professionals who use the arts as part of their professional practice, in which

166 *Applied Theatre: Women and the Criminal Justice System*

art is clearly a therapeutic tool and is not for artistic outcome. But I believe, if you are working as an artist, you cannot be working as a therapist – you are looking through a different lens. In Somebody's Daughter Theatre, our sole purpose is to create; we know fantastic things can happen but that is not our starting point. We do not start out to heal. We set out to create the best theatre, art, music we can, and we know that, because the arts are all about journeys, about arrivals at places that can only be navigated by heart and soul, there will be not only a fantastic production but also transformative personal outcomes:

> You don't have to be a doctor to save lives because [a] doctor maybe save[s] your physical [body] but I feel you guys actually look after our souls. I think I was lost and I think my soul [...] deteriorated by the harsh world, by my past, by my childhood, my look[ing at] all the things that had happened to me. But then I got to meet you guys and the dignity that was stripped off me, I regained it.
>
> And you were talking to all the girls and I was actually judging, I was like, oh you know we are criminals, [...] ferals, [...] junkies – why are these people wasting their time with us? Because we were fighting. We couldn't even get along. I thought we can't produce a production, it's going to be a nightmare. But then ...
>
> When I saw the girls onstage performing and I had goosebumps and I had tears in my eyes and I was like, oh my god if *us* women have this sort of opportunity [in] our life we wouldn't be in jail. We would have achieved so much in life you know.
>
> It helped me [...] it made me feel, 'Alright, if this is how joy and happiness feel like, I want to be part of this, I want to belong' you know. And I felt that I was belong[ing] to something big with Somebody's Daughter Theatre.
>
> Fatima

We know that so many we have worked with have gone on to do things that had seemed impossible. The words of 'Dizzy Lizzy' in a performance in the late 1990s still echo: 'There are pieces of me missing and I want them back.' This woman, who had been in and out of prison for some fifteen years, upon release went straight to a Buddhist meditation centre, eighteen months later was ordained by the Dalai Lama and now, nearly twenty years later, is still a Buddhist nun who runs a Buddhist centre in Australia. The arts were the bridge for this: the path she stepped onto post-release came from her creative journey. But we did not set out to do this; the creative process

Somebody's Daughter Theatre Company

167

opened new pathways in heart and spirit and soul – that is what made it possible.

As an artist, you are the ferryman. Our work is to create the best art, music and theatre we can with the community we work with, without any agenda. The only proviso – and this is important – is that our work does not strengthen an individual's emotional connection to the cycles of abuse and disadvantage. This is very subtle. There is no end to the stories that destroy the hearts, souls and bodies of those we work with, and often individuals feel very safe in those deep wells of emotional chaos. Our work as artists is to move beyond that chaos, not to cement or strengthen it, and it is a skill that is crucial for the community artist.

Often, I have worked with an individual in improvisation where a very emotional and painful event/chapter in life is captured. The individual feels very comfortable in this space and may want to stay there. Improvisation, and even rehearsal, can become a space of feeding emotional trauma or helping to keep someone stuck in unresolved emotional chaos. In the drama process, there must be movement from this space. Therefore, one of most important principles of our work is that we are always working with the same expectation we would have if we were working with professional actors. Sure, it might take longer and, because it is a prison, there will be a level of chaos and unpredictability that would not be encountered or tolerated 'professionally', but that is part of your job description – to work *with* these forces, not to be drawn into them, or to drown in them.

As in any creative work, there will be emotional crisis and great moments of self-doubt for everyone. This goes with the territory of artistic endeavour. In the devising of a show there will be the exploration of feeling – present, past and future – searching for character motivation, experimentation with characterization, the continual need to place the actor's journey in context and the continual search for storyline but this is all part of the artistic process, not therapy. It is the journey every actor, every ensemble, takes, that every new devised work takes. Our work is to get to the shore of opening night and to bring an audience into the heart and soul of the world we 'play' in. Hence skills work; voice, movement, improvisation, etc. are the bedrock of what we do every workshop. We do what we'd do with any group of actors. Anything less shows a great lack of respect. This is not 'therapy' but skills development: the tools needed for performance.

Theatre is about voice. This is very important for those who don't have one. Having your own voice, not someone speaking for you, about you and defining who you are (workers, lawyers, judges, psychologists or policy-makers), but speaking your own truth and being heard. In Somebody's

Daughter Theatre, a lot of time is spent on voice work, on articulation, on singing. A lot of time is spent on breathing, finding your own breath, finding your centre. To breathe deeply puts us in contact with what we're really feeling. For many we work with, this has never been safe – to stay with what they are really feeling.

Much of the work is bodywork. Abuse goes with the territory of most of those with whom we work – young and old have been abused. How often the words echo: 'Fly away, numb myself ... I must leave myself, never enter my body.' So many find it difficult to stay in their body that it is safer to 'disconnect' from feeling, from touch, from physical connection. Theatre work is about being totally inside the body – reclaiming your own body – feeling your cells come alive; trusting your body, trusting someone to massage your body. This work is extremely potent in an environment where your body is not your own – where it can be invaded with strip searches, handcuffed, observed through cameras.

Change comes from the individual's own journey, and that journey through the arts is using all of yourself, not just your head which has so many negative tapes playing that it's hard for another voice to be heard. Through the creative process, those voices can be challenged, dulled and, if not stopped, then muted. Standing in the drama circle, there is a lot happening when someone 'comes to the line' – that is, when they say 'yes' to being part of something that is bigger than them. Empathy, reflection, trust – moving from just being in the mind to the very cells of your body.

Lessons I have learnt

- As an artist working in a prison environment there are challenges which cannot be ignored.
- There is the unpredictability and chaos of the prison world. While on one hand it is very regulated, it is a world of constant readjustment.
- Humour and good will are needed at all times.
- This is not only for the community of women you are working with but also negotiating with management.
- Energy is very real, and working creatively you are working with invisible, but very tangible, energies.
- It is important that oppressive, depressed energy does not prevail. Our job as artists is to raise the vibration level, lift energies, create a space of allowance not restriction.
- Many that we work with feel safe with conflict: in fact, many are expert at creating conflict and divisiveness, especially if under pressure.

Somebody's Daughter Theatre Company

- Humour is a secret weapon that means that it is a constant challenge and necessity for the artists to be energized. This means that both the company, i.e. Somebody's Daughter Theatre, and the individual artist must take responsibility for this.
- Company members need to be nurtured and cared for. This means continual debriefing, massage, ocean retreats – whatever it takes to refuel, refind your own centre, build up your own vibration – some would say, 'stay in contact with your own song or source'.
- The human psyche is fragile: it is too easy to absorb another's pain, to feel inadequate, overwhelmed, powerless, to overidentify, to want to make the journey for someone when they alone can do it.
- It is essential to ensure that there is 'debriefing', discussing, processing so that you can remember that a 'hit out' is not about you, that angry words, tantrums, are not about you.
- It is important that you don't start chafing against prison regulations, to always remember it is not about you and the restriction on your freedoms for the short time you are in the prison: it is about the women you are working with, who can't walk through the gates and leave the prison as you will at the end of the session.
- Or that you don't feel 'guilty' about your life or that you don't try and 'save' someone.
- That you don't fall into becoming the martyr, the saviour or the guru.
- Another great challenge is belief – the belief to keep going – to believe that you will meet the deadline when it feels nothing short of madness to keep going forward.
- Any production requires great leaps of faith and trust and fearlessness.
- Every production is a challenge for the prison and it is so important to respect this: the challenge is constantly balancing the demands of prison protocol and the demands of an artistic outcome. Often it means choosing which battles to fight and which to leave.
- 'Art' is so much a prison is not, so much that abuse and violence is not – transcending, uncontainable, inspirational, mysterious, free to roam and dream and find parts of yourself – for 'your soul song to sing yourself back home'. Please don't diminish or try to contain or limit its power in any way. It is wondrous and limitless.

Being in prison had not transformed me. It had not cured me. I was punished and I lost everything. My life had stopped but the rest of the world had been busy getting on with its. There was less room for me now than there had been in the first place. However, had I have not gone to prison, I would never have been introduced to the arts. Being in those couple of plays gave me something to be proud of. For once in my life, I had people feeling what I felt, and seeing what I saw. I was able to express my fears, my dreams, my grief and my remorse – yes, I had remorse. And that audience listened very carefully, and their response was gratitude and empathy. I found a purpose. I will share my stories, and maybe I will play a part in creating an awareness of women just like us, woman from the inside. And one day those of us who have been relegated and neglected will be remembered as somebody's daughter.

Cath Brigal

Extract II from *Killers* (1980)

Jacqueline Holborough

The Prisoner Did I wash my floor this morning? Well, of course, I wash my floor every morning. Some people are born floor washers in life and some are not. In my case there is always a smear or two. Some missed bit of fluff under the bed to be discovered on routine inspection. Such things are a symbol of decline, sparing no expense we must employ and train more people to seek out the fluff under the beds. But, madam, I've lived quite happily all these years with fluff under my bed.

And look where it's got you – you filthy little liberal. You dirty, deranged delinquent. That pile of shit has dragged you into the sewers where you belong. But – we are here to save you. We can put you back on the road to recovery – and we will!

There's nothing wrong with me.

Nothing wrong with you, you say? Stick out your tongue. Constipation?

All the time.

Good. Health excellent. You can go.

What about my mind?

What about your mind?

I want one.

You want a mind? Mad are you? Insane? Feel resentment, do you?

I don't feel anything.

What – no resentment? Swallow this liquid three times a day. We must keep you down. Keep you in your place. Strap you to the floor if necessary. You must be made to feel resentment.

All right. I'll try. I hate. I hate you. I hate you all. It's no good. You'll have to give me time. I can't just switch on resentment like that. I haven't got

172   *Applied Theatre: Women and the Criminal Justice System*

over being amused yet. Are you listening? One key, two bolts and a few thousand volts to keep my door locked. Am I meant to take this seriously? Not one, not two but three sets of bars at my bulletproof window. Looking onto the fences, the walls, the cameras, the scanner lights ... barbed wires, dogs ... And all this to contain eight and a half stones of frightened female. Is there some subtle message here? Some expectation of greatness yet to come. Should I prepare myself? Must I be ready to live up to all of this? Will the day arrive when I shall be required to smash through tons of concrete and steel. Rip down gates. Tear up tarmac. In my desperate desire to devastate. Danger alert – number six on the threes is Proving Us Right situation. All officers to underground shelters immediately.

This extract is a monologue, a direct address to audiences, towards the end of the play when The Prisoner has experienced months of incarceration. It is an imagined conversation between herself and Mrs Thomas, a prison warden, who embodies the institution, its regime and regulations.

For information about *Killers*, please see p. 142.

8

The Meeting Place: Collaborative Learning in a University–Prison Partnership

Rachel Conlon

This chapter focuses on the work of the York St John University (YSJU) Prison Partnership Project (PPP), an ongoing partnership between the university and two local prisons in the north of England: HMP New Hall, a closed female prison in Wakefield, West Yorkshire and HMP Askham Grange, an open female prison in York, North Yorkshire. The partnership was born, in 2013, out of the desire to provide a creative arts collaboration between higher education and the prison service, facilitating weekly drama and arts provision in prison. This chapter establishes the context for the partnership, introduces some projects that the PPP has undertaken, addresses the benefit of sustained collaboration and how issues of motherhood, identity and voice have arisen through it: it provides insight into the often hidden impactful work in the meeting place between university and prison, students and prisoners.

My understanding of the potential for a relationship between a university and prison stretches back to 1991 when, as a final-year undergraduate theatre student, I entered HMP Styal in Cheshire to take part in a drama project with my then theatre lecturer, Allen Owens, who was working in the prison. As I entered this unfamiliar space I realized that I was in an environment that housed a rich diversity of women from a wide demographic and socio-economic background. I watched them and they watched me: assessing, imagining what we were like and wondering why we were there. During those early days, getting used to the barred windows, acclimatizing to the noise of the wing and the stare of the officers, I started to focus on making moments of theatre and using drama as a tool for change. I began to stand beside the women, realizing that some of their stories of womanhood rang true to me, too – they were very quickly becoming less 'other' to me. This was a defining experience, a moment that I look back on and know that it was a beginning, a shifting point in my thinking, a door opening that would be hard to shut again. I am now Senior Lecturer at YSJU and director of the PPP.

YSJU has a strong community spirit realized through strategic priorities such as social justice, inclusivity, mental health and well-being and social

174   *Applied Theatre: Women and the Criminal Justice System*

innovation. In the development of the PPP, I wanted to share those values with women in prison and with women in the city of York who had experience of the criminal justice system. Through outreach and partnership work, we wanted to turn the university 'inside out' and offer our rich resources (staff, students, facilities) to the wider community to bring together two communities which wouldn't normally meet. The university now opens its doors to women Released on Temporary Licence (ROTL) from an open prison, engaging in resettlement activity as well as women post-release who can access staff expertise, student collaboration, campus performance opportunities and spaces, technical equipment and library resources. In addition, the students learn off-campus, in the prison, so that this experience will empower and inspire them, providing pivotal moments – not unlike my own – that drive them to shape the communities where they live and work in the future.

I am interested in the mutual benefits for the students and women with lived experience of the criminal justice system working together. The intention is that *both* communities are equally impacted by a transformative learning experience which emphasizes creative collaboration and addresses issues of social concern: it is vital that this is a mutually enriching experience, rather than a unidirectional one of benevolence from the university to the prison. By doing so, it provides the conditions of what my colleague Nick Rowe has described as the creation of a 'healing campus'. It attempts to heal the 'fracture' between women with experience of the criminal justice system and their community and the social and cultural fracture that exists around gender and offending. At the centre of the PPP is an arts practice which seeks to merge these two worlds. The result, as the following examples demonstrate, are opportunities to create dialogues that explore perspectives of women, both in the criminal justice system and outside, beyond adopted media myths and societal stigma.

Theatre making is collaborative – it was, therefore, imperative to nurture the developing collaboration between the two institutions and to envisage a shared purpose for the work. We co-created the aims and objectives of the project through an open discourse around the practice, supporting the prison in its understanding of ways of working in the arts and supporting the university (including staff and students) in the ways of the prison regime. Aiming for the arts to be celebrated and not feared, we wanted the work to be accessible and high quality, while being mindful of the prison regime and restrictions. Trust, open dialogue, being prepared to shift and attune along the way and to maintain a healthy respect for both institutions were crucial. Key to the success of the project was working closely with the remarkable Michelle Daly, Head of Industries at HMP New Hall, and, under the eye of two forward-thinking female Governors, Diane Pellow and Susan Howard, we held the experience and safety of the women prisoners and university students and the relationship between the two communities at the heart of the work.

This chapter highlights specific moments during the PPP over the past five years that illuminate the range of our practice and how it adapts to the needs of participants, developing collaborative learning that reaches beyond the university, beyond the prison, informing wider societal understandings about women's criminalization. Each of the four sections that follow focus on a particular model of practice: sustained, weekly drama work with vulnerable women as part of a programme of creative learning and support in a closed prison for all categories of prisoner; the development of a creative songwriting and singing programme with women in an open prison preparing for resettlement; a multipartner collaboration and film project focusing on the impact of incarceration on mothers and their children; and a collaboration with the Donmar Warehouse on Phyllida Lloyd's acclaimed Shakespeare Trilogy (2012–16), which played to audiences in both theatres and prisons, in London, New York and, through its broadcast on film, to wider audiences internationally.

I. Sustained weekly drama practice at HMP New Hall: 'I see myself as a different person now'

HMP New Hall sits in a valley outside Wakefield. It is not seen from the road as it lies in the sump of the landscape, hidden and out of view. Our drama programme runs in Rowan House, a unit that supports more vulnerable residents. Referrals are made by the first-night centre, education induction and via the trauma-informed, safer custody and safeguarding teams. Any staff and personal officers can also make referrals. Rowan House offers holistic daytime and evening activities; one of these is the drama project I run with YSJU undergraduate- and masters-level theatre students, with support from two fantastic graduates, Jessica Robson and Casey Fox, who co-facilitate the project and have established their own theatre company, Through the Gap. This programme offers introductory and intermediate drama groups for twelve weeks, three times a year, with women moving along the programmes as they need or wish. Facilitating a weekly arts practice enables us to develop a deep, respectful and relational approach, travelling alongside the women from week to week as they navigate the topography of imprisonment. Our sustained presence allows an immersion into the prison culture, its rhythms and its atmospheres. Over time we have become acutely sensitive to the organizational practices and what's needed to deliver creative and educational work within it.

176   *Applied Theatre: Women and the Criminal Justice System*

Women arrive in New Hall by prison van bringing their histories with them: their crime and its aftermath. Their time in prison is temporary – some will be anchored here a long time and for others it is a fleeting mooring, filled with not knowing and uncertainty. I am constantly motivated by the resilience and strength these women call upon. Through the drama workshops, they share fractured and disjointed personal narratives of life, histories of victimization, mental ill health and addiction. Drama's focus on narrative enables a more developed narrative picture to emerge. Experiences of trauma can lead to resistance, grief, sensitivity and fragility as the many women begin to acknowledge what they have endured: trauma which may have shaped past chaotic drug-filled lives adopted to anaesthetize emotional pain, sabotaging relationships with others and themselves, and dictating, for some, a life lived on the street. Poverty's relentless presence has hardened them to feeling that they are worthless, and survival has dictated behaviour. As one woman explains:

> He was such a violent man and he controlled and beat me on a daily basis. I became homeless, living on the street and I was badly addicted to heroin, crack and diazepam. I was always arguing, fighting and getting arrested. One day I just snapped, I lost my baby and I lost my children.

The repeating narratives of child sexual abuse, sexual violence, inter-generational neglect and abuse, domestic violence, and of state systems failing them, have unremittingly cascaded from the women over the years. For some, they wear their pain as slices to their skin or hair that has been cut into in moments of anger. For others, desperation sits just underneath the surface and seeps into conversations or presents itself as anger, disjointed thought or hopelessness. However, some women are steely and quiet, determined to push down every emotional disturbance as it rears its head.

I trained as a drama therapist, and while therapeutic strategies inform my practice, the programme in Rowan House is not drama therapy: we do not aim to seek out women's trauma, but if a woman wants to talk or disclose, she does. Empathic and distancing processes, embodiment and dramatic projection are reflected upon within the facilitation. Embedded in the programme is the proposition that there can be calm; that there can be light as well as darkness in our emotions; that in the Drama space you are safe; that creativity can support the journey travelled through prison. Vulnerability and an opening up to truth is an excruciating process to move through, but fruitful in what it can enable. One resident observed:

> Trust and confidentiality have been important, we said powerful things in the creative writing and acting and we sort of put ourselves in a

The Meeting Place   177

vulnerable position doing it, but it felt good, it gave me confidence. It gives you ownership over your creative ideas and work. I felt secure in the group and I began to trust myself and others, when we worked together in the sessions. That was and felt powerful.

While there is a broad consensus evolving recognizing the need for a distinct approach to working with women in the criminal justice system, this has always been crucial to the work of the PPP: our arts delivery is gender-responsive and trauma-informed. The values of trauma-informed practice, designed by the 'One Small Thing – Becoming Trauma Informed Initiative', are central to our woman-centred arts delivery and to the prison in how it works with the woman in its care: safety, trust, choice, collaboration and empowerment. We consider trauma when planning and facilitating, avoiding triggering trauma reactions or retraumatizing an individual, supporting participants' coping strategies and trauma symptoms. Gender-responsive environments and programmes consider personal safety and are respectful of the realities of the women's lives and histories. How the women present themselves after systematic and continuous disadvantage needs an attuned arts process that offers a healthy relational approach, boundaries and care. One woman reflected on taking part in one of the drama programmes:

I'm on antidepressants and I have off days in prison, but on the days we have drama, I wake up knowing that I am looking forward to drama. Medication doesn't give you friends, a group to be part of, a community. Drama gives me these things, it gives me a family feeling, it keeps me busy and my head busy, it gives me a boost.

The women become motivated and the act of creative sharing offers a catharsis and a sense of possibility. Theatre writing and making can provide that in a relational form that emboldens self-reflection, creativity, person-centredness and potential for change. These principles are fundamental to the ethics of the provision, to the fertility of the arts process. A strong motivational force for change can restore confidence and self-worth. When reflecting on participating on two programmes of drama activity, one woman stated:

Coming to drama has raised my confidence; I've now become a mentor on my wing and a wing painter. I'm much calmer now; I give things a go because I feel much stronger. I see myself as a different person now and I see others as different, too. When you get more confident, you can then work with others. I talk more to other people on my wing, I smile more often and my well-being is better and I'm putting myself into more things. I know drama isn't a medical cure, but it really helps me with my depression and my mental health.

Interpersonal skills, empathy, awareness, group problem-solving and rehearsal for life role-playing all have a clear purpose, building on prisoners' existing strengths and potential, encouraging emotional capability and impulse self-regulation. They act as a catalyst for positive cognitive and identity transformation, seeking meaningful personal change and supporting desistance thinking. On considering her pathways on from the drama programme a resident identified:

I'm in the intermediate drama group now, when I first started drama I couldn't read out in front of people. The benefit of having confidence now is that you can take that confidence out of the drama group into the rest of your life, I've been thinking of going to college when I leave prison.

Empathic and positive student–prisoner relationships create an environment that fosters positive reinforcement and growth, trust-building and fun, as the students and prisoners travel on a positive creative journey each week together. By explicitly co-creating an educational, learning community that nurtures a sense of commonality, connectedness and acceptance through dialogue, learning and creativity, we create a learning community that is individually, socially and institutionally transformative. One student reflected on this relationship and the learning developed through it:

Working off university campus with the YSJU Prison Partnership Project enables me to develop my practice in a prison within a creative process that puts aside the label of 'prisoner' and focuses on the exploration of our creativity as artists together. We work together with the women as equals in the creative process, enabling us to see through the stigma associated with women in prison and recognize how similar we really are.

II. Creative writing, song and resettlement at HMP Askham Grange: 'Wanting a relationship with my family again'

At HMP Askham Grange, the drama programme is situated within a resettlement framework. All prison education and work-based learning is geared towards release, and our work engages with narrative of journeys

The Meeting Place

beyond the prison and what's needed in order to navigate them. Some are reconnecting with children and families; some will not have seen civilian life for a long time; all are experiencing a taste of freedom mixed with absolute fear of rejection and stigma. We hear of women Released on Temporary Licence (ROTL) having panic attacks in shops; others on home visits contemplating sleeping in a bed with someone again after years of bunk beds in cells; some feeling awkward and disjointed as they re-establish the role of mum to children that have been cared for by gran. Women on day release navigate the complexity of working for organizations not knowing whether or not to share that, when they go home after work, they are going back to a prison. For others it is too dangerous to resettle back in the community they came from, and they are attempting to build an infrastructure in the new town that they now go out to work in.

HMP Askham Grange was once a grand family home, built in 1886 as the country residence for a British politician, Sir Andrew Fairbairn. The openness and quietness of Askham Grange can be deafening after the orchestra of noise in closed prison: no bars, no locked cells, a more fluid regime. There is an air of optimism and positivity which can feel alien after the bleakness of closed prison conditions. The drama and singing programme at Askham is open to all and runs on a Tuesday night in the ballroom. With its wooden floors, ornate pillars and long windows that look out onto green countryside and tall trees, it feels other worldly within the context of prison. The ballroom has a sprung floor and raised stage, a space where performances can be shared with the whole prison community.

Askham Voices was created to provide a weekly provision of prison community singing and creative writing workshops, funded by the North Yorkshire Police and Crimes Commissioner. We heard repeatedly from the women in the drama group that there were women in the prison who had remarkable singing voices; they would sing in the showers, in the dorms and in the canteen. Each week, more women came. Some would appear at the ballroom door – peering in; some would sit on the side and listen; others would bring their toddlers from the mother and baby unit and they would dance around the space, watching their mums singing. Before we knew it, we had a core group of women who came every week. We would wheel the piano from the chapel into the ballroom and fill the space with singing voices, beautiful women's voices, strong, powerful and tender female voices. The echoes could be heard throughout the prison, and officers on the night shift came and listened. Gradually the women brought their writing, often clutching bundles of sheets of paper: love songs for their children, apologies in verse to their victims or angry rants to men that had failed them. It was powerful to witness their drive and energy to perform, their wish to stand

180   *Applied Theatre: Women and the Criminal Justice System*

and sing in front of others, to be heard. When the women sang, people listened with care. A strong sense of accomplishment and connectedness was established. Letting sound and voice out of a body that can feel like it wants to hide is an act of hope, of faith in being heard. Many women were due for release and to be reunited with their families, some frightened of what lay ahead and others displaying newly emerging determination and resilience. Through the process, the women were giving their selfhood and creativity permission to identify their needs.

Working with YSJU theatre student and songwriter, James Aconley, we planned a performance for the prison and YSJU communities. The women would sing individually and as an ensemble. Often on a Tuesday evening, the Governor, whose office was situated above the ballroom, would come down before she left for the night and sit and listen. One night, she asked the women if they would like their children to come to the performance. This question was met with heightened emotion, disbelief, fear and flashes of self-doubt, but ultimately with an overriding yes. It offered a moment where mother and child – small children, teenagers and adult children – would reunite, not in the formal nature of a prison visit, but in a performance: a moment with other children watching their mothers sing. The thought of it was moving and the sense of responsibility overwhelming. A process of careful consideration decided who would be invited, what could be sung, what needed to be spoken and what was to be voiced at another time. How would the children get there, who would bring them, what in their songs did they want them to hear and would they be able to bear it? Some women decided that their children should not attend. The women who were in contact with their children on the outside of prison spoke with the mothers who were not – we will sing to your children, too, said the mothers who were not in contact with their children, we will sing with and alongside you.

III. Motherhood and prison: 'Keeping mum'

I was commissioned by Barnardo's Children Affected by Parental Imprisonment (CAPI) service to create a short film highlighting the effects on children of parental imprisonment and the need for maintaining parental and family ties. Following a detailed planning phase, with Barnardo's and the family service at HMP Askham Grange, we decided on three phases of creative engagement and delivery for the project, *Keeping Mum*. The name highlighted the societal keeping quiet/'keeping mum' about experiences of children with mothers in prison and the impact of incarceration on the role and efficacy of motherhood.

Motherhood and childhood are ever present in the discourse with women in prison: there is a longing that aches through their words when they speak of their children, or of their own abandoned childhoods. Some, whose mothers or family members are now looking after their children while they are in prison, have concerns as they remember their own younger lives punctured by confusion with periods of neglect and chaos. Each woman presents different coping strategies for managing loss and disconnection from their children. Some remain actively involved with their children through positive communication and by having a strong support system in place for their children. For others, however, they live with the worry and anguish of their children being taken into care, or that their children have been told that 'mummy is working abroad or on a long holiday'. We hear of 'motherhood' and its experience from both points of view, from the perspective of the child and of the mother. For others, the state system becomes the corporate parent to their vulnerable children, and they shut down and switch off all communication as an act of self-preservation, feeling that this will be best for the children.

Different dads in different towns, and many mothers of these dads, are temporary guardians for children whose mothers are imprisoned. Some know where their mothers are and others who do not. Older children look after, or parent, younger siblings while negotiating exams, emerging into adulthood or jobs. The impact on these children and the complexity of the relationship between imprisonment and motherhood are acutely felt in a female prison. Anniversaries, birthdays, pivotal school achievements and flashes of positive moments with their families on visits are clung to. Many women say they want their children back, that they love them and that they have a right to family life. A few others acknowledge that they are not sure if they can, or if they know how to, be the mum that they think they should be, to offer shelter, safety and love and to meet the needs of their children. As one woman thoughtfully stated, 'I'm working on myself bit by bit, day by day, I'm even starting to like myself and maybe even love myself again. But I'm waiting, waiting for time to pass, waiting for parole, waiting to be free, wanting a relationship with my family again.'

In the first phase of *Keeping Mum*, we ran an extensive series of drama and creative writing workshops with women over a six month period, to elicit stories and shed light on the narratives of their children. Women were offered the opportunity to participate through self-referral. It immediately became clear that difficult stories of motherhood brought this community together. We discovered that the stories of their children varied according to many factors: the child's age, family dynamics, geographically where home was, the length of their mother's sentence, their crime and what support systems were

182   *Applied Theatre: Women and the Criminal Justice System*

or were not in place. While conducting the research, we were acutely mindful of the potential impact on the participating women of being asked to talk about the trauma of being separated from their children. In recognition of this, my work took on a close relational approach, enabling the women to recognize the role that relationships play in shaping their lives. We explored the thoughts and feelings they had for themselves and each other in the group process, when exploring themes of motherhood and childhood through one-step-removed theatre images and role play. Together we created large-scale visual character images crafted through collage and metaphor mapping. Text, colour and descriptions were layered onto the character body images to embody where the women carried their children – metaphorically in their arms, hearts, minds – and to communicate what emotions lay next to these visual sites of narrative. Detail became critical to the accounts, the things that they would notice, ponder on, or the elements that spoke so acutely of their separation and the impact on their children. Working closely and carefully over time with Claire Malarkey, the Family Support Worker from Barnardo's, was fundamental in understanding and creating a safe and holistic process that highlighted children's stories, sensitive to the women's needs and vulnerabilities. We considered the ethics, ownership and intentions of the work, and the politics of female imprisonment, when facilitating a process that had a public agenda and end outcome that would be shared beyond the intimacy of the drama space. The creative process needed to be reflective, fluid and with the possibility to shift and attune.

Towards the end of the creative engagement process, I invited the playwright, Laura Lomas and Imogen Ashby, then Head of Engagement from Clean Break theatre company, into the process. Clean Break, who we often collaborated with, was set up in 1979 by two women prisoners in HMP Askham Grange, who believed that theatre could bring the hidden stories of imprisoned women to a wider audience. Laura's brief was to write the script for a short film with the women working alongside her, creating three female characters who would represent an amalgamation of all the women's stories. We worked with the women to write sections of text, placing themselves into the narratives of their children, inhabiting the complexity of the situations presented when offering analysis of the impact of prison on their children's day-to-day lives. Across a series of one-to-one and group sessions with the women, Imogen, Laura and I facilitated the women to illuminate their images and writing. The women's stories occupied the territories of the internal and external worlds of their children, including accounts of the children's sadness at the separation from their mother, fear of what was happening to them while they were in prison and the emotional impact of prison visits. External factors effecting the children were highlighted also: bullying, community stigma, family transience and tensions and carer pressures.

As we approached filming, Barnardo's was notified by the Ministry of Justice (MoJ) that the women would no longer be able to speak their own stories directly to camera due to security restrictions in accordance with their sentencing. It was crucial that we found a way of representing the women's narratives authentically and honour their children's experience. It was decided that the best way forward was to work with women who were graduates from Clean Break theatre education programme, enabling us to work with actors who were mothers with experience of the criminal justice system. We were then faced with another challenge: the MoJ again revised their decision and said we were no longer allowed to film the actors in the prison and were given permission only to take photographs of a prison holding cell and a prison corridor. We worked with film-maker Ross Anderson, Director of Dustfarm productions, to create a film shot in a theatre studio at YSJU, and then edited this together with photos of a prison cell and corridor to create an 'as authentic as possible' final product.

Children affected by parental imprisonment are one of the most vulnerable groups in society, and the impact of maternal separation can be severe and long-lasting. Barnardo's, YSJU and Clean Break all use *Keeping Mum* when working with women, children, families and professionals to raise awareness of the impact of imprisonment on children and how their needs can be met and supported. Without the women at HMP Askham Grange and their openness, honesty, creativity and desire to represent their children effectively, this film would not have been made.

IV. The Donmar Warehouse Shakespeare Trilogy: 'I feel like I have a voice'

Between 2012 and 2017, the Donmar Warehouse situated three of Shakespeare's plays in a female prison setting, with an all-female cast: *Julius Caesar*, *Henry IV* and *The Tempest*. What made their project unusual and ambitious was an accompanying desire to carry out considerable ethnographic research into the prison context in collaboration with the PPP's drama groups. This was an opportunity I grasped wholeheartedly, as it mirrors the objectives to create mutually beneficial relationships between the university and prison. This project was a rich learning environment for all the participants: the prison residents, PPP's theatre students and the Donmar company. This mutuality was vital. The Donmar project spanned many aspects; here I outline moments from the making of *Henry IV*.

184   *Applied Theatre: Women and the Criminal Justice System*

The journey that artistic director Phyllida Lloyd and executive producer Kate Pakenham took, following an introduction to me via Clean Break, nurtured a deeper understanding of the terrain of prison, authentically mapping its topography within the productions. Working in parallel, through a carefully cultivated process, we interrogated these texts to unearth a voice that challenged the perception of women in prison and questioned issues surrounding class, diversity, freedom and justice. The Trilogy intentionally challenged wider assumptions regarding the 'ownership' of Shakespeare through the diversity of the performing company. As Kate identified:

> Setting the productions within a women's prison intentionally pushed the challenge of cultural ownership and diversity beyond gender, putting the words of our greatest writer into the mouths of the most voiceless women in our society. It was important to us creatively to ensure that we were doing so with the greatest possible authenticity, sensitivity and respect.

Through the course of the project, we saw women who had never previously considered reading Shakespeare, let alone standing up and performing it, develop a new desire for learning. For others, a fleeting past interest in theatre was awakened in their curiosity about Shakespeare. As one woman put it: 'I always used to think Shakespeare was boring, but I get it now.'

Through careful negotiation, following co-led weekend drama residencies, we were given permission by the prison to continue working with the Donmar Trilogy company and engagement team, holding weekly phone link-ups between the drama group I was running in HMP Askham Grange and the rehearsal room in London. Every Tuesday night, we would sit in the Governor's office and for two hours talk with Phyllida and the Donmar actors on the phone, working through character development and scene structure. Scenes were performed by the Donmar company and we listened intently, the women stopping and directing the actors to rerun sections, or asking them to qualify their reasons for playing a scene in such a way. There were moments in the rehearsal process when a shift in the development was needed, and the women provided the nudge that was required, sharing experiences of hierarchy, power and relationships in prison to enable the actors to unlock an understanding of their characters' connection to one another and to the prison system. The women facilitated an emerging construction of the actors' prison characters and how they resonated with the Shakespeare character they were playing. Themes of loss, addiction, forgiveness, loyalty and honour were interrogated. The actors' desire to make sure that they were not merely presenting a simplistic view of women in prison, their desire to do justice to

The Meeting Place 185

the women that they had met and listened to through the work of the partnership, was powerful.

The residents were amazed by the Donmar's commitment to highlighting the impact of imprisonment and the criminalization of women, and delighted at how the actors had listened in the weekend residencies to the fresh insights of prison life that they provided. One resident, when reflecting after a phone link-up, stated, 'At the weekend residency they listened to us, because I can hear [...] how they have taken our comments and experiences and they have considered them when thinking about the characters and the play.' The women felt valued, and that their opinions mattered; they were instrumental in the development of the work in this collaboration. When moments such as these happened, the women would leave the drama group empowered and full of vigour: 'I feel like I have a voice, my views feel valued, I think they really are interested in what I had to say,' said one resident; 'I feel an investment in this project, I enjoy giving my insights, giving my perspective enables me to see how far I have come from when I first came into prison,' said another. When the Trilogy company restaged their production of *The Tempest* in HMP New Hall, one woman responded, 'WOW! That was simply stunning, moving, entertaining and emotive. I was enthralled from beginning to end. The story made sense, the language was beautiful. I cried, I laughed, I ached.'

This brief account presents just one of the many strands of the Donmar's extensive and ongoing creative engagement with the PPP. Through our partnership work and with support from the prisons, we have enabled film screenings of the plays to be shown to the women in prison following extensive drama residencies and engagement programmes. Together we co-created meaningful discourse around gender politics, socio-economic imbalance, female empowerment and transformation. The Donmar Warehouse Shakespeare Trilogy aimed to create a step change in terms of excellence, leadership and accessible opportunity for marginalized prison communities. Positive, respectful and supportive relationships and collaboration between the PPP, its students, the Donmar staff, artists and the women in prison were key to the success and longevity of this project. The women were treated with respect and value, and all strived to deliver inclusive, high-quality art that would inspire, educate and motivate prisoners. The result was an innovative and truly significant arts initiative.

Conclusion

As a practitioner, I seek to investigate women's personal and collective narratives and to explore the relationships women navigate between the

186   *Applied Theatre: Women and the Criminal Justice System*

inside and outside of prison. My work is driven by a social justice and feminist agenda offering the potential for change, giving voice and transformation. Through creative group workshop processes, narratives are shared and pathways into crime reflected upon, facilitating a deeper understanding of self, community and social justice. By co-creating theatre between women prisoners and university students, they participate in an arts practice that encourages hope and an equal voice in the learning experience; self-esteem and confidence can be improved as both communities see each other not as homogenous groups, but as individual people and artists. The partnership enables collaborative arts-making to happen outside the mainstream traditional theatre or educational learning space, and examines life beyond the prison walls in respect of freedom, education, family and community.

Many women, by the time they reach prison, feel silenced, invisible and forgotten due to their gender, socio-economic position and oppression through living in entrenched patriarchal communities. In all its purpose, the PPP seeks to develop the women's ability to speak, to not let themselves be silenced, to lay strong roots of resistance and resilience and to enable new creative ways of being.

Extract II from *Inside Bitch* (2019)

Conceived by Stacey Gregg and Deborah Pearson, devised with
Lucy Edkins, Jennifer Joseph, TerriAnn Oudjar and Jade Small

This list was compiled from workshop material created by the company in
response to the question: what do you associate with ideas of prison?

Bullying
Pretty girl
Lesbians
Drugs
Horrible people
Horrible food
Tracksuits
Trading
No TV
Better than I thought
Guilty
Basic, standard, enhanced
Tattoo
Bag in at visits
Women raping women
Holiday camp
Inmate having an affair
Prisoner beat up in a shower
Phone in cake
Butch prison dyke running wing
Rats and cockroaches
Days like Roman numerals
Bread and water diet
Passing drugs on visits
Escaping prison
Pussy sucking
Fighting over chicks
Swallowing and shitting things out

188 *Applied Theatre: Women and the Criminal Justice System*

Spitting in food
Drugs
Decrutching
Suicide
Peter thief – stealing from each other's cell
Swooping – picking up cigarette butts
Depression and mental health
Knickers on radiators

40–1

For more information on *Inside Bitch*, please see p. 124.

9

Acting Out: An Interview with Sherrin Fitzer

Ashley Lucas

Sometime in early 2012, I received an email from a woman I had never met asking for a copy of my unpublished play. This woman, Sherrin Fitzer, told me that she worked in a women's prison in the Midwest (USA) and that there was a theatre company of incarcerated women with whom she wanted to share my script. Would I please send it to her, and might it be possible for the women to perform the play?

At the time, I was teaching theatre as an assistant professor at the University of North Carolina at Chapel Hill (UNC), some 800 miles from the prison where Sherrin works. I had written an interview-based play called *Doin' Time: Through the Visiting Glass*, which, by the time of Sherrin's first email, I had been touring as a one-woman show for eight years. My father served twenty years in a Texas prison and, both during the writing of the play and in the year Sherrin emailed me, he was still incarcerated. The play is a series of thirteen monologues about people who have family members in prison. Sherrin had heard about *Doin' Time* through a resource list sent out by the Dead Man Walking Play Project as she was searching for new material for the theatre troupe at her prison.

I responded to Sherrin immediately, saying that I would gladly send her the script and hoped that it would be possible for me to attend a performance, should the women choose to produce the play. Sherrin talked to the women – a delightful group whose official moniker is the Acting Out Theatre Co. Acting Out was founded in October 2001 and, by the time I encountered them in 2012, they were a cohesive ensemble with a history of self-governance. They decided that if I was willing to come to the prison, they would rather see me perform the play and perform something else for me. The women read *Doin' Time* and decided to write their own monologues about visiting with their families during their incarceration.

Thus began a writing collaboration that lasted for several months. The women wrote monologues, which Sherrin typed and emailed to me. I gave them feedback and critique on their writing, which they used in their revisions of the script. My UNC colleague Joseph Megel, who had directed my one-woman show, agreed to travel with me to the prison for the performance.

190   *Applied Theatre: Women and the Criminal Justice System*

We edited together a version of the play in which the women's monologues were woven in between mine. While we rehearsed in North Carolina, the Acting Out company rehearsed inside the prison. My mother and my Aunt Nancy decided to fly from Texas to meet us there. They had followed me to Ireland and many other places to see me perform this play and were not about to miss my first theatrical collaboration with incarcerated women. The four of us finally met Sherrin at the gates of the prison in September 2012.

After nearly half a year of corresponding with one another about the play, Sherrin and I greeted each other like old friends. It felt much the same to meet the women whose extraordinary writing I had come to admire. We rehearsed for a day and a half, under Joseph's skilled and thoughtful direction. The women had clearly worked hard with Sherrin prior to our arrival, and they proved to be extraordinarily talented and giving actors onstage. On the afternoon of the second day, an audience of about two hundred incarcerated women, prison staff, my mother, Aunt Nancy and a few outside guests watched us perform. I always hold a post-show conversation with the audience after performances of this play, because so many audience members have never before had an opportunity to discuss what happens to the families of prisoners. The women in this audience expressed admiration and gratitude for the bravery and eloquence of the incarcerated performers. They told stories of their own families and wept over the fact that my mother and aunt loved me enough to be with me that day in the prison. Many of their own families were ashamed of their incarceration, and more than a few women said that they were moved by the fact that my family supported my work in prisons. The women in the audience and onstage praised Sherrin for her long-standing dedication to the theatre programme and her hard work to make events like this possible.

In the five years since that performance, Sherrin and I have remained friends and travelled together to conferences in Indiana and Puerto Rico to speak about prison theatre. In 2013, I moved to Ann Arbor to accept a job at the University of Michigan, six hours' drive from the prison where Sherrin still works. This proximity has enabled me to visit several times to see Acting Out performances, and for Sherrin to visit the Prison Creative Arts Project, a programme I direct at my university. Acting Out has now produced more than sixteen plays by a diverse group of playwrights, including Shakespeare, Toni Morrison and members of the company. The following interview was conducted via email exchanges in August 2017:

AL   *How did you first decide to start working in a prison?*

Acting Out   191

SF   I had a friend who ran a college programme at the prison where I work now. I also had friends who taught in different prisons. I went in to talk to college classes as a volunteer from the Rape Crisis Center and the AIDS Task Force in Bloomington, Illinois. I also went into the prison as a judge for a Battle of the Bands because of my experience in music. Oh, it was so cool! They put prison bands on a bus and brought them here from all over the state.

I loved the time I spent there so much. I found the students engaging and engaged. I have always believed in helping people. When I got my master's degree in English and my friend offered me a job teaching, it felt like the right place to be.

I began working in prisons as a contract worker in 1991, for various community colleges. I taught college English – composition, drama, women's literature, journalism, speech. I began at Logan Correctional; it was co-ed then. I also taught at maximum security male prisons, federal prisons and all-female prisons. I loved the work so much that when an opportunity came for a full-time job, I jumped at it.

AL   *Why is working with incarcerated women (as opposed to men) important to you?*

SF   As I said, my first teaching job in a prison was in a co-ed classroom. I taught many classes at all-male prisons. Although the men are amazing as well, I guess I do prefer working with women. This could be because of my feminist beliefs. It could be because women prisoners have it worse than male prisoners in some ways. I believe they are an even more invisible population. There is still a stigma in society about women who get incarcerated and leave their children. They are judged more harshly than men. I can relate to women more because we share similar experiences. So many of the women have experienced trauma – rape, incest, domestic violence. Yes, I think it is because of my feminist beliefs.

AL   *Once you were working in the prison, what made you decide to start doing theatre with the women?*

SF   I do not think that I 'decided'. We had a warden who ordered my mentor to begin a theatre troupe. He was as specific as to tell us he wanted the subject matter to be about violence against women. My mentor asked me to be involved. There were many different staff members involved – the chaplain, psychologist, leisure time services staff, someone from the business department. After the first or second production, I was the person running the troupe. I would like to think that, had he not ordered it, I would have

192 *Applied Theatre: Women and the Criminal Justice System*

eventually begun a troupe myself. For the first performance, we chose women who we knew. Now I hold open auditions.

AL *What does theatre do for incarcerated women that it might not do for people who live in freedom?*

SF Theatre in prison opens up a world to women that they may have known nothing about before they were incarcerated. Many women, because of substance abuse, have no idea what they like or what they are good at. Joining the troupe often surprises them when they discover that acting is something they have a talent for. It allows them to transcend the prison environment, allows them to be someone else, to be somewhere else. Performing gives them confidence and boosts self-esteem. I have had women tell me that, by playing a certain role, they have been able to work out personal issues that they had. They have fun – sometimes theatre is the one thing that they look forward to all week. Working with people from outside the prison makes them feel seen, feel human.

AL *What was the first play that you did with the women?*

SF *Poof!* by Lynn Nottage, along with a series of monologues about violence against women and a Tracy Chapman song 'Behind the Wall'. We performed the monologues and the song first – then the play.

AL *Who chose the name Acting Out? How did that happen?*

SF It has been so long that I cannot remember for sure. I have always been delighted with the name. I think the staff who were involved may have come up with it, and the women liked it.

AL *You have brought quite a few outside theatre artists into the prison to collaborate with the women. Tell me about one or two of your most successful collaborations and how they came about.*

SF I believe that our collaboration with you and our collaboration on *Through the Fire* have been the most successful. *Through the Fire* was a script compiled by Kathryn Moller and Maureen May, adapted from interviews of nine survivors of abuse. They originally produced it in Colorado, and then came here for weeks to do it with our women. My counsellor [on staff at the prison] did research on the Internet and found Kathryn. We just called her up. Kathryn directed the production here in 2004. Stacey Sotosky filmed it.

Acting Out 193

We managed to get an Illinois Arts Council Grant to pay for part of the expenses.

AL *How many women are in the troupe today? How often do you get to rehearse?*

SF I have twenty women in the troupe right now. We rehearse for two hours two times a week. Now that we are getting close to a performance, we will increase that to maybe four times a week. We have to do a costume fitting, blocking, tech and dress rehearsals.

AL *Who does costumes for your productions?*

SF I do. For most of them. We draw from our Out Next Week Boutique [a resource at the prison to provide clothes to women who will be leaving soon]. I borrow them from people or buy them myself. Sometimes, if an outside director is here, they bring something in – Kathryn did.

AL *Are there any limits on what kinds of costumes and make-up you can use?*

SF I can't really think of any. Occasionally, security was concerned about wigs, but they have let us use them, as well as facial hair. Of course, modesty is an issue. We have to keep a very accurate inventory of what we are using so none of it makes it out into population. Their main concern is not doing anything that would aid in an escape attempt.

AL *How did you decide to produce the play you're working on now –* Our Country's Good *by Timberlake Wertenbaker? How does this play resonate with the women?*

SF I saw *Our Country's Good* years ago at Illinois State University (ISU) and loved it. I taught it in my drama classes. ISU did it again and brought the cast in [to the prison] to perform some of it for the [Acting Out] troupe some years ago and got their feedback.

It is a play that I always thought would be amazing to do in prison. Once I shared it with the troupe, they agreed. It's a theatre-lover's play that shows the transformative and transcendent power of theatre. It also – unfortunately – debates issues surrounding criminality that we are still debating today:

Whether being a criminal is innate or taught?

Is theatre beneficial for convicts or a waste of time?

194   *Applied Theatre: Women and the Criminal Justice System*

Are [prisoners] able to be rehabilitated?
If so, how?
The women love the play and relate to it very much.

AL   *How has being a part of this theatre company had an impact on your life and your job?*

SF   The theatre troupe sustains me during rough times at work. It has allowed me to meet amazing people like you and the many other people who bring theatre to prisons – Curt Tofteland [Shakespeare Behind Bars, Michigan, USA], Tom Magill [Educational Shakespeare Co., Belfast, Northern Ireland], Sabra Williams [Actors' Gang Prison Outreach Program, Los Angeles, USA], Johnny Stallings [Open Hearts Open Minds, Portland, USA] and on and on. I have been able to travel and present at conferences. I feel as if I have a family across the United States – and the world. It has challenged me. I have not been trained in theatre, so I have stumbled through directing and other aspects of production. Directing Toni Morrison's *The Bluest Eye* was one of the best things that I have been a part of. Now I get to put on *Our Country's Good*, which is a play that has always moved me greatly. Bringing other theatre people, like you, Janet Wilson [ISU], Kathryn Moeller and Stacy Sotosky, has been an amazing experience. I am able to have the thrill of watching how theatre impacts the women [in the prison].

AL   *Who gets to see the performances that Acting Out does? How have audiences responded?*

SF   For the most part, it is the other women [in the prison] who see the performances. I have tried to bring their families in, but so far have not been able to get that approved. We have guests sometimes, like you or other professors who have worked with the women previously. Faculty from ISU. For *Our Country's Good*, for example, the two women who worked with the women on their dialects will be coming in.

AL   *You're doing dialect work with the women. That's a level of training not offered to many college theatre students. Is this the first time that you've had professionals do specialized voice or dialect coaching in the prison?*

SF   Connie de Veer has worked with the women two times on dialect. She is a delightful woman. I am blessed to have Illinois State University near. They have been very generous. The head of the department, Janet Wilson, is the person who came in for a summer and worked with them on writing and

Acting Out 195

performing *A Theatrical Ritual by Incarcerated Women for Incarcerated Women*. The Illinois Shakespeare Troupe had come in to perform and do workshops with the troupe over ten times.

AL *How has that experience been for you and the women in the troupe?*

SF Most of the women LOVED it. Some feel a bit intimidated by it. For this production, if the dialect was interfering with their acting, I told them to forget it or just pick certain phrases to use with it. So you will see a variety of competencies in this play. It just seems to come more naturally for some. They have a blast when working with Connie.

AL *Should every prison have a theatre troupe?*

SF YES, and the troupe agrees wholeheartedly.

Inside a Cloud (2016)

Sabrina Mahfouz

Carly   I'll tell you what it is, babe.
My dressing gown, I love it.
It's seen me through two babies,
wearing it in the hospital when it got too hot.
Wearing it while I was swearing at my man for being so crap.
Clenching it when the sweat was pushing me to another planet.
Wearing it again when I held them close,
when they crawled up my chest, like little lost lambs.
Now, it hangs there, staring at me.
Reminding me of all the things I'm missing out on.
All the days I won't get back, my babies like little lost lambs
but without a chest to climb up and find some place they know.
So it has to go.
I can't see it, but I can't throw it.
I want you to take it, just keep it somewhere.
You don't have to wear it, just let it breathe a bit.
Let it see the sun in the park maybe.
You could lay it on the grass for a picnic.
Maybe you know, if you can.

In 2016, Clean Break, in collaboration with Music in Prison – The Irene Taylor Trust, ran a residency at HMP Styal. The play, *Inside a Cloud,* developed from a collaboration between the women and Sabrina Mahfouz. In this extract, Sophia is about to be released from prison, and her friends are throwing her a leaving party, giving her tokens to take with her.

10

'There Is Still Life in Me, Despite What I Have Done': Assuaging Woundedness through Collective Creativity

Katharine E. Low and Clara Vaughan

Introduction

In May 2012, we facilitated a three-day process of creative play in the female section of Sun City – the ironic nickname for the Johannesburg Correctional Centre. The aims of this pilot project were to encourage the women to think about, and share their hopes for, the future and to consider their role models in life. This was done with the intention of exploring the topics which helped them 'keep going' during their sentence, bearing in mind their extremely difficult daily circumstances and the resulting impact on their well-being and ability to 'cope'. Based on this process, and drawing from interviews conducted with the women who participated in the project, in this chapter, we consider questions about what occurred in specific moments of the process and offer the suggestion that, in those moments, the women were able to deepen their connection to themselves, and to each other, in a way that was productive to their well-being.

Acknowledging Wendy James' argument that understandings of well-being are culturally and historically dependent (2008: 69–79), for the purposes of this paper we are informed by views of the woundedness of South African society as suggested by South African thinkers such as Mamphela Ramphele and Desmond Tutu. We propose that, in this context, understandings of a person's well-being are linked to notions of dignity, human interaction and witnessing, which is a challenging concept in a prison context.

We argue that, by taking part in drama activities, there is an opportunity to be witnessed and to be recognized as an individual, which is crucial in an environment in which people are deliberately de-individualized and treated as homogenous. This has particular implications for female inmates due to the oppressive conditions found in the prison, which we will address in more detail shortly. Working in a context with high levels of experience of woundedness and where well-being is lacking, our argument is that the theatre project created a space for collaborative creativity which assuaged some of the peripheral effects of woundedness that the women were encountering. Although this space is both transient and temporary, we argue that it enabled the women to feel 'well' in that they both were perceived and perceived each other in multiple and layered ways, connections were made and they were acknowledged. We argue that this has significant value in that moment and that this is as important as longer-lasting 'effects' which are both difficult and tenuous to argue for. While we are not claiming to have affected a permanent change, the inmates experienced a temporary shift of consciousness and experience. This returns to our intentions for the project, where, working within the system, we wanted to encourage women to find ways of coping with their oppressions. We believe that people cannot make political or fundamental changes for themselves unless they are feeling 'well' and that the individual is as important as the collective, particularly in prison contexts. The fact that the women felt visible and valued is important, and that is where the worth of this work lies for us.

In this chapter, we explore these ideas to set out an argument regarding the importance of dignity and creative collaboration in theatre-making within a prison setting and the possible implications in relation to improved well-being. We will first note the contexts of the practice and our theoretical framework before analysing what occurred in the space.

Contexts

At the time of the workshops, Clara Vaughan, a South African freelance facilitator, director and performer, was based in Johannesburg, and Katharine Low, a South African socially engaged theatre practitioner, was based in London. We are both white feminist women, working with participants who were predominantly black. While we designed and led the project, we were assisted by six applied theatre students – five from the Royal Central School of Speech and Drama in London, and one from Sibikwa Arts Centre, just outside Johannesburg. One of the aims of the project was to provide a model of professional practice for the applied theatre students, who would shortly be running a project of their own. We were not the first facilitators to 'do drama' with the women at Sun City. Rhodessa Jones has run regular theatre projects there since 2006 as part of the Medea Project.[1] However, the intention and focus of our process was fundamentally different in two ways: first, unlike Jones, we did not focus on *why* the women were in prison – what

Assuaging Woundedness through Collective Creativity   199

crime they had committed. Secondly, we were not working towards a public performance for an outside audience: our project was process-oriented, the only performances being between, and for, group members.

South African prison context

Before 1994, mass incarceration – the penal system – was a tool for racist subjugation used by the apartheid state (Gillespie 2008: 69). There is a symbolic and material resonance between the apartheid system and the institution of prison – many of South Africa's struggle heroes and current leaders were unjustly imprisoned, and even murdered, for political dissent. It is striking then that, since 1994, when the first democratic elections were held, the prison population has actually grown by 35 per cent,[2] and women are one of the fastest growing prison populations (Biggs 2016: 4).[3] South Africa has, by far, the highest rates of incarceration on the African continent, and is currently eleventh in the world in its use of imprisonment (World Prison Brief 2016). It is also striking that the prison system continues to punish, disproportionately, the same people who were most violently assaulted and impoverished by the structural violence and injustice of the apartheid system – poor black people living in townships. In other words, the penal system targets those most wounded by South Africa's past and unequal present.

When the post-apartheid South African government came to power, it faced the challenge of showing control over the 'crime wave' that came with the fall of apartheid, while fulfilling its mandate of liberation and transformation (Altbeker 2011). With post-apartheid concerns of moral regeneration and nation-building, there has been a rise in discourses of rehabilitation rather than punishment, reframing the prison as a benevolent, even parental, institution transforming bad citizens to good (Gillespie 2008). Even its name has changed, from the 'Department of Prisons to the 'Department of Correctional Services' (Gillespie 2008: 73). Despite this, today's prisons remain somewhat militarized, a legacy of the apartheid government's military training of the prison wardens by the army before they began work at prisons (Centre for Conflict Resolution 2004).

Women make up a tiny part of the prison population: statistics from March 2015 indicate that female prisoners account for only 2.6 per cent of the total 159,563 inmates, and there are few female prisons, which means that many of the female inmates are often imprisoned far away from their families and any community links that they might have (Institute for Criminal Policy Research 2016). While there exists some research on women in South African

200   *Applied Theatre: Women and the Criminal Justice System*

prisons (cf. Gillespie 2008; Young-Jahangeer 2005, 2013), it is limited in comparison with research conducted with male prisoners. The South African Department of Correctional Services does not have a policy framework for the specific needs of female prisoners, particularly in health care (pregnancy, menstruation and child care). This is despite the Department of Correctional Services' signing of the UN Rules for the Treatment of Women Prisoners and Non-Custodial Measures for Women Offenders treaty in 2010 (Manaleng 2014). According to the women who are incarcerated in Sun City, to survive you have to stay strong, focused, wary of whom you trust and talk to and take care not to reveal too much. Considering that South African prisons are infamous for their overcrowding, this cannot be easy: the official capacity of the prison system is 120,000 inmates, and currently the official occupancy level stands at 132.7 per cent (Institute for Criminal Policy Research 2016).

Comprised of three prisons, Sun City has a capacity of approximately 600 inmates in the female prison (Haffejee 2014); however, at the time of writing in June 2016, there are 960 women incarcerated there, including 309 women awaiting trial – that is to say, 61.3 per cent over capacity (Correctional Services 2016). Between 2.30 p.m. and 7 a.m. the following morning, the women are held in cells of between thirty-six to forty-two women. These are compact rooms with brick latticing instead of glass in the windows, freezing in the Highveld winters. Each room has one shower, one toilet and two sinks along one wall, with rows of cots distributed throughout the room. Relationships between inmates and members (as wardens are called in South Africa) are tense, as the inmates are often infantalized, treated as young teenage girls, an act which challenges their agency and adulthood. An inmate, Lauren,[4] commented: 'Some members are nice. Others try to break you – they don't deal with you individually, they deal with you as a group.'

Since 1996, when the Correctional Services 'allowed recreational activities to be introduced [into prisons] for the first time' (Young-Jahangeer 2005: 143), there has been an increasing use of theatre in prisons from both local practitioners, such as Miranda Young-Jahangeer's (2013) and Chris Hurst's work in Durban's Westville Prison; Alexandra Sutherland's work in a prison in Grahamstown (2013); the long-standing Centre for Conflict Resolution's Prison Transformation Project in Pollsmoor in Cape Town; and international projects such as the Medea Project run by Jones, which has been located in Sun City since 2006 (Biggs 2016). However, in the context we have described, drama programmes can be co-opted to literally showcase the rehabilitative effects of prison (Gillespie 2008: 71). Prisoners frequently perform plays and dances for visiting officials and special events, their bodies inscribed with new meanings of obedience, happiness, health and well-being, despite the

Assuaging Woundedness through Collective Creativity   201

reality of harsh conditions and overcrowding. This has the effect of making the issue of crime a matter of problematic or immoral individuals, rather than an issue of structural inequality, despite the clear socio-economic patterns evident in incarceration statistics (Gillespie 2008: 71). It could be argued that projects such as Jones', in which prisoners recount or re-enact the crimes they committed that put them in prison, are a part of this discourse, as the prisoners perform confession and remorse.

We argue that our project, rather than being a contribution to the rehabilitative capacity of prison, was a process that assuaged some of the inmates' woundedness caused by being incarcerated. Thus, while we are aware of the rehabilitation narrative or encouraging a 'positive change' perspective which can surround prison theatre practice (Buell 2011; Baim, Brookes and Mountford 2002), we would like to suggest that, in these workshops, something more subtle than 'betterment' or 'rehabilitation' was occurring. We propose that, during the different activities, spaces or moments of engagement, opportunities emerged for the women to see each other as multiple and complex beings, not solely inmates. This is highlighted in one of the women's comments, when commenting on the difference between this workshop and her other experiences of theatre: Lauren said, 'You are alone, as an individual, [it is about] your views. You are you. It justifies you as a person.'

It is well known that prisons can be dehumanizing environments, and there are psychological implications linked with institutionalization, particularly for women (McAvinchey 2011; Thorn 2010). As Thembi described it, 'Sho – it's like hell: misery. [I'm] angry every day; violent, aggressive, short-tempered, [but I'm] also soft-hearted, emotional. [I] cry easily.' Prisons are complex structures in which relationships are regularly contested and inmates are not treated as individuals. Often, as Maud Clark describes it, 'there are beliefs and expectations that go with the label prisoner – crim, junkie, murderer – that separate these people from being woman, lover, mother, sister' (2004: 102). Indeed, as Californian community arts in prison practitioner Judith Tannenbaum (2002) argues, inmates are often already perceived in a particular way:

> For a moment, think of the worst thing you've ever done. Whatever it is, remember it well. Now imagine that this act is all you're known for. Imagine that everything in your world is designed to treat you as a person defined by that act. Any other fact of your life – any act of love, kindness, compassion, intelligence, creativity, joy, humor – is irrelevant. You are only a person who has done this worst thing. That's it, that's you, from now till forever.

202 *Applied Theatre: Women and the Criminal Justice System*

Yet such a definition of a prisoner, i.e. that they are defined only by their crime, appears inconsistent with the South African constitution which enshrines the right of prisoners to detention conditions that are 'consistent with human dignity', particularly for women (Centre for Conflict Resolution 2004: 163–4). We would argue that the environment the women live in limits their dignity as there are rare opportunities to be seen as a 'multiple' and complex human being, an individual, which is an idea that Mamphela Ramphele has considered in more depth with reference to the South African psyche.

Theoretical framework

Ramphele, a medical doctor, social anthropologist, former Vice Chancellor of the University of Cape Town, anti-apartheid activist and a member of the Black Consciousness Movement, creates a link between the woundedness of South Africa as a nation and the lack of spaces to view and speak to each other as individuals. Speaking about all South Africans, Ramphele has argued: 'Our woundedness as a nation, the divisions that we carried into 1994, are persisting like a wound deep down, with a little scar on the top' (2012a). Recounting the impact of apartheid's social engineering, Ramphele points to traditional literature to argue that human beings need to be connected to other human beings. This correlates with the African philosophy of Ubuntu, encapsulated by the Zulu proverb, 'umuntu ngumuntu nbabantu' which translates literally as 'a person is a person through other persons'. Similarly, Desmond Tutu points out that: 'We are humanised or dehumanised in and through our actions towards others ... My humanity is caught up, bound up, inextricably, with yours' (Tutu cited in Kronenberg et al. 2015: 22).[5] All of this is also contextualized by Emmanuel Levinas' understanding of alterity in which he proposes:

> Our relation with him certainly consists in wanting to understand him, but this relation exceeds the confines of understanding. Not only because, besides curiosity, knowledge of the other also demands sympathy or love, ways of being are different from impassive contemplation, but also because, in our relation to the other, the latter does not affect us by means of a concept. The other is a being and counts as such. (2006: 5)

What Levinas is describing is the moment where we recognize that the self is always formed in relation to another, where the other cannot be an object of knowledge. Yet, if we do not recognize this – if we try to demean, infantilize or dehumanize the other – this fractures us as a society, community or organization. We can then become, in Ramphele's term, 'wounded' or are, in Tutu's context, dehumanizing each other. If we consider this within the South Africa context, apartheid fractured connections: it was a systematic devaluing of particular cultures and languages that still impacts how people see themselves and others today. Indeed, these concepts of dehumanization, lack of alterity or woundedness can also be applied to a prison context. Acknowledging the impact of apartheid on South African society, Ramphele draws strong parallels to a person's well-being, arguing that woundedness results in people engaging in suicidal tendencies or self-sabotaging behaviour, such as engaging in unprotected sex in the era of AIDS (2012b).[6] Her thesis is that when people recover their dignity, they begin to look after themselves (2012a). She makes a key link between the act of acknowledging and being acknowledged, and the impact of this on a person's well-being and dignity.

It is important to note, however, that Ramphele is making an argument about finding ways of improving South Africa's national sense of well-being. Yet, well-being is a problematic concept, prone to misuse or morality judgement by policy-makers or, as Alberto Corsín Jimémez describes it, 'well-being is a holder of limits: an unstable and fragile resting place for the political' (2008: 4). Indeed, Ramphele is using this in the political sense as she proposed in 2012 that South African woundedness can be resolved through the promotion of active citizenship (2012a, 2012b).[7] Nonetheless, acknowledging this theorization, we argue that the criteria for woundedness is heightened in prison and exacerbated for women. Indeed, as Nina Billone describes it, 'Criminalised women experience a distinctly gendered form of civil death' (2009: 264). In essence, the small sizes and numbers of the prisons, distance from home and family, a lack of space for dignity, the infantalizaton of the women by the members and the fact that the relatively small population of women is often overlooked in the distribution of resources (Biggs 2016) are reasons why our conceptualization of dignity and well-being are important for our analysis.

Well-being is a social construct which melds together individual's and community's understandings of their own health. Perceptions of well-being should be considered as incorporating all aspects of health, including physical, emotional and spiritual health. This is in addition to encompassing the notion of social connectedness, including societal influences, such as links to a community or social isolation, and cultural and economic status. Considering this, Ramphele's argument bears similarity with social anthropologist Nigel Rapport's research with hospital porters in which he describes well-being in the following manner:

Well-being comes to be understood as physical, intellectual and emotional opportunities to interact with fellow human beings, over a period of time, in ways that are valued by actors and reinforced by others.

2008: 108

Rapport furthers his explanation by noting how well-being is linked with 'having the resources to participate as a full member of a social milieu' (2008: 108). A lack of well-being, conversely, is when people are deprived of the 'conditions of life' that enable them to take part in society and perform their roles (Townsend 1987: 130, cited in Rapport 2008: 108). For us, Rapport's description of a lack of well-being is a prisoner's experience, in which their punishment is not to have the freedom to be part of their community and perform their multiple roles as individuals. Furthermore, in the very structure and running of the prison, it is emphasized to them that they are not individuals. Indeed, as demonstrated above, at present, the South African Department of Correctional Services does not detain inmates in conditions which are 'consistent with human dignity', in terms of both physical and emotional well-being.

Considering this, the notion of dignity becomes vitally important. In the inaugural Mike White Memorial Lecture at the Wellcome Trust in June 2016, poet Fiona Sampson considered the role of creativity and the creative arts in health and care. In her lecture, acknowledging the 'elastic' nature of the concept, Sampson argued that '"dignity" appeals to a notion of human-ness as more than the sum of its parts' (2016: 4) and that:

the principle that dignity is fundamental to *what we are* is *not* an appeal to good manners. It *is* a capacious (re)definition of being human: one that leaves us growing room and that says, in effect, nothing more or less than that 'humans are intrinsically valuable'.

2016: 5–6, emphasis in original

Here Sampson's theorization of dignity is a fundamental framework for articulating what we believe can be temporarily achieved through the interactions found in collective creative practice. Acknowledging the dignity of, and offering dignity to, the other is, in fact, recognizing that individual's value and worth.

If we place these ideas within the context of Sun City, or any prison, there are strong resonances: it is essentially a prisoner's experience – their punishment is not to have the freedom to be part of their community and perform their multiple roles as individuals. There is little dignity held or offered to each other. At Sun City, Sibongile explains: 'Sometimes we treat each other like shit. Sometimes the members [wardens] really make us feel like inmates, they don't give us respect.' The daily lack of respect is coupled with the lack of space to yourself. In the prison, there is no privacy or dignity. It is, as the warden commented, 'a careful life', a precarious life, in which there are few 'physical, intellectual and emotional opportunities' to interact with each other. In these circumstances, it could be argued that the women's well-being is fragile as they have no space to be themselves nor to recognize their multiple roles. The environment they live in limits their dignity as there are rare opportunities to be seen as individuals. Furthermore, in the structure, running and existence of the prison, it is emphasized to them that they are first, and most importantly, criminals.

While both apartheid and the criminal justice system are dehumanizing practices, drama can create humanizing spaces, where, through creative practice, we can be both individuals as well as seeing the 'other' as unique and multiple and having different connections. We argue that, within these theatre-making settings, theatre enables the opportunity for the idea that 'I am because I see you and because you see me' through collective creativity. In particular, as we will argue next, this comes about through opportunities for witnessing each other and taking careful risks.

The practice: Witnessing each other and seeing myself

Touch and collaboration are fundamental to theatre process; this was the conceptual through line that wound together the series of theatre, music and visual arts activities that we designed, some of which form the basis of our analysis here. The first is a postcard to the world, a simple activity which, interwoven with other touch and memory games, led to great hilarity and moments of sharing. Each participant created a postcard representing themselves, with the tagline: 'This is what the World needs to know about me.' The postcards were 'posted' before being received by another participant, whereby each woman created an image in response to their card. In small groups, they then devised short performances, integrating all their responses. These showings were both electric and moving. One group developed a short, jivey dance routine, with each woman taking turns to share her moves to copy, demonstrating increasing levels of skill, strength and dexterity. Another performance ended with the women 'sunbathing' on the beach (in fact, the patch of sun in the courtyard), singing '*Tell the World, I'm coming home*'.

The act of interpreting and reading other's ideas is crucial for beginning to step away from boundaries and recognize the multiplicity of each other, through performing and witnessing the performance of multiple roles:

206   *Applied Theatre: Women and the Criminal Justice System*

mothers, daughters, lovers, friends, dancers, singers and all manner of strong women. This, we argue, is one of the ways in which the theatre activity provided opportunities for different forms of interaction than the women would have had previously experienced. Jessica Berson, writing about a US-based female prison dance and performance project, observes that '[t]he collaborative work of creating a performance piece grants inmates permission to speak and be heard, to touch each other, and to play, all of which can contribute to emotional growth' (2008: 92). This echoes closely with Rapport's definition of well-being, but crucially what Berson draws attention to is the fact that, in constrained settings, the act of playing and creating together can create spaces in which the women can speak and be heard by each other.

The second strand of activities we discuss is a process of creative writing where the participants began by listening to Paloma Faith's 'Upside Down', a song about a woman who has survived living in an 'unforgiving place' and lives her life in an 'upside-down' manner. In response to the song, we went through a process of free writing, swapping pages, before each choosing particular phrases from their writings. Taking those words, each group created a poem. In another exercise, the participants wrote a letter from their eighty-year-old self to themselves today, offering advice or encouragement, whatever they felt their older self would want to say to their younger. Once written, they chose to share the letter, or not, in small groups. In both activities, the women created works in which they expressed aspects of who they are, their thoughts about life, inside and outside prison, what they love and what they miss and, particularly in the letter exercise, what they dream of for the future. In their letters, the women expressed how proud they were of themselves, and their tone was encouraging: 'there is so much for you to achieve', 'forgive yourself, and start living', 'I write this letter to say how proud I am with myself' and 'I want you to know that you can put aside your fears'. While there was pride and encouragement, the letters also hinted at difficult times both in the past and which might lie ahead: 'my kids are not married to abusive men, but good men', 'prepare yourself for the outside world' and 'please stay away from those peers you are having, they are no good and please control your anger coz it might harm others'. The letters moved from poignancy and morals to affection: 'I love you' – the women heard each other's letters quietly.

In each instance, as they created a particular viewpoint of themselves, they also acknowledged their multiple identities: they were more than the singular identity of 'incarcerated women'. Rapport's notion of well-being, linked to physical, emotional and intellectual opportunities to interact with others, is synonymous with what can occur in applied theatre practice such as this. A space was created in which dignity prevailed: the women were attentive,

Assuaging Woundedness through Collective Creativity   207

actively listening and responding to each other, visibly enjoying the process, with laughter and elated suggestions. For example, when Sabrina, who believed she could not sing, improvised a song out of the poem, she was supported by her group members in front of an awed audience, who had never seen her so uninhibited.

Crucially, part of recognizing the other comes through the act of witnessing, which in this context we argue is an act of humanizing by seeing the other as having multiple identities. This idea is informed by our earlier theorizing around the notions of woundedness, ubuntu and alterity. Witnessing is an approach; a way of listening to, and receiving from, another person. It implies an openness, a respect of the other, a carrying of the 'weight' of the other. We subscribe to the idea that my witnessing of you is giving you the space to be you. Accordingly, in each instance, as they created a particular viewpoint of themselves, they also acknowledged the multiplicity of themselves, in the sense they were not only incarcerated women. In that shared experience, they were supportive of, and responsive to, each other. As one women commented, 'there was laughter, dancing and concentrating' – actions which all require some form of stimulus from, or interaction between, another other to happen. This hinted to us the fundamental difference in the manner the women might usually interact in their cells. In these shared experiences, it felt as if it was a less constrained environment, as there were opportunities to interact differently both with each other and with the warden. We would argue that part of the ease of the interactions came from the experience of being witnessed.

Drawing on Peggy Phelan's view that witnessing enables the lost and the departed 'to continue to live', Caroline Wake proposes that 'the function of performing witness is to enable and engage with subaltern speech and to render visible those subjects who might otherwise remain invisible' (Phelan 1999: 13, cited in Wake 2008: 188). Accordingly, if we consider the prison environment, the moments in which women spoke about their imagined dreams, their feelings of prison, their thoughts of being outside, made these women visible, not just to us as 'outsiders' who heard their ideas but also to themselves and among each other. In hearing each other, in making themselves visible, we argue that all the women, including the warden and ourselves, acknowledged and witnessed the 'other'. Tim Etchells argues that 'to witness an event is to be present at it in some fundamentally ethical way, to feel the weight of things and one's own place in them' (1999: 17). Similarly, Salverson notes: 'Witnessing is also about impossible tenderness' (2006: 154). Here, we read this idea of tenderness as the space to listen and the desire to be attentive and responsive to each other, a state which was facilitated through the workshops. For example, in both descriptions, the witness offers to feel

208   *Applied Theatre: Women and the Criminal Justice System*

the significance of the other or to acknowledge this. The significance is everything from hearing a woman's pain of leaving her children to be cared for by others to carrying the guilt for what she has done.

Salverson's idea of tenderness is accurate in this instance – the offer to feel the gravitas of each other's ideas, thoughts, experiences was a tender one. Throughout the three days, there were few dismissive remarks or disparaging laughs, rather the atmosphere was tender, chaotic and energetic. At times, it was also 'soft', for want of a better word, in the sense that, when we listened to the poems or heard the letters, we clustered around; it was intimate, personal and receptive. And this was important for the women. For example, Sikelelwa explained that 'When I came back from the workshop, I was me – no bitterness inside. I forget I was in prison, but when I got back to my cell, I remembered.' While Sikelelwa notes the experience of being herself, she also draws attention to the temporary nature of the experience, which is important to recall before making transformational statements about the impact of these workshops.

Yet, for the inmates, however fleeting this experience may have been, it still remains important in the sense that, for short periods, they felt like themselves, they interacted with others as themselves, they reached a level of well-being in that they participated as 'full members' and established connections with each other. In short, they had dignity, 'growing room' and had established further 'connectedness' with a few people, which was a step towards bolstering their well-being and assuaging their woundedness. This resonates with the idea of ubuntu that 'who and how we can be as human beings is always being shaped in our interactions with each other' (Kronenberg et al. 2015: 23).

Taking careful risks: Seeing the 'other'

We have argued that, in these shared moments of performance-making, the women were beginning to witness each other as individuals and were affirming each other in their representations. However, this interaction is not always an easy one. Indeed, Julie Salverson argues, drawing from Levinas' notion of alterity, the representation 'must firstly always leave room for the other to breathe' and, secondly, by 'being available as a witness [requires us] to disturb our own sense of ourselves, and to risk bringing that shaken self to the table' (2006: 149–50). It is risky, particularly in highly controlled environments, to perform each other's roles or ideas, to open yourself to experience other people's views without constraining the other.

There is a finality in the imposed label of prisoner for both the inmate and those who label. Thus, to allow themselves to be seen as individuals, the inmates needed to lower their façades – the 'prisoner' persona that many adopt

Assuaging Woundedness through Collective Creativity   209

as a protective measure against bullying or abuse. While the persona has a defensive function, it also serves to isolate the inmates even further; thus, in an environment that has already separated them from existing support networks of family and friends, they are also isolated from each other, despite the lack of privacy or space. Young-Jahangeer speaks of this lowering of façade as positive risk-taking behaviour, in that it provides an opportunity for social cohesion and healthy human interactions (2005: 9). This is illustrated by one of the participants in the process, who said in the follow-up interview:

> I'm an angry person, when people are talking to me, I'll be harsh to them. Since you people came, my anger is just down. Now I give people advice – before I told them, 'Go and ask someone, I'm not the advisor.' Now people are people, we must help each other. Because one day it will be me.

It is not only the inmates who maintain a protective façade, however. The members must also wear a persona that maintains their authority. After all, it is through the wardens or members that the practice of 'corrections' – the interpretation of policy – is enacted (Gillespie 2008: 77). So, inasmuch as the inmates seldom get a chance to be seen as individuals, neither do the members. While the inmates wear uniforms that de-individualize them and lower their status, the wardens wear uniforms that also de-individualize them and raise their status. During the second or third warm-up game on the first day of our workshops, one of the members, Jeffreys, who had been standing slightly behind the circle, unobtrusively joined it. We were surprised when she joined in – from her demeanour, we would not have dared suggest it. While the inmates were inclusive and facilitated a space for her, at the beginning, her participation did not last long: one of the first exercises we facilitated was Boal's Columbian Hypnosis, and Jeffreys was partnered with an inmate. She stopped playing when it was the inmate's turn to lead and, in the reflection afterwards, she said she found it 'humiliating'; she had experienced a loss of status in that moment and was uncomfortable.

Michel Foucault's description of the relationship between the body and the state is particularly apt when considering a prison:

> the body is also directly involved in a political field. Power relations have an immediate hold upon it, they invest it, mark it, train it, torture it, force it to carry out tasks, to perform ceremonies, to emit signs.
>
> 1979: 25

The inmates have little power over their own bodies – the 'regime of incarceration' (Lawston 2008: 9) – when to sleep, wake up and eat is determined

210   *Applied Theatre: Women and the Criminal Justice System*

by the members, the representatives of the state. This, the perpetuation of the powerlessness of the inmates, is reinforced by the members in the day-to-day living in the prison (Young-Jahangeer 2005).

Consider this in relation to the physical dynamics, the relationship of bodies, in Columbian Hypnosis. Played in pairs, the follower must gaze at the leader's palm and maintain the same distance from it with her head, while the leader moves her palm, taking the follower on a physical journey through the space. This is a step away from the formalized power dynamic of everyday prison life, in which it is usually the member who determines the physical movements of the inmates, not the other way around.

Despite the discomfort of this, from that moment on Jeffreys participated fully in every activity, explaining afterwards: 'I enjoyed it so much, I forgot I was at work. I forgot the prison environment.' This is particularly insightful in terms of Jeffreys' engagement, as in later parts of the process she made far more risky decisions, engaging in a series of tasks that revealed her as far more than a member. She occasionally expressed doubts about this; 'risk-taking', for her, was a dangerous business, creating a tension between her participation in the drama and her position in the prison as an institutional figure of authority. She said that, as a member, she cannot be 'overfriendly', and that it was dangerous for the inmates to know too much about her. Yet she also expressed pleasure in finding out more about the inmates: 'It changed, it made me realize they are more than what you perceive. Everyday things that you won't necessarily find out by just talking.' She never chose to sit out again and, in conversations where you had the voluntary option to speak about a creative process, she always chose to do so.

By the last day, her integration into the group was markedly different to the first. We asked the participants to create an amulet symbolizing what keeps them going while they are inside, by decorating a small chipboard heart with various art materials. This was a powerful exercise that everyone really invested in, creating hearts representing children, love, God and memories. Jeffreys' heart was pink and silver – there was a small circular mirror in the centre surrounded by a softness of pink feathers, and the outline was bordered with silver and gold sequins. The adjectives that come to mind, in looking at the heart, are feminine, girlish, delicate, soft, sensitive, playful – a vivid contrast to the professional, quite distant persona that Jeffreys usually presents to the inmates. Perhaps most significant is the name she wrote on her heart (in pink glitter). This was not her surname, which is the name commonly used for her in the prison, but her first name, Rose, short for Rosaline. A name that is extremely apt for the heart she created, and symbolic, perhaps, of the progressive depth of self she expressed during the drama.

Assuaging Woundedness through Collective Creativity   211

When Jeffreys wrote 'Rose' on her heart, she was sharing a part of herself, an aspect of her identity that we imagine the inmates had not seen before. Furthermore, this was a choice she made herself, indicating, despite a certain sense of conflict, a willingness to sacrifice some of the power of her 'member' façade in order to be witnessed. It is not only the disempowered who crave to be seen more fully, who wish to be acknowledged as individuals, who benefit from being recognized as an identity beyond what is institutionally imposed. It seems that there was something to be gained for Rosaline as well for herself.

We believe that, in taking part, Jeffreys was occasionally able to let go of her role as Sergeant and be 'Rose', playing, creating and performing with the other women, which in turn led to temporary moments of transgression, sitting squashed together on a bench, a shared hug between inmate and warden. Furthermore, her reflection of the inmate as individual was, in our view, recognition of the other as being more than their perceived status in prison (while still acknowledging the power structures that remain in the space). Yet Jeffreys' comment on her recognition of the individual or other as being more than what you see also applies to her – she will have been seen differently by those inmates who took part in the workshop with her. It is possible that this witnessing of Jeffreys as being more than a warden momentarily established connections between the inmates and herself, which is important in creating a space for, and to celebrate, a person's dignity in such constrained settings, and which would have also had an impact on her personal sense of well-being in that environment.

Conclusion

In her account of the theatre and art made in the concentration camps and the internment camps during the Second World War, Anne Dutlinger (2001: 5, cited in Balfour 2004: 2) explains that, while it did not save lives, 'the act of making art ... helped to sustain hope, a sense of the self, and the will to live'. It is developing this 'sense of the self' which we believe should be the key ideology of theatre in prisons. It is about humanizing the circumstances of prison life, creating a space where prisoners can rediscover their multiple roles in life and refuse to be defined and labelled by a sole, 'worst' act. It is about refuting the myth that prisoners are different from 'normal' people (Clark 2004: 101) and that the labour of the prison staff can be complex and challenging for them.

This resonates strongly with the recurring comment we heard when we went back to the prison a week later to conduct interviews about the

212   *Applied Theatre: Women and the Criminal Justice System*

programme, which was 'I forgot that I was in prison'. Several women said this, including Jeffreys. However constrained their bodies were in space and time, we would argue that they found what Baz Kershaw calls 'a fissure in which to forge at least a little freedom' (2004: 35). Freedom, we suggest, from the dehumanizing and wounding label of 'criminal', as they acknowledged, and were acknowledged by, others in a multiplicity of roles, thus helping each other sustain their senses of individuality and humanity. For us, this was a step towards assuaging their woundedness as dignity was offered to each other and held by individuals.

We are clear about the impact that collective creativity can have, yet we also recognize that these impacts are temporary. We are conscious of not overclaiming the impact or the value of the work. We hear and acknowledge theatre professor Laura Edmondson's warning against the 'academic sugarcoating', or the overemphasis, of the transformative or transgressive impacts of such theatre interventions (2007: 7–8). Yet we also need to recognize the subtlety of such interventions, particularly if we recall the warden's experience. Considering Ramphele's notion of woundedness and Rapport's concept of well-being, we argue that, in the experience of being witnessed in these actions, momentarily these women had dignity, and they were able to be more than an inmate. These experiences, coupled with the opportunities to reflect on their hopes for the future, were, we think, important for the women. Their lives did not change, they remained in prison, but small connections were made, and briefly they participated as 'full member[s] of a social milieu', as complex and multiple individuals who are valued or are 'intrinsically valuable'.

Acknowledgements

We would like to thank all the women incarcerated in Sun City who participated in our project, and the staff who assisted our project and enabled the work to take place. We acknowledge the research assistance in the form of a grant from the Research Office at the Royal Central School of Speech and Drama. Finally, we thank the Sibikwa Arts Organisation, Phyllis Klotz and Lehlohonolo Dube, and the Central students who worked alongside us.

Notes

1   For more information about Jones' Medea Project which has been running since 1992, predominantly in the US but also in South Africa, please see Rena Fraden's book (2001) and Nina Billone's article (2009) on the practice.

Assuaging Woundedness through Collective Creativity   213

2   This calculation is based on a comparison of the World Prison Brief figures from 1995 (prison population total: 118,205) and 2015 (159,563); data is from the Institute for Criminal Policy Research (2016).
3   In 1994, the Department of Correctional Services reported an average of 2,867 women in prison, compared with their figure for 2015 of 4,118.
4   All the participants' names have been changed.
5   While we are conscious of the problematics of using the term 'ubuntu' it is not as a trope from white, Westernized practitioners. Rather, in this context where 'ubuntu' is often a commonly referred to philosophy which determines how communities are/were supposed to work together, it is important to employ the term as it helps us to make visible the very real oppressions faced by the female inmates.
6   This idea is similar to Antony Altbeker's reasoning for the level of crime in South Africa. Altbeker, an independent policy researcher in crime and policing, argues that the 'precariousness of life in poverty', coupled with the ensuring emotional stress, leads to situations which stimulate/encourage violent crime (2011: 62).
7   Ramphele's work on this concept in 2012 was the precursor to the establishment of her failed political party, Agang, in June 2013, aimed at challenging the ANC leadership (Molele 2013).

References

Altbeker, A. (2011), 'Crime and Policing: How We Got It Wrong', in M. du Preez (ed.), *Opinion Pieces by South African Thought Leaders*, 27–32, Johannesburg: Penguin.

Baim, C., Brookes, S. and A. Mountford (2002), *The Geese Theatre Handbook: Drama with Offenders and People at Risk*, Winchester: Waterside Press.

Biggs, L. (2016), 'Serious Fun at Sun City: Theatre for Incarcerated Women in the "New" South Africa', *Theatre Survey* 57: 4–36.

Berson, J. (2008), 'Baring and Bearing Life Behind Bars: Pat Graney's "Keeping the Faith" Prison Project', *The Drama Review* 52(3): 79–94.

Billone, N. (2009), 'Performing Civil Death: The Medea Project and Theater for Incarcerated Women', *Text and Performance Quarterly* 23(4): 260–75.

Buell, B. (2011), 'Rehabilitation through the Arts at Sing Sing: Drama in the Big House', in J. Shailor (ed.), *Performing New Lives: Prison Theatre*, 49–65, London: Jessica Kingsley.

Centre for Conflict Resolution (2004), 'Prison Transformation in South Africa', in M. Balfour (ed.), *Theatre in Prison: Theory and Practice*, 161–75, Bristol: Intellect.

Clark, M. (2004), 'Somebody's Daughter Theatre: Celebrating Difference with Women in Prison', in M. Balfour (ed.), *Theatre in Prison: Theory and Practice*, 101–6, Bristol: Intellect.

214   *Applied Theatre: Women and the Criminal Justice System*

Correctional Services (2016), Johannesburg Female Centre of Excellence. Available online: http://www.dcs.gov.za/AboutUs/COE/centre/GP%5CJHBFemaleCC.aspx (accessed 16 June 2016).

Corsín Jiménez, A. (ed.) (2008), *Culture and Well-Being: Anthropological Approaches to Freedom and Political Ethics*, London and Ann Arbor: Pluto Press.

Edmondson, L. (2007), 'Of Sugarcoating and Hope', *TDR: The Drama Review* 51(2): 7–10.

Etchells, T. (1999), *Certain Fragments: Contemporary Performance and Forced Entertainment*, London: Routledge.

Foucault, M. (1979), *Discipline and Punish: The Birth of the Prison*, London: Penguin.

Fraden, R. (2001), *Imagining Medea: Rhodessa Jones and Theater for Incarcerated Women*, Chapel Hill: University of North Carolina Press.

Gillespie, K. (2008), 'Moralising Security: "Corrections" and the Post-Apartheid Prison', *Race/Ethnicity: Multidisciplinary Global Contexts* 2(1): 69–87.

Haffejee, I. (2014), 'The Women and Babies of Joburg Prison', *JHB Live*. Available online: https://www.jhblive.com/Stories-in-Johannesburg/article/the-women-and-babies-of-joburg-prison/5902 (accessed 1 August 2019).

Institute for Criminal Policy Research (2016), *World Prison Brief: South Africa*. Available online: http://www.prisonstudies.org/country/south-africa (accessed 21 July 2016).

James, W. (2008), 'Well-Being: In Whose Opinion, and Who Pays?', in A. Corsín Jiménez (ed.), *Culture and Well-Being: Anthropological Approaches to Freedom and Political Ethics,* 69–79, London and Ann Arbor: Pluto Press.

Kershaw, B. (2004), 'Pathologies of Hope in Drama and Theatre', in M. Balfour (ed.), *Theatre in Prison: Theory and Practice*, 35–51, Bristol: Intellect Books.

Kronenberg, F., Kathard, H., Rudman, D. and E. Ramugondo (2015), 'Can Post-Apartheid South Africa be Enabled to Humanise and Heal Itself?', *South African Journal of Occupational Therapy* 45(1): 21–6.

Lawston, J. M. (2008), 'Women, the Criminal Justice System, and Incarceration: Processes of Power, Silence, and Resistance', *NWSA Journal* 20(2): 1–18.

Levinas, E. (2006), *Entre Nous: On Thinking-of-the-Other* (translated by M. Smith and B. Harshav), London: Continuum.

Manaleng, P. (2014), 'Women in Prison: Ignored and Neglected', *Saturday Star*, 8 March. Available onlime: https://www.iol.co.za/news/south-africa/women-in-prison-ignored-and-neglected-1.1658349#.U4SuqHJdWSp (accessed 26 May 2014).

McAvinchey, C. (2007), 'Possible Fictions: The Testimony of Applied Performance with Women in Prisons in England and Brazil'. Unpublished PhD Thesis, QMUL.

McAvinchey, C. (2011), *Theatre & Prison*, Basingstoke: Palgrave Macmillan.

Molele, C. (2013), 'Aganga Launch: Ramphele's Scathing Attack on Zuma', *Mail & Guardian*, 22 June. Available online: https://mg.co.za/article/2013-06-22-agang-launch-rampheles-scathing-attack-on-zuma (accessed 28 June 2013).

Ramphele, M. (2012a), 'Woundedness and South African Society', Business and Keynote Speaker presented at The Country Club Johannesburg, Johannesburg, South Africa, 7 June 2012.

Ramphele, M. (2012b), 'Walking over the Wounded', *Mail & Guardian*, 28 June. Available online: https://mg.co.za/article/2012-06-21-er-the-wounded (accessed 5 July 2012).

Rapport, N. (2008), 'On Well-Being, Being Well and Well-Becoming: On the Move with Hospital Porters', in A. Corsín Jiménez (ed.), *Culture and Well-Being: Anthropological Approaches to Freedom and Political Ethics*, 95–114, London and Ann Arbor: Pluto Press.

Salverson, J. (2006), 'Witnessing Subjects: A Fool's Help', in J. Cohen-Cruz and M. Schutzman (eds), *A Boal Companion: Dialogues on Theatre and Cultural Politics*, 146–57, London and New York: Routledge.

Sampson, F. (2016), 'A Speaking Likeness: Poetry Within Health and Social Care'. Mike White Memorial Lecture, held at the Wellcome Trust, London on 14 June. Available online: http://www.creativityandwellbeing.org.uk/sites/default/files/Sampson%20A%20Speaking%20Likeness%20on%20poetry%20and%20healthcare%20June%2014%202016.pdf (accessed 30 June 2016).

Sutherland, A. (2013), '"Now We Are Real Women": Playing with Gender in a Male Prison Theatre Programme in South Africa', *Research in Drama Education: The Journal of Applied Theatre and Performance* 18(2): 120–32.

Tannenbaum, J. (2002), 'Human Beings Together', *Turning Wheel* (Summer): 26.

Thorn, L. (2010), *Release: Women in Prison Write about Self-harm and Healing*, Bar None Books.

Wake, C. (2008), 'Through the (In)visible Witness in Through the Wire', *Research in Drama Education: The Journal of Applied Theatre and Performance* 13(2): 187–92.

Young-Jahangeer, M. (2005), 'Bringing in to Play: Investigating the Appropriation of Prison Theatre in Westville Female Prison, KwaZulu-Natal (2000–2004)', *South African Theatre Journal* 19: 143–56.

Young-Jahangeer, M. (2013), '"Less Than a Dog": Interrogating Theatre for Debate in Westville Female Correctional Centre, Durban South Africa', *Research in Drama Education: The Journal of Applied Theatre and Performance* 18: 200–3.

'Dirty Rule Makers', *Voices from Prison* (1987)

Lynn, Clean Break

dirty rule makers
the cold feet of steel
steel steel steel
steel keys sneaking
creeping dirty
peeping tomming
dead eye peeking
no reasoning. Follow
the ruling ruling
ruling. Don't ask why
No questioning. Only
following following
orders. Haven't I
heard that somewhere
before before before ...

For information on *Voices from Prison,* please see p. 56.

11

The Stella Adler Studio Outreach Programme at the Rose M. Singer Center for Women at Rikers Island Correctional Facility: An Interview with Joanne Edelmann and Tom Oppenheim

Caoimhe McAvinchey

The Stella Adler Studio, in the heart of Manhattan, is a world-renowned centre for actor training that has, since 1949, been guided by the principle that growth as an actor and growth as a human being are synonymous. The Studio has evolved into an important cultural centre, developing an ambitious programme of arts events and programmes that reach far beyond the walls of its studio, working in public schools, correctional facilities and with community partners. The mission statement is strident in its articulation of the imperative for theatre artists to be critically aware and to participate in social justice, 'to create an environment with the purpose of nurturing theater artists and audiences who value humanity, their own and others', as their first and most precious priority while providing art and education to the greater community'.[1] Since 2014, the Stella Adler Studio has run an outreach programme at Rose M. Singer Center for Women at Rikers Island Correctional Facility, a jail complex on the outskirts of New York City. The following interview with Tom Oppenheim, Artistic Director of the Stella Adler Studio, and Joanne Edelmann, Master Teacher of Movement who leads the women's work at Rikers, took place in the Stella Adler Studio, West 27th Street, New York City on 21 April 2017.

CM *The Stella Adler Studio has an extraordinary portfolio of work. When did you decide to collaborate with the women at Rikers and how does this programme of work sit within the wider frame of the work of the Studio?*

218   *Applied Theatre: Women and the Criminal Justice System*

TO   I took over the Stella Adler Studio in 1995 and my primary objective was to make sure that the Studio would not degenerate into a wax museum devoted to Stella, which I've seen happen at other institutions that have an inspirational founder. It had to be a living, breathing expression of her spirit, which I also took to be the spirit of her father, Jacob Adler and the Yiddish theatre, and Clurman and the Group Theater. They were both devoted to theatre as a means to uplift and edify the people of their community, theatre as a social force, as an educational force. They were art theatres with real social purpose. Stella was in both and developed techniques with the imprint of the spirit of that tradition. Central to this was a vision of an actor as an ever-evolving, culturally aware, socially engaged human being. If you study her technique, the essence of the spirit of her technique that's connected to this tradition is insight – growth as an actor and growth as a human being are synonymous. From that came the mission of the Studio to create an environment that nurtures theatre artists and audiences so that they value humanity, their own and others', as their first priority, while bringing art and education to the community. What I surrendered was Adlerian dogma, but by surrendering the dogma I connected much more deeply with the spirit of Stella and that whole tradition. There were curricular ramifications to that and being able to connect a faculty that may or may not have studied with Stella and maybe teach her technique or don't teach her technique, but who harmonize with this idea of an actor. And then there were also extracurricular ramifications, much of which was the creation of something called the Harold Clurman Art Series, a series of different cultural events: a poetry centre, a music centre, our own professional theatre company, a movement theatre company, a playwright division.

Much of that was an effort to communicate with our acting students the idea that as actors they're members of the family of artists first and foremost, that they're more beholden to artists than they are to agency casting directors, that there's an ancient art form with a primordial purpose and that's what we want them to commit their lives to. And then, in addition to that, there's the sort of passion for social justice, both in me, but also in that tradition. This produced the Stella Adler Outreach Division, with a dual mission to confront the educational and economic social inequity in America by offering free training to people that can't afford tuition or can't get acting training, while providing our tuition-based students with a model of social engagement. For many years the primary programme was called Adler Youth, an after-school programme where New York City high-school students come here and train for free, three times a week for two years, possibly longer.

I always had an interest in bringing the benefits of acting training and of theatre to people who wouldn't necessarily find their way here, the kids that

The Stella Adler Studio Outreach Programme 219

we train in the Adler Youth, I describe them as the theatre nerds of the inner city. They're highly driven young people, they are on free lunch, which means they subsist, a family of four on $22,000 a year, so they're decidedly living at the poverty level but they find their way here and they study from 4.30 p.m. to 6.30 p.m., three days a week, and we feel very responsible to them. But we wanted to bring the training to people that, for one reason or another, wouldn't get here. There was an interest in bringing acting training and theatre to jails and prisons, and Tommy Demenkoff had that kind of previous experience, so that was the road that led us. We developed a programme called *Outside In*, which happens here for three hours on Sundays, for people we meet at Rikers and Phoenix House, a drug rehabilitation programme. The programme, *GOSO*, which stands for *Getting Out and Staying Out*, is an alternative to incarceration and is also plugged into Rikers, and people get to train for free. We feel compelled by virtue of our mission to do it and we feel that it feeds the mission.

JE We've been working at Rose M. Singer Center, the women's facility at Rikers, since 2014. Tom Oppenheim asked me to do there what I do here – teach an actors' class that culminates in a movement project. The movement project is simply an extension of who the people are in front of me. I don't go in with any preconceived notions of what we're going to do until I meet the group. The basis of my work happens on the floor. One thing I discovered immediately with teaching at the women's facility on Rikers was that I can't ask the women to work on the floor. It's filthy. Even after we washed the floor and were able to work on it, I realized that the floor for the women was a place of abuse: they were thrown on the floor, they were raped on the floor, and so asking them to sit on the floor is traumatic, asking them to lay down on the floor is even worse. I had to really change my idea of how to warm them up, everything has to be standing. They're not in good physical shape, they eat terrible food, they don't have any exercise, they gain a lot of weight, they become immobile. Some of the women have jobs, but most of them don't. As Rikers is a holding pen, a jail, the women really have nothing, they're just sitting around. So, what do I do? I bring a lot of poetry, which the women love. I was told that perhaps they wouldn't understand it, because, again, the perception is that these are not smart women, that they're not creative women: the truth is they're not formally educated women. Poetry transcends that.

Recently we brought these two wonderful actors who performed scenes from August Wilson plays, and although these women may never have heard of August Wilson and certainly had never seen a play of his, they knew exactly what was happening. They understand everything and they're very insightful.

220   *Applied Theatre: Women and the Criminal Justice System*

The poems are gifts. I want to give them something in their hands, so the pieces of paper of poetry I give them are printed on the Stella Adler stationery. They love it, they love the quality of the paper.

So, I bring in poetry, we read the poetry, and I bring in music and it is always music that they're less likely to have heard before. Philip Glass, Steve Reich, contemporary music, classical contemporary music. We brought in Olatunji, African drumming, and they adored that – it's very intricate. So, I work with poetry, music and then we start moving. I don't give them choreography per se: I will say something like, let's wipe your hands, and that's the beginning of the movement sequence, and then I ask, what should come after that? and what should come after that? That's how we create movement sequences. Often the stories that are told within the movement projects are about what freedom is and how you can't lock up the imagination. We talk a lot about Federico García Lorca's theory of duende. Duende is a momentary burst of inspiration, the blush of all that is truly alive, all that the performer is creating at a certain moment. And they will frequently, if they do something which wasn't in the piece, they'll say to me, well my duende came and [laughs] it made me do something else!

CM   *How long does each project last? What's the arc of activity?*

JE   I'm there every Wednesday. I always say to the women, you're a student of the Stella Adler Studio, it just happens to be here, we don't know what you have been accused of doing and it is not our business: that's not how we see you. And on Wednesdays during this time you're a student at the Stella Adler Studio. I bring in a lot of poets, actors, singers, musicians, New York University students, and they perform for the women and then they work with the women. But come June, I start looking at the group of women and thinking, what's the piece going to be about this year? Where are we going to go? For example, this year we did a lot of work on Hamlet's 'To be or not to be' soliloquy, so I have an idea in my head that someone will come out and say, 'To be or not to be', and then the group comes out and says, 'That is the question', and that this may then somehow lead in to an August Wilson scene from *The Piano Lesson*.

We have had poets-in-residence for the last couple of years; one was Sonia Sanchez and we used her incredible haikus. They're also easy to memorize. I don't want the women to have the anxiety of memorization, also we never know who's going to be there. There might be some woman who memorized everything and is really terrific, and boom, she won't be there the day of the performance. This has happened. So that means all of the women have to know all of the poetry. I have a teaching partner that comes with me and that

The Stella Adler Studio Outreach Programme 221

person is on book and so I say to the women, don't worry if you forget what to say. These women have never performed before, and they're in this large gym with the commissioner, the captains, the officers, about eighty other inmates come to watch, the poets and forty or fifty people from the Stella Adler Studio. Paula Washington was our MC this year. Can you imagine, your first performance in front of all these people? The first year when the women came in to be part of the audience, they were really tough, they just sat there – what is this going to be? The women performing had pink shirts on and skirts. The other inmates were laughing at the women. Then, all of a sudden, they stopped laughing and they leaned in: it's magic in the theatre.

CM   *How do you come up with the various titles?*

JE   We couldn't do a proscenium piece of theatre because the staff don't like for people to sit behind each other, and so we did it in a circle. We said, this is the circle. And it became *The Circle* and then it was *Our Circle*. After this project, I was talking to the women and I said, you have to know who you are to be an actor. And one woman said, we know who we are, we are murderers and thieves. And I said well, that is what has happened to you at a certain point in your life – we can't measure your life by the one awful thing you've done, that's not your whole life and so we need to heal. So, the next piece was *The Healing Project* and then this was followed by *The Compassion Project* – a call to see people for who they are right this minute.

CM   *The women living at Rikers feel part of a community beyond it – they are part of the Stella Adler Studio community that stretches across geography and time. Even though they can't come here, to West 27th Street, they are part of the studio. There is something fundamental about continuity – over time, over years – both the organization and the individuals within it.*

TO   One summer there was a woman giving feedback after a project. She was trying to articulate what the experience of this five-week journey was and she said, I've been able to express myself in here in a way that I was never able to express myself out there. The woman observed that if she had the opportunity out there [beyond Rikers] to explore herself in a way that she was in Rikers, she may never have ended up in here. And you feel that with so many of them. So that's my real interest and why I'm grateful for *Outside In* and what I continue to ask myself: you see them in a moment, you see that they're these glorious human beings, but it's quite clear that they don't see it. Maybe they see it briefly, but it gets snuffed out, it's so hard to sustain it. But

222   *Applied Theatre: Women and the Criminal Justice System*

it's a lifeline. How can we increase the number of experiences and then provide them with the opportunity to be on a positive road?

JE   One of my favourite things is to watch the officers watch the women, and they get such a kick out of them. And I know at some point we would like to give a class to the officers, because the officers then see the women so differently. [...] Last year one of the officers was going to be in the performance. Because the women wear skirts during the piece and then, at the end, they take their skirts off, are back to their uniforms and go, he was going to collect the skirts and say, 'See you next week.' And we rehearsed it, we rehearsed it, 'See you next week.' 'No, that's not right.' 'See *you* next week.' 'No, that's not good.' And the women were saying to him, you know, this isn't just about you, you just have one line! And it was really great. But then, at the last minute, the warden said, 'I don't think so.'

TO   In our New York University (NYU) fourth year we do one-hour versions of Shakespeare plays and bring them to schools in the South Bronx. It's an effective and complicated programme. That year I was directing *Twelfth Night*, and Christa, a colleague, was doing a different show, *Comedy of Errors*. The performance fell on a rehearsal day so we thought instead of cancelling the rehearsal we would just bring the group. So we brought eighteen NYU students, VIPs and board members. There's a long bridge that leads to Rikers and there was enormous fear and trepidation going in: the warden was there and various Department of Corrections brass and then fifty inmates walked in. It was a very disparate group of people and lots of nervous energy and fear. And then, these women came in and they started to do their work and the women started giggling, like the way kids giggle at each other, and I thought, oh god, I hope it doesn't go in that direction. But the women really owned their piece, enormous self-belief, and they commanded the audience. So, you started to feel laughter, but it was appropriate. And you could hear the NYU students. They were fourth-year students and they were seeing some of the exercises that they did as first-year students – they could see the common vocabulary. And the piece lasted thirty-five minutes, but at the end of it the whole room was together. You felt like it was Dionysus, saying, 'You're all the same.' That's the thing. We're not separate people. It was a great, great validation of the value and magic of theatre.

CM   *And Rikers is committed to the continuation of the work?*

TO   The Department of Corrections is, yes. Though there was some news that the Mayor agreed to close Rikers in the next ten years. The commitment

The Stella Adler Studio Outreach Programme   223

is there from the Commissioner and Deputy Commissioners who invite us in and are happy we're there. What I feel is that we have a punitive philosophy with respect to incarceration in America, so they invite us in and we feel we change the environment there. I think they're caught between, in America, degrading and punishing inmates as opposed to reforming inmates.

CM   *Every jail or prison has its own politics. When I was working in Northern Ireland, the prison population there was, post-Good Friday Agreement and the release of political prisoners, very small. It is possible to work with the entire female prison population if it's thirty-four people. During one particular theatre, photography and sculpture project with Janetka Platun and Rachel Hale, we had a real sense, at the end of the first day, that it was going to be okay, that the women had bought into the idea of the project, and that it was ok not to know for sure where it was going to get to. But the next day when we turned up at the prison, none of the women came to workshop. When we spoke with the officers, they said they didn't know what was going on but that the women didn't want to come to the project. We finally persuaded the officers to allow us to go to the wing and talk with the women. The women said that when the officer came round he said, 'Are you going to this drama thing? No-one else is.' The top level says yes, the education department says yes, but individual officers may not be so supportive – some can be obstructive . . .*

TO   We have exactly that same experience: people from the Commissioner down are very cooperative and then there's a gap between that level and then the day-to-day people who are there.

JE   It depends on who the officer is. Sometimes the women will say that the door opens and they'll say, 'Drama', and close the door. There are lots of other drama organizations. Or they'll open the door and they'll say, 'Stella Adler', and close the door. But what I do is I give them a list of the women and I want the officers to open the door and call each name. And then for the women who are in individual cells, the door's closed, they don't hear. There's one woman that I can't get to because she's in an individual cell, so I sent an email to the warden and sure enough, that woman showed up this last time. But it's tricky, I don't want to be a pain-in-the-ass teacher, I want the officers to be on our side, and they are, so I can't be too demanding.

TO   Because of the violence there, the women have to be escorted.

JE   In the women's facility, I have seen more violence in the last couple of months than I have the entire three years.

224   *Applied Theatre: Women and the Criminal Justice System*

CM   *Do you mean violence playing out in the workshops, or violence on the wing?*

JE   What I see is the women coming in wearing these black mitts because they scratch the officers, and then they're shackled. I'd never seen this until recently. When we did a Black History Month celebration, it was just unreal. The women came in to watch it with these black mitts, shackled ankles and wrists, all smiling, 'Hi, how are you doing?' And they're shackled and you're talking to them just the way I'm talking to you. 'Hi, I'm so glad you're here, here's the poem', and they're shackled. We're in the dark ages. Not like Norway. We're not anywhere near them.

CM   *Norway is pretty extraordinary – when people have been convicted of crimes the state, instead of saying you're beyond society, says we are all society. But if things are so disrupted and volatile, where violence is so quick to potentially arise, what does this mean in terms of the actual practicalities of working at Rikers?*

JE   It's so quick and I can see that the officers are trying to protect us. When we bring in the students I know it's hard on the officers – it's maddening for the officers to be looking after us, I know that. The women used to be able to move freely, except for the women who are in protected custody. Now everybody has to be escorted so they are just sitting there waiting. And then sometimes an officer goes to pick them up and then there's an alarm and the officer can't get them. There's so many things ...

TO   ... lots of variables. But obviously, it would be productive for us to be able to communicate. If there were a culture of reform, of rehabilitation, of true rehabilitation we could all get together on it. It feels like the mission of the Stella Adler Studio would be useful for them.

* * *

Since the interview in April 2017, there were many changes which impacted on the Stella Adler Studio's work at Rose M. Singer Center. Joanne has provided the following postscript:

September 2018 marks the fifth year for the class at Rikers Island, RMSC's Adult Women's Movement Theatre/Poetry/Music class. In that brief period of time the class has moved from working with women in several of the housing units to one. Currently, we are in Unit 2 East A. The class is held in the eating area next to where the women sleep in a 'ward'-style area. The tables and chairs are bolted into the floor. There is a fairly large empty area that allows us to move across the floor. The women keep the area clean. There are windows. And light. In some ways this makes the gathering of women easier, as we (not the male teachers) are permitted to enter where the women sleep and invite them to participate or to watch class. We, therefore, do not have to rely on anyone to escort the women to a common area. The downside of this arrangement is that we no longer have a mix of women in the class. And this is unfortunate, as it offered opportunity to get to know and work with other women in the facility. It afforded variety in a place where mostly each day is the same. However, it seems that no matter where the class is held the structure remains the same. That is – it is fluid. The teachers in the housing unit are able to assess the mood of the women and act accordingly. At times we listen to music when the women are particularly down or upset. Recently I saw *Carousel* on Broadway and brought in the soundtrack. The women were transformed by listening to Josh Henry and most especially by the voice of Renée Fleming. Currently we are working on *Antigone* to be performed in the autumn of 2018. On a personal note I must say that each week I see how bringing poetry, plays and music to the women is like bringing food to the starving. It nourishes them. Gives them strength. Brings laughter and love into a place where there is little to none of that served.

Note

1   https://stellaadler.com/about/core-beliefs.

21.23.6.15 (2018)

Sandrine Uwayo

A Voice   to the adult you I never got to know
to all of you ze, I apologise
the 21-year-old boy the 15-old girl, the 23-year-old boy AND THE boy
who will on one day be 11, 13, 17. But right now, is only barely beginning to
comprehend, Understand and ask for me.
TO the 6 OLD YOU,
most of all
I APOLOGISE.
Here is what I should have said when you came of age
nobody and I mean nobody is entitled to your body
you are   bold,   beautiful,   kind,
miserable,   ugly   mean   scared   suicidal   lonely
strong   you have urgency,
you have LIGHT
                        spirit   resilience   a voice
nobody will ever love you as much as you,
you are frail
Frantically lost   barely keeping your head above water
but   you,   you are surviving
more and more each day you keep on living
Speak and give testament to the future
Inspire Generations
Legacies
You WILL not be defined by your gender, sexuality, race, background
Above all you are NOT a political weapon.   to use for or against YOU

Scream if you want to
cry when you hurt
give and receive love to your heart's content
advocate for as much or as little as your heart contents
Run fast   slow down   Take in the beauty around you.
                                        be bold.   boundless.

Get lost   but remember to take a torch with you, so you can always
come home to me.
Be Impatient and unsatisfied with life.
Be restless   demand more   BE, HELPLESS unguarded   defenceless
Be ugly on purpose
Have many, many lovers so you can learn how to love in return
Be hurt
Teach and be taught tough lessons
Write prose
Content Shakespeare   Inspire ANGELS to make THE DEVIL . . .
                     SING
Simply come to me at the end of it all. Lay your head on my lap and tell
me your worries AND HURT
I am finally able to give you a home.
ready to listen.

Sandrine was a member of Clean Break's Brazen Programme for young
women. She wrote this piece while attending the Writers' Circle, facilitated
by Deborah Bruce.

12

In Their Shoes: Participation, Social Change and Empathy in Open Clasp's *Key Change*

Kay Hepplewhite

As the audience settles for a performance of *Key Change*, we are presented with a stage, bare except for a woman in a grey tracksuit, sitting at the side, playing pop tunes on a CD player and reading a magazine. Gradually four other women, also in the uniform tracksuits, join her. They hang out and chat. There is a physical closeness between them: they are at leisure but not at home. Lining up with their backs to the audience, they ask each other 'Ready?' and the play springs into action. The actors speak in strong north-east of England regional accents, addressing the audience directly with physicalized narrative. We are invited over the walls and, for the next sixty minutes, our 'inside' guides introduce us to the hilarity, tender sensitivity and stark reality of their life in prison.

The actors use rolls of masking tape to mark out the prison boundaries on the stage floor. We are shown the layout of the pads (cells), the location of the showers and the precious but frequently broken payphones. As the tape is held up, we fleetingly see the fences and razor wire that separates prisoners from us, the audience. An early scene sets the tone for this volatile world, where the women are queuing to phone their families. Not all of the phones are working.

'She thinks I'm in Spain,' explains Kelly as an aside to others while she covers the receiver. Kim describes sweetly how 'Nana' can't see a picture down the phone. She then shouts, in humorous contrast to those waiting impatiently, 'Do you mind? I'm on the fucking phone to me granddaughter!' An argument builds and the confrontation ends with Lucy becoming the victim of every woman's anger and frustration as she is shockingly beaten by the others. Loud music pounds throughout this scene, and two women end up in segregation. We see that it can be dangerous to stick up for your rights on the inside. The lively banter of prison life is gone, but Lucy and Angie go on to build a supportive friendship.

Throughout *Key Change*, the audience witnesses each woman in the lead-up to her prison sentence: we see experiences of sexual abuse, domestic

230   *Applied Theatre: Women and the Criminal Justice System*

violence, homelessness and resulting drug use and theft. The women's stories illustrate the complexity of issues underpinning their involvement in the criminal justice system. We are shown how life for many involves prescription and illegal drugs as alleviation from, and the cause of, their life in prison. We hear a rich description, without judgment, of the pleasure and escape provided by heroin: 'it's like a thousand orgasms and everything tingles ... you feel protected ... and safe.' The character Angie's first heroin use starts at the funeral of her baby; she needs emotional support and the drug provides a warm numbing from her loss.

Later in the play, the beating we witnessed earlier is repeated in a flashback, but, in this scene of domestic violence, Lucy is punched and kicked by her husband in front of their children after she confronts him about his infidelity. She is so scared she wets herself. She turns to theft when she struggles to support herself and her children after they flee their violent home. This story is just one, woven among others, that illustrates life before prison and the circumstances that contribute to offending.

Extremes provide *Key Change*'s most resonant images. The woman being viciously beaten contrasts with the sensuous flight of origami birds made from letters received by the women in prison. The birds are animated in a synchronized flock flying across the stage and watched intently by the women, uniformly earthbound in their drab grey. Their gaze suggests envy at the birds' freedom and lightness, and a longing to be home with the senders of the letters. It is a lyrical interlude amid the intensity of prison life, communicating the pain that women experience when separated from families and children. The spare aesthetic of the play illustrates the toughness of prison life but also the vulnerability of the women prisoners. The fluidity of style shifts between drama, storytelling, hilarity and intense physicality. There are sections of tightly choreographed movement and scenes of grim realism.

The play, *Key Change*, formed only one part of an extensive project for Open Clasp Theatre Company. Alongside this crafted theatre-making for public audiences, the company develops careful participatory theatre practices with women and girls, with the objective of personal, social and political change. *Key Change* was the result of a substantial project (2014–17) for the all-women theatre company, telling the real stories of women from HMP Low Newton. The original play was first commissioned to be made by, and presented to, the women prisoners, and then to tour men's prisons with a cast of professional actors. Later, the company performed in theatre venues in England, Scotland and the USA, with additional audiences in women's prisons. A film of *Key Change* broadcast worldwide in 2017 for UN's days of activism against gender-based violence. These events are the most publicly visible aspects of *Key Change*.

In Their Shoes   231

This chapter goes on to reveal the less visible work inside prison and explore the politics of collaboration that resulted in the production. Open Clasp's work is characterized by a careful fictionalization of women's experience, framed within a sociopolitical analysis. The company offers an interesting example of participatory arts practice with women who are marginalized and, in this case, criminalized, raising issues of representation, social change and empathy that are analysed in the chapter.

Interviews with writer and Artistic Director Catrina McHugh MBE and director Laura Lindow inform a critical reflection of *Key Change* and outline how, although experienced as community practitioners, the project in prison challenged their previously established understandings of the politics of collaboration. The chapter will critique the practices of Open Clasp, engaging with debates about the ethical use of personal story in performance-making to evaluate the company's feminist, emancipatory objectives. The role of empathy in collaborative drama-based activities in community contexts also supports analysis of intersubjective aspects of the company's work.

The work of Open Clasp Theatre and the *Key Change* project

Open Clasp has been making theatre for, with and about women since 1998, when founders Catrina McHugh and Kathryn Mace completed Northumbria University's drama degree in Community Practice. A feminist agenda informs performances and workshop approaches, as well as the company's objective of social change, encouraging audiences to 'walk in the shoes of women … most disempowered in our society' (Open Clasp, n.d.). The company stages plays and facilitates workshops about the concerns of women and girls in working-class communities while making partnerships with social agencies and support organizations. For example, they have worked with women seeking asylum, the LGBTQ community and those who identify as sex workers. Rarely going into a community foregrounding an issue, the company frequently finds that domestic violence comes to the fore in the work. *Jumping Puddles*, a collaboration with Frantic Assembly (2014–15), was informed by work with young women. *Rattle Snake*, a play and interactive workshops (2016–17), worked with Durham Constabulary to train front-line police officers in understanding the complexities behind coercive controlling behaviours. *Don't Forget the Birds* (2018) is the first-hand account of what happened after release for Cheryl Byron, one of the original 'inside' cast of *Key Change*, performed with her daughter Abigail.

232   *Applied Theatre: Women and the Criminal Justice System*

Open Clasp's performances present a sharply focused reality through fictional portrayal based on true-life narratives. The work is a dialogue between professional and participatory work, personal biography and social issues, which produces a style that blends dramatic representation and authenticity. The creation of the play *Key Change* was typical of Open Clasp's approach, premised on building relationships with participants over an extended period. First, community groups work creatively to explore experiences and debate issues, drawing on their own realities within drama workshops. The materialization of characters does not lead the project at this stage, however. The resulting play is based on issues and experiences but represented fictionally by McHugh as the writer, a process that allows for truthfulness but at one step removed from exposure of personal details or direct autobiographical portrayal. The scripted drama then goes on to be performed by a professional company in theatres and, typically for all the work of Open Clasp, also in community venues, often played back to the women whose lives are depicted in the play. In some projects, the groups make their own community performances.

Key Change was written by McHugh following a series of workshops with women in HMP Low Newton. Originally, Open Clasp gained access through Dilly Arts, an organization with well-established prison links. The Open Clasp workshops used approaches drawn from drama in education such as hot-seating and 'role on the wall' (see Neelands and Goode 2000: 22) where a character is devised from the contributions of the group. Drama techniques, such as 'thought tracking' (Neelands and Goode 2000: 91), are also represented within the final performance in the prison visit scene, discussed below. Fictional characters are filled out and given a 'timeline' of their life experiences, with their narratives developed over successive workshops. McHugh's playwriting blends the narratives to create a scripted dramatic fiction that is not verbatim, but remains true to life, supporting anonymity but allowing for participants' own experiences to be represented in the play. Passages of text are frequently poetic, allowing for choral performances and inclusion of non-realistic modes of presentation in the aesthetic style of *Key Change*.

The first incarnation of *Key Change* was presented (perhaps incongruously) in the prison chapel, as the only space large enough to hold the gathered audience of staff and women prisoners. Some of the workshop participants performed; other roles – where women had left prison or were not well enough to perform – were substituted by actors who had been part of the final workshops. The performance made a significant impact on both the audience and those taking the steps to act, many for the first time. The relationships between the company and the women performers/workshop participants were carefully handled, and sensitive management of the drama

In Their Shoes 233

processes aimed to offer a positive, even therapeutic process for the women sharing their stories. McHugh reflects on the impact on the women performing the play:

> They'd left that performance high. And I often talk about it now, they were no longer the offender, they were the actor. They were the theatre-maker. And they walked around the prison and people saw them in a different light. And they were the women who had created this amazing show that everyone loved.

The play went on to be performed by Open Clasp's professional actors (two had worked with the women inside) in a tour of men's prisons. The women prisoners were consulted from the outset about what they wanted to say to their male equivalents in relation to their stories. Primarily, they wanted to tell them to stop hurting women, but McHugh also recalled a debate:

> And the women had said, in the very beginning, when we just talked about what was going to be created: 'We don't want the men to feel like we are making them feel bad, that they are the bad people, and finger-wagging at them. And to demonize them.' Because they also understood that men could equally be victims, that they could equally be survivors, that some of their brothers or their fathers [may be victims], but also understanding that some of them are perpetrators as well. So I made sure that, within the script, there was the voice of males.

The play included a character of a male school friend, reunited with one of the women in the transport on its way to prison. The audience are informed that he was also the victim of child sexual abuse. This sensitive moment is followed by a finely balanced comedic sequence where the women act out a rebellious schoolboy and teacher in a classroom incident. Responses of the audiences in the men's prisons showed how they identified strongly with the characters in the play, seeing themselves as children, watching their mothers being hurt, but also identifying themselves in the representation of the male violence against women.

The content of the play was also required to be carefully negotiated with prison authorities, potentially major contributors to many negative experiences represented in the play. McHugh reflects on how this sensitive relationship with the prison impacted on her writing:

> There were challenges [...] about the women's viewpoint of the prison and the governor's viewpoint of the prison. And there was some

234   *Applied Theatre: Women and the Criminal Justice System*

compromise to be had around the script, which was challenging for me as a writer [...] Behind the scenes there were still questions about whether [...] the governor would let [the play] happen.

As well as issues of censorship, McHugh noted the challenges to rehearsing within the hierarchical structures of a prison:

There's things in that situation which wouldn't happen in any other situation. You wouldn't have an officer come in, walk straight up to the stage and take an actor away without talking to the director.

This incident sharply brought home conflicting values between the theatre workshops and how the power structures in the prison were 'performed'. Differing worlds had to be carefully managed in the relationship formed in the *Key Change* project for the play to be performed in prison and on the outside. There were issues about the portrayal of prison life – for example, allowing the play to show the drug smuggling that is acknowledged to exist. McHugh expressed respect for the governor's stance on the project:

And he let it happen ... we asked him to hold his breath ... we needed his endorsement ... I think having a company like Open Clasp was brave of them. And they've let us back into the prison now as well.[1] And I understand what conversations need to be had. It's a funny line to tread, because we're there to advocate for the women, but we also understand we're within an institution.

At the first public showing at Newcastle's Live Theatre, McHugh recalls the proximity of the women prisoners. She felt that, although the prisoners were not there physically, they informed every aspect of the production, breathing through the characters and in the words that they said:

then it was like the women had come over the razor wire [...] and they were onstage. [...] We had a post-show discussion with the governor. People from the prison were there. And there was a woman who had been in prison and she'd heard it on BBC Radio Newcastle [...] and she was just in bits afterwards. And she was going: 'This is great,' then she came back in the evening.

The play went on to be widely successful. It won the prestigious Carol Tambor Best of Edinburgh award following Northern Stage hosting the play at Edinburgh Fringe Festival in 2015, subsequently performing in the New York

Theatre Workshop. The play toured Open Clasp's circuit of community audiences in the north-east of England and UK theatre venues. To complement the theatre tour, the company sought out prison audiences in Edinburgh (Scotland) and Connecticut (USA), who also found points of connection with the material. The play was also performed at the House of Commons, as part of an event organized to lobby Members of Parliament for alternatives to prison sentences for women.[2]

Representing the voices of women prisoners

There is a huge disparity between the lack of voice typically afforded by society to the women offenders whose stories are told and the wide-reaching platform of the performances of *Key Change*. Throughout the project, Open Clasp collaborated with women who have experienced prison, along with prison staff, support organizations and academics. A company aim that 'the voices of those women are heard by audiences including policy-makers' (Open Clasp, n.d.) informs this approach. The play sets out to also represent social issues that shape the experiences of the women prisoners. How effectively did *Key Change* communicate a social message through representing the 'voices' of the women the company worked with inside the prison?

In a model that is challenged by Open Clasp's way of working, criminologist Ngaire Naffine (1997: 49) writes about how female criminals are more frequently talked *about* in literature and media presentations and rarely talked *to*. This can lead to perpetuating myths and stereotypical presentations in dramatic forms. Naffine claims that social compulsion to 'act out' femininity is additionally enforced by prison 'types' we are used to seeing in film and television, resulting in clichéd images of female offenders in dramatic reconstruction. Audiences are already familiar with stereotypical roles that are difficult to counteract: the troubled or troublesome who offend either through need or greed.

In *Key Change*, the foregrounding of women prisoners' experiences (and sometimes violent responses) challenges the audience's presumptions and, at the same time, echoes society's preconceptions of women criminals. The women are presented as survivors and victims of circumstance rather than aberrant wrongdoers. The audience are shown how easy it is for some, struggling to cope with life's emotional and economic challenges on the outside (often created by domestic violence), to turn to solutions of drugs or theft that result in prison sentences. However, Open Clasp's play about women in prison does not discuss their crimes, focusing more on societal structural injustices visited upon them and inferring the support they need.

236 *Applied Theatre: Women and the Criminal Justice System*

Throughout the play, we see that some women in prison can turn a corner in their lives – for example, the character of Kelly comes off heroin and we hear about a domestic violence course. But rehabilitation is complicated by a need for change on the outside. To reduce offending, it is argued that the *social* sources of crime need to be tackled, as the backgrounds and circumstances of women are inextricably linked to their crimes. Criminologists report that a blend of social issues, individual circumstances and immediate psychological factors can contribute to the lead-up to the crimes of female offenders (Gelsthorpe and Morris 2008: 140). Personal difficulties and welfare problems contribute equally. There is recognition in official reporting of the additional influences on women's offending and sentencing, including their economic position, mental health, physical and sexual abuse, responsibilities to children and others (Gelsthorpe and Morris 2008: 141). Women are more harshly punished by a prison sentence, a view that underpins any social message that may be taken away by audiences for *Key Change*.

Key Change makes careful aesthetic choices to present a balance of emotional content with the message that crime is a social issue. Resonating with Open Clasp's objective for their theatre to be for 'personal, social and political change', Lyn Gardner reviewed *Key Change* in the *Guardian*, stating 'Don't get the wrong idea: this is art, not social work' (2015). Stylistic choices are deliberately used in the play to create emotional distancing, and foreground the social and political issues experienced by the individuals. Conventions of 'acting out' are used, such as direct address and externalized commentary on internal emotions to present a *distanced* telling of the stories of the women. The play does not depend on naturalistic dialogues but draws on choreographic techniques, montage and direct address. Episodes rather than fluid narrative are explored, playing with timescales through use of flashback to show cause and effects of prison, such as the use of drugs and violence. There is a dramatic arc, but no tidying up of storylines nor any easy resolution to women's problems.

Social issues about prison are incorporated in *Key Change*; links to outside prison such as letters, phone calls and visits, which are so vital to the women, are shown to be a mix of yearned-for connection and yet painful reiteration of reprimand. Criminologists note how the impact of imprisonment affects the wider family and can additionally punish women. Rosemary Sheehan and Catherine Flynn explore how financial, physical and geographical pressures complicate children's relationships with imprisoned mothers, and how the environment for visiting parents is not child-friendly (2007: 229). There is a significant impact on the lives of children whose mothers are imprisoned, and resulting childcare can place strains on other relationships within the family.

A prison visit in *Key Change* illustrates how relationships with close family members are endangered and how communication is impaired by prison. The mother of the prisoner is angry with her daughter for creating a difficult situation and refused to give her refuge from a violent partner. The two young daughters appear awkward and estranged in a cruel reminder of their mother's punishment in the prison environment. The prisoner is disempowered by her incarceration and life outside is damaged in a double sentence, inflicted both on prisoners and those they love most. This chastisement is held in the actors' portrayal of the bodies of the children, using minimal gestures and looks. The scene is presented with a drama technique of 'voice on the shoulder' or 'thought-tracking', where an actor speaks for the mother and daughter, indicating an inability to voice what they really mean in the precious but agonizing visit. Each dialogical exchange is followed by a pithy statement of subtext from the actor, emphasizing unspoken feelings of loss.

As audiences, we are invited to see the performance as a (re)presentation. In a Brechtian sense, emotions are distanced to analyse a social construction of the women's lives. Moments of the acting out, such as the beatings, are stylized and slowed down, then portrayed realistically. We are guided to hold back from pity on an individual level and to see the portrayal as socially illustrative. Each scene serves to show the personal impact of prison, but always as a representation of wider, socially framed experience.

In their shoes: Debates of representation and appropriation

Recalling Open Clasp's aim, to 'walk in the shoes of women … most disempowered in our society', this section considers risks of representing, and the role of empathy in portraying the lives of women prisoners in *Key Change*. During the autumn tour 2016, McHugh and Cheryl Byron, one of the women in HMP Low Newton who originally devised the play, were interviewed for BBC Radio 4's *Women's Hour*. Byron's testimony passionately explained how the workshops with Open Clasp provided her with an opportunity for positive reflection on issues and experiences in her life. Interviewer Jane Garvey asked whether the company were 'farming' for stories, a suggestion that McHugh fiercely resisted. In her blog (2016) she wrote a response:

Farming suggests a detachment, and an intention to pick and sell. Open Clasp's methodology is collaborative and democratic; working with women to create the best theatre we can to change the world.

238   *Applied Theatre: Women and the Criminal Justice System*

To aid analysis of this risk of 'pick and sell' of personal stories, it is useful to consider debates around ethics within participatory theatre practices. Alison Jeffers writes about working within theatre with refugees, a comparably vulnerable group. She discusses the dilemmas of representation when connecting personal narratives to an objective of social/political change: 'How are theatre practitioners to honour the experiences of the participants in projects and to challenge prejudice against those participants without resorting to demonstrations of victimhood?' (2012: 143). Even when the prisoners are not representing their own stories to a public audience, it is possible to transfer the same argument to the context of *Key Change*, where careful selection in the portrayal of the women prisoners' narratives was also demanded.

McHugh describes how they decided to suggest the underpinning issue of child sexual abuse that had been a present – although not explicitly discussed – feature of the workshop processes in prison: 'You knew that this had happened in it, dramatically. The father, you know, he kind of breathes into her ear. He strokes her breast, slightly. And you know, straight away. But that was it.' Even though a very small moment in the performance, this gesture is significant for the audience's understanding of the character Angie's anger and use of heroin. The inclusion was thoroughly considered by the writer and director.

Lindow was aware of an opportunity to 'confront' issues in the play that were evidently impacting on the women, such as sexual abuse and domestic violence, but also debated their portrayal:

> It's a question – how do we, as a society, talk about it? And how, in all of the complications that the issue brings up, how do we then create theatre that allows an audience to become part of that without putting people through something unnecessary, voyeuristic, punishing in ways that are inappropriate?

Lindow saw her role as 'interpretive', suggesting careful thought about how painful issues were shown in the play. She was concerned with aesthetic issues of presentation to an audience:

> We're trying to find the right artistic language so that an audience can really receive what it is that the women are communicating. It's not that we're invisible. But it is about the art, it is about the art as functional. And if you're moved then that should be in the appropriate place because you've felt something that's relevant to the stories and the experiences that the women are talking about.

In Their Shoes   239

Lindow acknowledges the artistic role as not being 'invisible', indicating choice in the aesthetic style she developed for the play, one that allowed the issues to be communicated amid the emotional content. Dramaturgical choices were influenced by the close involvement with the women's own ideas: 'And it's very powerful and it's very beautiful to work with. Because it just pushes aside this sense of story, which you can get quite tied up in ... it creates a real honest dynamic in the work.'

Open Clasp's process of consultation and consistent relationship with the group (as far as possible, due to some prisoners' release) aimed to make sure they were happy with how the stories were presented. Before a new version of *Key Change* with professional cast went on to be performed to men's prisons and public theatre audiences, the play had to first pass the company's self-imposed veto of being previewed by the women who devised the work. How did the women want to communicate a blended version of their stories to audiences to ensure that the portrayals and messages, although fictional, were accurately presenting their life experiences? This process forms part of Open Clasp's ethical approach to retelling the stories of under-represented women and suggests how they seek to resist potential exploitation of the collaborative relationship by misclaiming an authenticity or appropriating ownership.

In this project, the women were adamant about aspects of the representation of characters and tone. More than with other projects using the same approaches with communities of women, McHugh's script was taken to task and the company was held accountable for truly representing their community collaborators in the professional production. Lindow recalls the first read-through, discussing one woman's response:

> She had arms crossed and legs crossed and you could see her foot going – and she was just going: 'You're not me' [...] It allowed us to really, really talk about impact. And the impact that they wanted to have. And they could really *own* that language then. Because they had heard and experienced an impact.

As a result of the previewing process, the women prisoners became critics and part of the play-making. For those who acted in the first version on the inside, they had also gained an embodied knowledge through witnessing the impact of their own performance on an audience. As the scene was drawn from her reality, the prisoner/actor who played the perpetrator of domestic violence needed to know that the company was capable of presenting it as *her* truth in the 'outside' play. Aspects of script, direction and the professional actors' performances were further adapted by Open Clasp and endorsed by

240   *Applied Theatre: Women and the Criminal Justice System*

the women prisoners, giving them greater agency before the play was toured by the company's actors.

Jeffers states, 'Participatory theatre practice is commonly accepted as a process based on encouraging agency in those who participate in it as well as those who watch' (2012: 143). She suggests that particular attention should be paid to theatre participants and duty of care is required. An ethical responsibility of workshop leaders in theatre processes with any non-professional groups includes attention to the vulnerability of the workshop participants. This requires particular skills on behalf of the practitioners, and McHugh emphasized a close understanding of the prisoners' experience for all members of the company working in the prison. She outlined the director's role as more than just shaping the performance with the women prisoners:

> Laura's job is to keep the room safe. Laura's job is to get the women to a place where they could perform to their peers ... she knows the journey, she knows the conversations the women have had. She knows the heart in the room ... She kept all the women safe and she kept the actors safe as well. And the actors kept the women safe you know, because the actors that we worked with are really capable.

The company values sophisticated expertise for everyone involved in the project. McHugh discussed the skills needed and one of the professional actors who went on to perform the play on the outside, working for the first time with Open Clasp's methodology:

> Instinctively she's great. She doesn't see the women as other. And that's really important for the facilitators, not to walk in with a patronizing manner ... They've got to be in the room – and the politics of it ... sitting with the women as equals and thinking about what is it that these women have experienced, what we as women generally experience. Or what is unfair in the world and what's unjust in the world. And you want them to have a sense of humour. And to be empathetic and to be funny and to get up and to have a laugh. And for the women just to feel very comfortable with them.

McHugh's comments itemize the multifaceted skills for a facilitator in this context, made up of a blend of political perspective and an appropriate rapport with the participants, drawing on personal qualities including humour and an ability to empathize.

Empathy is inferred in the second part of Open Clasp's mission statement that combines 'social debate' with encouragement for audiences 'to walk in the shoes of women' (Open Clasp, n.d.). Amy Coplan's (2011) analysis from a psychological perspective suggests that 'in the shoes' of others is the most frequently occurring type of empathy due to a natural egocentric bias that we all share. Coplan (2011: 5) stresses the importance of specificity in any discussion of empathy, because of its potential for many different interpretations and meanings. She suggests there is a risk that any 'self-oriented perspective-taking' (2011: 9) may lead to presumptions of understanding of the other (2011: 10). Further factors must be in play to gain full experiential understanding of the narratives of others through empathy, including an awareness of self as distinct from other (2011: 13).

It may be risky to make claims on behalf of others, even those we may feel empathy for, such as women in prison. This theory from psychology can be juxtaposed alongside a feminist perspective through social debate, such as proposed by Open Clasp. As women, we can share understanding. But is it sufficient to *feel* for the women whose stories a theatre company are communicating or do we also need a sociopolitical perspective, such as can be argued to be present in *Key Change*?

Within an exploration of feminist ethics, Daryl Koehn notes that empathy can enable us to 'enrich our moral discourse' by attending to what the other may think, feel or experience on 'her own terms' (1998: 57), thereby provoking shifts in the way we think, even to overcome prejudices. This 'vicarious experience' (1998: 57) can make a contribution to a sense of individuals as unique agents. She claims that an 'ethic of empathy ... celebrates difference because it has the capacity to challenge us and to enlarge our view of the world' (1998: 58). This resonates with the display of personal experience in the women's lives in *Key Change*. If we feel for the women in prison in Open Clasp's play, we may test preconceptions and step towards doing something to change what is seen as unjustified.

This use of empathy goes some way to challenge oppressions, but Koehn also suggests recourse to guiding principles and encouragement of shared 'ethical responsibility' (1998: 72) are necessary to accommodate 'major paradigm shifts' (1998: 65). Empathy alone cannot provoke change: political analysis is also needed. Feedback suggests that audiences are moved by the play through 'vicarious experience' of the lives of women prisoners; whether major shifts, or indeed a 'key change', follow is a further question.

Promoting a 'Key Change' through the portrayal of women prisoners

Open Clasp state: 'Our unique approach and practice collaborates with women on the margins of society to create exciting theatre for personal,

242   *Applied Theatre: Women and the Criminal Justice System*

social and political change' (Open Clasp n.d.). For those involved with the *Key Change* project, there was a drive to promote change while working with real-life stories through the processes from workshop to performance. This chapter has explored issues arising when a theatre company aims for genuine collaboration with individuals and institutions. *Key Change* offers an example of participatory arts practice that also represents the lives and ideas of a marginalized group to a wider audience, aiming for 'personal, social and political change' within both audiences and workshop participants.

The work that makes up the *Key Change* project blends listening and negotiation using an empathetic approach, with careful consideration of how personal stories can be ethically re-presented in dramatic form. A final image from the director encapsulates how the work seeks also to honour the ownership of the material. Describing the company's role as 'conduits', Lindow emphasizes that it is her responsibility to remember 'whose the work is, whose the stories are. And keeping them with the performances as they go'. Lindow's imagery of 'conduits' is useful in suggesting a combining of social awareness and personal connection in the way it *channels* the originators of the work throughout the performance processes, recalling the source at all times, even when the work makes its journey over the wire from the prison setting to theatre audiences worldwide.

Notes

1   Open Clasp's follow-on project, *Sugar* (2017), was written following workshops with women in HMP Low Newton, Women's Direct Access Homelessness Service Manchester and women on probation attending a Women's Hub at West End Women and Girls Centre, Newcastle upon Tyne.
2   The performance of *Key Change* at the House of Commons on 25 October 2016 was hosted by the National Criminal Justice Arts Alliance, Clinks, Prison Reform Trust and Agenda (Alliance for Women and Girls at Risk). It aimed to inform parliamentarians, senior policy-makers and decision-makers who need to understand the complex lives of women who come into contact with the criminal justice system.

References

Coplan, A. (2011), 'Understanding Empathy: Its Features and Effects', in A. Coplan and P. Goldie (eds), *Empathy: Philosophical and Psychological Perspectives,* 3–18, Oxford: Oxford University Press.

In Their Shoes 243

Gardner, L. (2015), 'Female Prisoners Unlock Their Creativity', *Guardian*, 7 August. Available online: https://www.theguardian.com/stage/2015/aug/07/key-change-open-clasp-edinburgh-festival-review-northern-stage-summerhall-low-newton (accessed 20 July 2016).

Gelsthorpe, L. and A. Morris (2008), 'Women's Imprisonment in England and Wales: A Penal Paradox' in K. Evans and J. Jamieson (eds), *Gender and Crime: A Reader*, 136–45, Maidenhead: Open University Press.

Jeffers, A. (2012), *Refugees, Theatre and Crisis: Performing Global Identities*, Basingstoke: Palgrave Macmillan.

Koehn, D. (1998), *Rethinking Feminist Ethics*, London and New York: Routledge.

McHugh, C. (2016), Open Clasp's blog. 26 October. Available online: https://openclasp.wordpress.com/2016/10/26/not-farming-jane-garvey (accessed 30 October 2016).

Naffine, N. (1997), *Feminism and Criminology*, Cambridge: Polity Press.

Neelands, J. and T. Goode (2000), *Structuring Drama Work*, Cambridge: Cambridge University Press.

Nicholson, H. (2005), *Applied Drama: The Gift of Theatre,* Basingstoke: Palgrave Macmillan.

Open Clasp (n.d.). Available online: https://www.openclasp.org.uk/ (accessed 25 July 2016).

Sheehan, R. and C. Flynn (2007), 'Women Prisoners and Their Children', in R. Sheehan, G. McIvor and C. Trotter (eds), *What Works with Women Offenders,* 214–39, Cullompton: Willan Publishing.

Index

Acting Out (USA) 22, 189–95
affect 107–9, 112–15, 153, 156
    affective economies 108, 115–17
    affective labour 21, 107, 117
    and gender 112–15, 117–18
Aljwaida women's prison (Jordan) 18
audiences
    carceral traditions around
        spectatorship and criminality
        145–6
    penal spectatorship 4–6

Bad Girls 3, 124
Berlant, Lauren 143, 148, 149, 150,
    153, 159
Black *quare* activism 21, 56–76
Bond Street Theatre 19
Bridging Boundaries Arts
    Intervention 17
Brown, Michelle 4, 5

Cánovas, Elena 13–14
carceral imaginary 22, 143–61
carceral society 22, 144, 157
carcerality 22, 149
casework 143–61
Children Affected by Parental
    Imprisonment (CAPI) 180–3
Clean Break 2, 12, 15–16, 22, 24, 110,
    120, 143–61, 182–4
    21.23.6.15, Sandrine Uwayo
        226–7
    Charged, E.V. Crowe, Sam
        Holcroft, Rebecca Lenkiewicz,
        Chloë Moss, Winsome
        Pinnock and Rebecca Prichard
        22, 142
    Decade, Jacqueline Holborough
        77
    Efemera, Ask-em Out 15

Inside a Cloud, Sabrina Mahfouz
    196
Inside Bitch, Stacey Gregg,
    Deborah Pearson, Lucy
    Edkins, Jennifer Joseph,
    TerriAnn Oudjar and Jade
    Small 2, 124, 187–8
Killers, Jacqueline Holborough 16,
    141–2, 171–2
Voices from Prison 56, 105, 162,
    216
Wicked, Bryony Lavery 35
*Come Listen to my Story of
    Wonderland* 19
Compagnia della Fortezza 9
coping 110, 112
Corston, Jean 1, 2, 6, 7, 8, 147
critical consciousness 38
cultural representations of women in
    prison 3–6, 124
Crowe, E.V., *Doris Day* 146, 151

Daccache, Zeina 9, 18, 19
desistance 24, 178
'disruptive' gender expression, 21
*Doin' Time: Through the Visiting
    Glass*, Ashley Lucas 23
Doing the Arts Justice, Jenny Hughes
    10, 189
domestic violence 7, 19, 42, 60, 147,
    176, 191, 230, 236, 238
Donmar Warehouse, Shakespeare
    Trilogy 11, 22, 175, 183–5
Dworin, Judy 17

economy of credibility 24, 26
Edelmann, Joanne 23, 217–25
Edkins, Lucy 124, 187–8
Ensler, Eve 17
evaluation 10, 17, 24–5, 119

Index

family members in prison 23, 189
feminization of poverty 6, 7, 41
fictionalized authenticity 23
Fitzer, Sherrin 189–95
Fox, Mary 110, 113
Fricker, Miranda, epistemic injustice 25–6

Geese Theatre Company 17–18, 37, 120
   Journey Woman 18
gender-based violence 43, 44, 46, 48, 230
gender sentencing 147
gender performance in prison 58
global corrections industry 1, 6
Graney, Pat 17
Gregg, Stacey 124, 187–8

Hag-Seed, Margaret Atwood 11
Harb, Hakeen 18
Heywood, Louise 17–18
higher education–prison partnerships 22, 79–104, 173–86
HIV/AIDS 43, 44, 46, 147, 191, 203
Holborough, Jacqueline 15, 16, 77, 141–2, 171
Holcroft, Sam, *Dancing Bears* 146, 150
HMP Askham Grange (UK) 15, 21, 22, 173, 178–84
human rights 49–51

indigenous women's over-representation in prison in Australia 21, 81–3
Inside, Philip Osment 11
intersectional injustices 1, 3, 6, 12, 13, 25, 26, 60

Jones, Rhodessa 12–13, 198, 200
Joseph, Jennifer 1, 2, 124, 187–8

Katimba, Dipo 19
kinship and prison networks 59

Lenkiewicz, Rebecca, *That Almost Unnameable Lust* 146
Lloyd, Phyllida, Shakespeare Trilogy 11, 175, 183–5
Logan Correctional Center (USA) 22, 191

McCormick, Susan 15
Mahfouz, Sabrina, *Inside a Cloud* 196
Makepeace, Effie 19
Medea Project: Theater for Incarcerated Women (USA) 12–13, 198, 220
Moss, Chloë, *Fatal Light* 146, 154
motherhood 46–7, 87, 118, 154, 173, 180–3

Nanzikambe Arts Development Organisation (Malawi) 19
National Criminal Justice Arts Alliance (UK) 10, 118
narrative
   biography and fantasy 125–40
   personal narrative and national politics 37–55
   at risk 150–8

Open Clasp Theatre Company 23, 229–44
Oppenheim, Tom 217–25
Orange is the New Black 3, 10, 124
Oudjar, TerriAnn 124, 187–8

Participatory Radio Drama 79–104
Pearson, Deborah 124, 187–8
Pinnock, Winsome, *Taken* 146, 151
political prisoners 9, 38, 223
popular criminology 4–5, 16
prison
   material conditions 2, 60, 141–2
   privatization of prison 7, 109
   uniform 58–9, 63–4
   work 109–12
Prison Creative Arts Project (PCAP) 190

Index

prison theatre 8–11
  Afghanistan 19
  Australia 18, 79–104, 163–70
  Brazil 21, 125
  Jordan 18
  Lebanon 18–19
  Malawi 19
  New Zealand 19
  South Africa 18, 37–55, 197–215
  Spain 13–14
  United Kingdom 15–16, 17–18,
    107–23, 173–86, 229–44
  United States of America 12–13,
    17, 57–76, 189–95, 217–25
Prisoner Cell Block H 3
Prichard, Rebecca, *Dream Pill* 146,
    149, 150
Punzo, Armando 9

quare activism 58, 64–5

Rafter, Nicole 4, 5
rehabilitation 8, 10, 24, 39, 60, 62, 199,
    201, 219, 236
Rose M. Singer Centre, Rikers Island
    Correctional Facility (USA)
    23, 217–25

San Quentin Drama Workshop 9
Scheherazade in Baabda 19
sexuality in prison 47–9, 57–76
Shakespeare in prison 11
social co-creation of criminal
    subjectivities 22
Small, Jade 124, 187–8

Somebody's Daughter Theatre
    Company 18, 163–70
Split Britches 22, 125–40
Staging Human Rights (People's
    Palace Projects, Peggy
    Shaw, Lois Weaver) 10, 21,
    125–40
Stigma 108, 147
Sticky, Sara Ahmed 5, 107–9, 112, 113,
    116, 117

Teatro Yeses (Spain) 12, 13–14
theatre
  for debate 40
  for development 39
  devising practices, 40, 61, 65, 110,
    125
  Popular Participatory Theatre 20,
    37–55
trauma
  aesthetics of injury 86
  trauma trails and transgenerational
    trauma 21, 83, 86–7
Troustine, Jean 11, 17

Uwayo, Sandrine 226–7

Weaver, Lois 21–2, 125–40
Wentworth 3
Westfield Female Correctional
    Facility 37–55
Within These Walls 3
World Female Imprisonment List 1
Woundedness, Mamphela Ramphele
    202–3

CPSIA information can be obtained
at www.ICGtesting.com
Printed in the USA
LVHW010352300821
696386LV00017B/2215